Organizational Theory for Equity and Diversity

Organizational Theory for Equity and Diversity covers a range of organizational theories as applied to educational leadership practice and research, exploring not only traditional perspectives but also critically oriented epistemologies, including Critical Race Theory; LatCrit, Asian, Tribal Crit, and Black Crit; Disability Studies theories; feminist theories; Queer Theory, and theories of intersectionality. Each chapter features teaching suggestions, discussion questions, and questions to help aspiring leaders critically analyze their leadership strengths and limitations in order to understand, apply, and integrate theories into practice. This valuable text provides aspiring school leaders and administrators with the theory and tools for creating equitable and diverse schools that are effective and sustainable.

Colleen A. Capper is Professor of Educational Leadership and Policy Analysis at the University of Wisconsin-Madison, U.S.A.

Organizational Theory for Equity and Diversity

Leading Integrated, Socially Just Education

Colleen A. Capper

 Routledge
Taylor & Francis Group

NEW YORK AND LONDON

First published 2019
by Routledge
711 Third Avenue, New York, NY 10017

and by Routledge
2 Park Square, Milton Park, Abingdon, Oxon, OX14 4RN

Routledge is an imprint of the Taylor & Francis Group, an informa business

© 2019 Taylor & Francis

Library of Congress Cataloging-in-Publication Data
A catalog record for this title has been requested

ISBN: 978-0-415-73621-3 (hbk)
ISBN: 978-0-415-73622-0 (pbk)
ISBN: 978-1-315-81861-0 (ebk)

Typeset in Aldine
by codeMantra

Contents

Series Editor Introduction

The series *Educational Leadership for Equity and Diversity* aims to publish the primary text for educator preparation courses. Educators in practice can also rely on the series for leadership development. This book, *Organizational Theory for Equity and Diversity*, extends the first book in the series, *Leadership for Increasingly Diverse Schools*, edited by George Theoharis and Martin Scanlan.

This text provides an entirely new approach to organizational theory by extending beyond typical organizational theory conceptions. The text provides prospective and current educators with an explanation of a range of epistemologies for organizational theory. These theoretical understandings can assist prospective and practicing educators and scholars to be able to identify the underpinnings of the various educational reforms, programs, initiatives, models, professional development, and federal and state policies to determine whether, and to what extent, these measures are oriented toward equity or not. Further, developing a deeper understanding of critically oriented epistemologies such as Critical Race Theory, Disability Studies theories, and Queer Theory, among others, can assist educators and scholars to determine the possibilities and limitations of equity-oriented efforts.

In the text, readers are guided to critically analyze their own leadership strengths and limitations from each organizational epistemology in a continued effort to better inform their current educational practices. As with all the books in the series, this valuable text will provide aspiring and practicing educators and scholars not only with the tools and strategies, but also the analytical thinking necessary for creating equitable and diverse schools that are effective and sustainable.

Colleen A. Capper, Series Editor
University of Wisconsin-Madison

Preface

This book is the first book in education and in the field of organizational studies that examines a range of epistemologies and applies these epistemologies to organizational theory and leading for equity. The book will help candidates in educator preparation programs and practicing educators to be able to understand, apply, and integrate a range of epistemologies and associated theories in ways that can help them to lead for equity and apply and generate theory in research toward equitable ends.

INTENDED AUDIENCE

I wrote this book for aspiring educational leaders and educational practitioners in the field. The book can be a core text in leadership preparation courses such as organizational theory, leadership for social justice, leadership for equity and diversity, and organizational change. The book could comprise a core text in teacher/educator preparation programs and educational policy, special education, educational psychology, and social foundation programs. The book can help prospective and practicing educators identify the epistemological foundation of education initiatives to be able to discern to what extent these initiatives are oriented toward equity or not. The book can also help prospective and practicing educators discern the epistemological underpinnings of education practices oriented toward equity to identify the potential and limits of equity practice.

KEY FEATURES

Similar to other organizational theory texts, this book addresses structural functional and interpretive epistemologies. However, this text also addresses a range of critically oriented epistemologies, including critical theories; Critical Race Theory and Black Crit; LatCrit, Asian, Tribal Crit; Disability Studies theories; feminist theories; Queer Theory, poststructural epistemology, feminist poststructuralism, and theories of intersectionality. The book applies these critically oriented epistemologies to traditional organizational theory concepts, including leadership, decision-making, and change. The book also considers how these critically oriented epistemologies can inform fresh theorizing about organizations and leadership toward equitable ends.

Grounded in Research

Each chapter opens with a description of the origination of the epistemology prior to its application to education. For each chapter, I conducted an extensive literature review of peer-reviewed empirical studies in education and educational leadership which relied on that epistemology from as far back as each literature database went through the end of January, 2018. In so doing, each chapter conveys the history of each epistemology within education and educational leadership, and the key scholars and empirical studies relevant to that history. The extensive citations and references that resulted within each chapter may then serve as additional reading for students and instructors who want to deepen their understanding of that epistemology for practice or research.

Organizational Theory and Leadership Development for Equity

This book contends that rather than learning about esoteric theories that may not be relevant to education today, examining organizational theory across epistemologies can inform leadership development for equity. Each chapter features an epistemology and guides readers to apply the epistemology to leadership development and practice in five ways:

1. Critically reflect on their own leadership via end-of-chapter discussion questions to guide that critical self-reflection.
2. Analyze a real case from their own experience that they have found troubling or unresolved with case analysis questions for each epistemology at the end of each chapter.
3. Consider implications for leadership, change, and decision-making.
4. Learn how education practice typically responds to diversity and difference.
5. Apply the epistemology to education such as the structure of the organization, the goal of education, curriculum, instruction, and assessment.

BOOK STRUCTURE

Chapter 1 opens with a brief history of my own journey with organizational theory and then presents an epistemological framework that guides the rest of the book. I provide a brief overview of each of the epistemologies featured in the book. The chapter concludes with clarifying the book's terminology.

Chapter 2, History of Organizational Theory and Equity in the Field. In this chapter, I detail seven reasons for the importance of understanding organizational theory for leading equitable schools. I also review the organizational theories that informed the field in the past and that currently inform the field and within the organizational sciences. I then analyze the past 18 years of empirical studies that address equity and educational leadership to determine the theories that informed that research or that emerged from the research.

Chapter 3, Structural Functional Epistemology. This chapter describes the history of structural functional epistemology, its key tenets, and how educators taking a structural functional epistemology react to diversity, difference, and equity. The chapter concludes with a set of educator development activities for educators to further understand structural functional epistemology, including discussion questions and questions to guide a case analysis and critically reflect on their leadership.

Chapter 4, Interpretivist Epistemology. This chapter briefly addresses the key principles of the interpretivist epistemology and how educators taking an interpretivist epistemology react to diversity, difference, and equity. The chapter concludes with a set of educator development activities for educators to further understand the interpretivist epistemology, including discussion questions and questions to guide a case analysis and to critically reflect on their leadership.

Chapter 5, Critical Theory Epistemology. This chapter charts the history of critical theory, including its history within the field of educational leadership. The chapter describes key principles and assumptions of critical theory and how these principles and assumptions inform leadership, change, and decision-making. I then consider how educators engaged in critical theory respond to diversity and difference. The chapter briefly describes the educational leadership for social justice movement – undergirded by critical theory – along with the limitations of the literature on social justice in educational leadership.

Chapter 6, Feminist, Poststructural, and Feminist Poststructural Epistemologies. This chapter briefly discusses feminist and poststructural epistemologies, then the bulk of the chapter addresses feminist poststructural epistemologies. I consider how each of these three epistemologies can inform organizational theory and what they can contribute to educational leadership for social justice.

Chapter 7, Critical Race Theory, Black Crit. This chapter argues for CRT as a framework to guide the practices of educational leaders to eliminate racial inequities in their leading of equitable, socially just schools. I draw from the CRT in educational leadership literature, supported by related literature and explicate implications for leadership practice to eliminate racism for each CRT tenet. From this analysis,

I developed a CRT Inventory for Leading to Eliminate Racism. The Inventory suggests questions to guide leadership practice for each of the CRT tenets. The chapter closes with considerations for organizational theory and leadership, change, and decision-making.

Chapter 8, LatCrit, Tribal Crit, and Asian Crit Theories. This chapter extends the previous chapter on Critical Race Theory to examine LatCrit, Tribal Crit, and Asian Crit theories in educational leadership. Within each section, the chapter defines and describes the theory and reviews its empirical application to education and educational leadership. The final part of the chapter explores the implications of these theoretical perspectives for traditional dimensions of organizational theory. I then consider how these theories can inform new dimensions of organizational theory and describe how these perspectives can support leading equitable schools.

Chapter 9, Black Feminism and Black Feminist Epistemology. This chapter identifies themes of Black feminism that may not only inform Black female leadership but also educational leaders of all races and genders in leading to eliminate inequities. I describe the key tenets of Black feminist epistemology and review the literature in educational leadership that has drawn upon Black feminist epistemology for the theoretical framework. I consider how this literature informs theories associated with leadership, change, and decision-making. The chapter closes with considerations of how Black feminist epistemology challenges equity leadership.

Chapter 10, Disability Studies in Education Epistemology. In this chapter, I first discuss how disability has been addressed in the field of educational leadership, followed by a review of the history of Disability Studies in education, its definition, and its central tenets. I then consider the implications of DSE for the field of educational leadership and how some current research in educational leadership can inform DSE. The chapter closes with implications of DSE for organizational theory, including leadership, change, and decision-making theories.

Chapter 11, Queer Theory. This chapter briefly reviews the educational leadership literature related to LGBT identities and the use, or not, of Queer Theory in that research. The chapter identifies and discusses tenets associated with Queer Theory gleaned from the literature, reviews the history of Queer Theory in the organizational studies literature, and considers hetero-organizational culture and structures and resistance and queerness in organizations. Related to intersectionality, the chapter also briefly discusses Queer of Color theory. The chapter closes with a discussion of applications of Queer Theory to organizational theories associated with leadership, change, and decision-making. The chapter includes questions for discussion and Queer Theory case analysis questions.

Chapter 12, Intersectionality and Individual and Organizational Identity Formation toward Social Justice. This chapter addresses the relationship between the individual identity formation (e.g., racial identity formation) of educational leaders and the social justice identity formation of educational settings as organizations. The chapter addresses how the identity formations of the educational leader and other stakeholders at the individual level inform the organizational identity of the educational setting as it evolves toward equitable ends. The chapter also considers intersectionality within individual and organizational identity formation, and includes an Identity Development Inventory to assess individual and organizational identity.

SUPPORT FOR LEADERSHIP PREPARATION AND DEVELOPMENT

This book provides many features to support leadership preparation and development. At the end of Chapter 2, readers are guided to write a case study of a troubling situation that they have experienced. Each epistemology chapter that follows then includes a set of Leadership Development Activities.

These Leadership Development Activities include a set of case analysis questions for each epistemology chapter that guides readers to analyze their case from that epistemology. The Leadership Development Activities for each epistemology chapter also include a set of discussion questions for whole-class or small-group discussions. Finally, each epistemology chapter also includes a set of questions from that epistemology for readers to analyze their own leadership from that epistemology.

Each epistemology chapter includes many practical examples that apply the epistemology to practice. The book also includes two Leadership Inventories for readers to critically reflect on their own leadership and on the equity practices in their settings (Chapter 6, Critical Race Theory Inventory for Leading to Eliminate Racism, and Chapter 12, Identity Development Inventory).

Finally, deepening their understanding about the various epistemologies can help readers consider appropriate epistemologies and theories for their research. Linking the epistemologies to practice, as this book does, will also help researchers engage the epistemologies in their research in ways to advance equity in the field.

Acknowledgements

Many thanks to Heather Jarrow, Senior Editor at Routledge, for her belief in the Leadership for Equity and Diversity series which I proposed to her along with this book. I am grateful to the Department of Educational Leadership and Policy Analysis at the University of Wisconsin-Madison for their encouragement and support to teach a course on organizational theory and critical epistemologies. Much appreciation to Brittany Hisa Ota and Heather Roth, graduate students who assisted in the final manuscript preparation. I am also indebted to the University of Wisconsin-Madison students in my courses, who are leading for equity in their schools and districts, and who are now professors; all have challenged and deepened me in my work far beyond what I could do alone, and for whom I have always felt a deep responsibility to prepare them to lead for equity and conduct research that makes a difference. It is to these students – former, current, future – that this book is dedicated.

CHAPTER 1

Introduction and Epistemologies of Educational Leadership and Organizations

My introduction to organizational theory occurred in my first doctoral course at Vanderbilt University with Professor Terry Deal and his four frames of organizations (Bolman & Deal, 2017). In my book on educational administration in a pluralistic society (Capper, 1993), I wrote about how the four frames were helpful in thinking about my leadership at that time in schools in the Appalachian region of southeast Kentucky. However, after reading William Foster's work on critical theory and educational administration (Foster, 1986a), combined with my Appalachian experience, I wrote:

> I knew that the literature and research (or "stories") I had studied in educational administration, both theoretically and practically, failed to address the range of "Others" I had experienced as a teacher, administrator, and researcher. I then learned … that the stories I had been told [in graduate school] were limited to structural functionalism or to a few "interpretive" stories, the latter via my training in qualitative research methods. (Capper, 1993, p. 2)

Thus, in my 1993 book, I advocated a multiple paradigm approach to educational administration that extended beyond Bolman and Deal's four frames grounded in structural functional and interpretive epistemologies to include critically oriented epistemologies such as critical theory and feminist poststructuralism (Capper, 1993).

Understanding a range of epistemologies can help leaders/scholars determine the epistemological underpinnings of various educational practices and, in so doing, identify the limits and possibilities of those practices toward equity. For example, relying on structural functional, interpretive, and critical epistemologies, I analyzed educational practices, including Total Quality Management (Capper & Jamison, 1993a) quite similar to the current school improvement "science" movement (Bryk, Gomez, Grunow, & LeMahieu, 2015), outcomes-based education (Capper, 1994b), and site-based management (Reitzug & Capper, 1996). I also analyzed the spirituality in education literature from a critical perspective (Capper, 2005) and from a combination of structural functional, interpretive, and critical epistemologies (Capper, Keyes, & Theoharis, 2000). In addition, we conducted a critical examination of community in spiritually centered leadership for social justice (Capper, Keyes, & Hafner, 2002). With my co-authors, we also identified the epistemological conflict that leaders can face in practice from structural functional, interpretive, and critical epistemologies (Keyes, Capper, Jamison, Martin, & Opsal, 1999).

In addition to structural functional, interpretive, and critical epistemologies, I incorporated poststructural and feminist poststructural epistemologies to analyze education practices, including outcomes-based education (Capper & Jamison, 1993b), the knowledge base in educational administration (Capper, 1995), how spirituality is defined in education and leadership (Hafner & Capper, 2005), and educational assessments and accountability (Capper, Hafner, & Keyes, 2001). I also critiqued practices that were non-traditional and critical, including a feminist, poststructural critique and analysis of non-traditional theory and research in educational administration (Capper, 1992) and a poststructural critique of the critical practice of community-based interagency collaboration (Capper, 1994a; Capper, Ropers Huilman, & Hanson, 1994).

When the postmodern epistemology began to be applied in educational leadership, many scholars from traditional perspectives lumped critical theory and poststructural epistemologies together. In response, I explained the differences between critically oriented and postmodern epistemologies and how these epistemologies could be applied to leadership practice (Capper, 1998). In that same publication, under the umbrella of critically oriented perspectives, I briefly described feminist theories, Critical Race Theory, and Queer Theory.

AN EPISTEMOLOGY FRAMEWORK

With this text, I extend this previous scholarship on epistemological analysis and implications for leadership practice by addressing Critical Race Theory, Black Crit, LatCrit Theory, Asian Crit, Tribal Crit, Queer Theory, Disability Studies theories, Black feminist epistemology, and theories of intersectionality, and how these epistemologies can inform organizational theory. To provide a guide to the epistemologies, I developed a figure to represent the epistemologies featured in this book and their relationship to each other (see Figure 1.1).

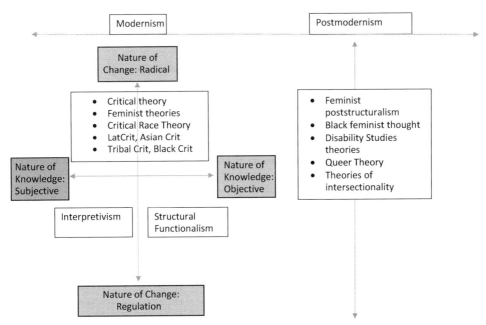

Figure 1.1 An Epistemology Framework

Arguably, drawing rigid boundaries around the epistemologies and arraying them in a heuristic requires many caveats. Using the words of Lather (1991), I recognize the limitations of such a framework:

> [I]ts system of analytic "cells" reproduces the very binary logic poststructuralism attempts to unthink; its movement is … linearity at its most bare-faced; its division of [epistemologies] is reductionist and dualistic; its central categories are reifications that are represented as pure breaks with the past … I could go on and invite you to do so. But I have found the chart a useful pedagogical tool. (p. 159)

In agreement with Lather, students have found the framework helpful as one way to identify the historical trajectory and relationship among epistemologies that they may be learning about in disparate ways in their graduate programs.

Whereas in this book I describe the unique aspects of each epistemology, the epistemologies vary in how sharply they can be defined and compared to one another. Accordingly, the parameters of the epistemologies continue to evolve and, because of the complexities of educational, organizational, and social life and the contested history of the epistemologies, any description of the epistemologies and their applications to organizational theory and leadership should not be considered final. Further, I selected these epistemologies based on their salience to organizations, leadership, education, and equity, but others could argue for differing typologies (English, 1993; Sirotnik & Oakes, 1986).

The epistemological framework begins with Burrell and Morgan's (2003) sociological theory framework aligned along two axes. The horizontal axis represents the nature of science or the nature of knowledge (i.e., epistemology, or how we come to know or entire systems of knowing) from objective at one end of the continuum to subjective at the other. The vertical axis represents the nature of change – at the bottom of the continuum the nature of change remains oriented to regulation; at the top end of the continuum the nature of change is considered to be radical toward social justice ends.

At this top end of the radical change continuum, Burrell and Morgan differentiated between the right quadrant of radical change associated with the objective nature of knowledge (radical structuralism) and the left quadrant of radical change associated with the subjective nature of knowledge (radical humanism). For our purposes, instead of parsing these differences, we will examine critically oriented epistemologies anchored in radical change that extend across the subjective/objective nature of knowledge.

To orient the reader to the differing epistemologies and to each associated chapter in the book, I next provide a quite brief overview of each epistemology, akin to riding a motorcycle through an art gallery. Each chapter that follows goes into detail about each epistemology.

Structural Functionalism

Beginning on the right lower quadrant, if the nature of knowledge is objective (horizontal axis) and the nature of change is oriented toward regulation (vertical axis), then the overarching epistemology and associated theories are structural functional (Chapter 3). The primary goal of structural functionalist epistemology focuses on efficiency. Bolman and Deal's (2017) structural frame, bureaucracy, top-down leadership, positivism, and quantitative research methods not oriented toward equity reflect the structural functional epistemology.

Interpretivism

In the lower left quadrant, when the nature of knowledge is subjective (horizontal axis) and the nature of change is oriented to regulation (vertical axis), then this combination describes the interpretivist epistemology (Chapter 4) – the goal of which centers on understanding. Theories of human relations, Bolman and Deal's (2017) human resources frame, and qualitative research methods that do not address equity all emanate from the interpretivist epistemology. Although interpretivist epistemologies with their focus on participation and human relations are often considered the antidote to structural functionalism, both epistemologies ignore privilege, power, identity, oppression, equity, and social justice. As described in Chapter 2, nearly all theories of organizations are grounded in structural functionalist or interpretivist epistemologies.

Critically Oriented Epistemologies

Moving to the top part of the change axis, the epistemologies located here are all focused on radical change toward justice and what I have termed "critically oriented epistemologies" (Capper, 1998, p. 354). Critical theory originated first among these epistemologies (Chapter 5). Foster (1986a, 1986b) initiated the application of critical theory to educational leadership. Theories of social justice, equity, and critical qualitative research methods originate out of critical theory.

Citing the limits of critical theory relative to gender and then race, feminist theories (Chapter 6) and Critical Race Theory (CRT) (Chapter 7) followed. Ladson-Billings and Tate (1995) applied CRT to education for the first time, and López (2003) considered CRT implications for educational leadership, the first scholar to do so. Most recently, Black Crit has emerged as one critique of CRT (Dumas & ross, 2016). All these epistemologies at the top end of the radical change continuum claim social justice as the ultimate goal (a term I will critique in Chapter 5 on critical theory). Importantly, all the debates between quantitative and qualitative research methods – the former anchored in structural functionalism, the latter in interpretivism – have ignored critical approaches to research methods that emanate from the radical change end of the continuum and critically oriented epistemologies.

In response to the limitations of CRT in legal studies, LatCrit and Asian Crit emerged, which were then applied to education along with Tribal Crit (Chapter 8). Building on the limitations of feminism and feminist poststructuralism, Black feminist epistemology emerged (Chapter 9).

The Modernism/Postmodernism Continuum

All the epistemologies discussed thus far – structural functionalism, interpretivism, critically oriented epistemologies, including critical theory, feminist theory, Critical Race Theory, LatCrit Theory, Tribal Crit, Asian Crit, and Black Crit Theory – are all grounded in modernist thought on the modernism/postmodernism continuum. Although all these epistemologies have fundamentally different origins and goals, they all share some commonalities. Modernism considers knowledge along a continuum from objective to socially constructed. Within modernism, power is conceived as all or nothing whether power is authoritarian (structural functionalism) or empowering (critically oriented) – a person either holds power or does not, a person either experiences oppression or does not. Educators in modernist approaches believe that individuals have an essential nature, which remains stable, fully aware, or in need of others to bring forth this awareness. Whether educators initiate change in a top-down fashion (structural functionalism) or as a result of considering multiple perspectives (interpretivism) or dialogue (critical theory), educators taking modernist approaches agree that change evolves in either incremental or radical ways, both linked to ideas of cause and effect.

Postmodern/poststructural epistemologies (though these terms differ, for our purposes consider them similar) were initially considered in educational leadership in the late 1980s and early 1990s (Anderson, 1990; English, 1998). Rather than working toward a goal in terms of change, a poststructural epistemology calls into question the end-point itself – whether the goal focuses on efficiency (structural functionalism), understanding (interpretivism), or social change (critically oriented epistemologies). With an interest in the complexities of decision-making and dissensus, a poststructural epistemology questions decision-making associated with dialogue and consensus that can oversimplify and mask power inequities and create an illusion of community. Rather than viewing power as all or nothing in modernist epistemologies, poststructural epistemologies view power as complex, plural, decentralized, and complex (see Chapter 6 which compares and contrasts feminist, poststructural, and feminist poststructural epistemologies).

Additional epistemologies emerged in response to the limitations of critically oriented epistemologies and postmodern epistemologies – all of which combine aspects of the two. Feminist theorists disagreed with many aspects of critical theory and postmodern philosophy; thus feminist poststructuralism emerged (Chapter 6). Given the timing of the emergence of poststructuralism, scholars of Disability Studies theories (Chapter 10) and Queer Theory (Chapter 11) have been strongly influenced by postmodern thought, and the tenets of these two epistemologies reflect that influence.

Theories of intersectionality arose with the work of legal scholar Crenshaw (1991). Although scholars in educational leadership are beginning to consider how educational leaders need to lead across student differences (Frattura & Capper, 2007; Scanlan & Theoharis, 2015), theories of intersectionality have yet to be applied to organizational theory and educational leadership for equity (Chapter 12).

TERMINOLOGY

In this section, I sort out the terminology related to organizational theory, including epistemology, theory, perspectives, and paradigm. I also problematize the terms diversity and social justice.

Paradigms/Perspectives/Epistemologies

Traditionally, scholars have referred to a constellation of theories as those which comprise a paradigm (Burrell & Morgan, 1982). In my earlier scholarship, I preferred the term "perspectives" to "paradigm" because, influenced by the work of Lather (1991) and Cherryholmes (1988), I found that the term "paradigm" itself denoted rigid, impermeable boundaries within the modernist tradition. I chose the term "perspective" at that time in agreement with Best and Kellner's (1991) definition:

> A perspective is a way of seeing, a vantage point or optic to analyze specific phenomena. The term perspective suggests that one's optic or analytic frame never mirrors reality exactly as it is, that it is always selective and unavoidably

mediated by one's pregiven assumptions, theories, values, and interests. The notion of perspective also implies that no one optic can ever fully illuminate the richness and complexity of any single phenomenon … (p. 265)

I now prefer the term "epistemology" in addition to "perspective." Epistemology has typically been defined as how a person comes to know or the nature of knowledge, but Ladson-Billings (1998) reminds us that an epistemology reflects an entire societal system of knowing and what counts as knowledge and who counts in creating that knowledge. For example, according to Anzaldúa:

> Theory, then, is a set of knowledges. Some of these knowledges have been kept from us and entry into some professions and academia denied us. Because we are not allowed to enter discourse, because we are often disqualified and excluded from it, because what passes for theory these days is forbidden territory for us, it is vital that we occupy theorizing space, that we not allow whitemen and women solely to occupy it. By bringing in our own approaches and methodologies, we transform that theorizing space. (Anzaldúa, 1990, p. xxv, in Solórzano & Yosso, 2001, p. 488)

Brayboy (2005) expands on the relationship between our personal identities and personal stories and theory:

> I once had an encounter with a colleague who told me that people like me "told good stories" and later added that because I told good stories, I might not ever be a "good theorist." I was struck by the seeming disconnect between community stories and personal narratives and "theory." I returned home to Prospect, North Carolina, one of the communities of the Lumbee tribe of which I am an enrolled member, and told several of my relatives and elders about my colleagues' comments. My mother told me, "Baby, doesn't she know that our stories are our theories? And she thinks she's smarter than you because she can't tell stories?" My mother clearly hit on the reason why locating theory as something absent from stories and practices is problematic in many Indigenous communities and in the work of anthropologists who seek to represent Indigenous communities. (Brayboy, 2005, p. 426)

Donnor and Ladson-Billings (2018) concur: "… we contend that all [emphasis in the original] scholars are 'telling a story'" (p. 196).

Thus, understanding different epistemologies is not as simple as "flipping frames" that Bolman and Deal (2017) advocate. The range of epistemologies I lay out in this book are not simple analytical lenses that one can easily put on or take off at will to understand organizational phenomena. Instead, each of the epistemologies captures an entire worldview, history, and systems, inseparable from an individual's intersecting identities. As James Banks (1993) more simply states, "all knowledge reflects the values and interests of its creators" (p. 4, cited in Scheurich & Young, 1997, p. 8).

Critical Theory and Epistemology

I also distinguish between what I term "critically oriented epistemologies" and critical theory (Capper, 1998, p. 358). Critically oriented epistemologies include all epistemologies at the radical change toward justice end of the continuum of change. Critically oriented epistemologies include critical theory, feminist theory, feminist poststructuralism, Critical Race Theory, LatCrit, Asian Crit, Tribal Crit, Black Crit, Queer Theory, Disability Studies theories, Black feminist epistemology, and theories of intersectionality. Some scholars advocate critical theory as the overarching epistemological umbrella over all other critically oriented epistemologies, yet as the succeeding chapters make clear, though nearly all critically oriented epistemologies share some commonalities, their history and details remain unique. To repeat Banks, even among critically oriented epistemologies, "all knowledge reflects the values and interests of its creators" (p. 4, cited in Scheurich & Young, 1997, p. 8). As explained in Chapter 5, critical theory was formed within the Frankfurt School of thought in Germany out of Marxism, developed by intellectually elite white males (sexuality unknown). Thus, to claim that critical theory speaks for all critically oriented epistemologies remains an affront to all identities and associated epistemologies who stand outside the white, male norm. Many of the succeeding critically oriented epistemologies arose due in part to the limitations of critical theory.

While epistemologies are an overarching knowledge system, scholars have created numerous theories within the epistemologies – primarily within structural functionalism and interpretivism. Nearly all organizational theories reside within the structural functional epistemology, and many organizational theories span structural functional and interpretivist epistemologies. Thus, epistemology is the overarching knowledge system umbrella with theories as smaller explanatory units within those epistemologies.

The epistemologies associated with critically oriented epistemologies all tend to be referred to as "theories." (e.g., critical theory, Critical Race Theory, feminist theory, Queer Theory, Disability Studies theories, etc.), and at the opposite end of modernism is postmodern theory. However, though their given name includes the term "theory," these "theories" operate as epistemologies. For example, critical race scholars refer to Critical Race Theory as an epistemology – as an overarching knowledge system (Delgado Bernal, 2002; Parker & Lynn, 2002).

The fewer number of theories within the critically oriented epistemologies relative to the plethora of theories within structural functionalism and interpretivism reflects perhaps the maturity of the field. A few theories have emerged within critical theory epistemology, such as Habermas and associated Habermasian theory (Foster, 1980), social justice theories (Rawls, 1986), and, relative to educational leadership, a theory of resistance in social justice leadership (Theoharis, 2007). Within LatCrit theory, Huber (2010) developed racist nativism. Over time, as scholars and educators continue to apply critically oriented epistemologies to education, organizations, and leadership, additional theories will emerge within these critically oriented epistemologies, as I review in the leadership for equity literature in Chapter 2.

"Paradigm Shifts"

Often, educators will argue that a particular educational practice represents a "paradigm shift," when, in fact, the practice may only represent a move from one theory to another within one epistemology – usually within either structural functional or interpretive epistemologies. Poplin and Stone (1992) further explain that claiming a paradigm shift:

> is [sometimes] misleading in that it creates the illusion that we are examining our ultimate paradigmatic assumptions, whereas in fact we are only referring to variation in theory within an existing paradigm, while leaving epistemological values and beliefs firmly in place. (p. 154)

This phenomenon is especially true in education where initiatives and practices are touted as "new" or "transformative" when in fact they originate out of the same structural functionalist or interpretivist epistemologies as previous failed practices. One goal of this book is that by understanding a range of epistemologies, educators will be able to analyze any existing leadership preparation program course, educational practice, book, or professional development opportunity and determine the underlying epistemology and the extent to which these phenomena address equity or social justice and further discern the limits and possibilities of work that claims to be "equity" work.

Equity/Social Justice

This text also problematizes the terms "equity," "social justice," and "diversity." In Chapter 5, I discuss the evolution of critical theory to social justice scholarship in educational leadership and I detail the limitations of both critical theory and social justice in the field. The term "diversity" has often been appropriated to primarily mean race without having to talk about race (Chapter 7), and without having to discuss any other aspects of identity and difference such as those related to sexuality, gender identity, ability, among others and their intersections. Yet, I deliberately chose the word "diversity" in the book title instead of the phrase "critically oriented epistemologies" as a symbol and substance to draw in a range of readers, including educators in practice.

Combining Epistemologies?

Scholars over the years have attempted to combine various epistemologies to view organizations and education. As previously mentioned, Burrell and Morgan (1982) developed a multiple paradigm approach to the study of organizations. Burrell and Morgan categorized organizational theory into four paradigms: structural functional, interpretive, radical humanism, and radical structuralism. Gioia and Pitre (1990) relied on Burrell and Morgan's framework to describe a multiple paradigm view of theory building, and Hassard (1991) demonstrated how to use all four paradigms in research on organizations. Sirotnik and Oakes (1986) grounded their rendition of critical inquiry in schools in a combination of structural functionalism, interpretivism, and critical theory. Popkewitz (1984) also explains these same three epistemologies and their utility for education research.

Scholars have also demonstrated how different epistemological approaches to a similar research topic can yield different understandings and interpretations of data. For example, Bensimon (1989) reframed her data analysis related to university leadership from structural functional/interpretive epistemologies to feminist epistemologies. Bensimon demonstrated how viewing data from different epistemologies not only reveals different findings, but also how structural functional and interpretivist epistemologies masked gender oppression. Lather (1991) analyzed data generated from journals and interviews with students in women's studies courses to juxtapose four epistemologies against each other and against the data, spinning four "tales": realist, critical, deconstructivist, and reflexive. Cherryholmes (1993) reframed research on reciprocal teaching of comprehension conducted by Palincsar and Brown (1984) viewing the data from four epistemologies: feminist theory, critical theory, deconstruction, and critical pragmatism.

Social theorists and education scholars are not unanimous in their support of Burrell and Morgan's (1982) four paradigm conceptualization of organizational theory or, indeed, in their belief that these paradigms even exist (Evers & Lakomski, 1991). Some theorists and scholars, including Burrell and Morgan (1982), give credence to the paradigms, but believe they cannot be used together to view a situation, that they are incommensurable (Foster, 1986a; Jackson & Carter, 1991; Parker & McHugh, 1991). These scholars argue that these four paradigms are incommensurable not only because they are constituted by differing epistemologies, ontologies, and methodologies and their associated language, but also because they have fundamentally different goals.

When I first advocated a "multiparadigm approach" toward educational administration (Capper, 1993), I believed that the four epistemologies I featured at that time (structural functionalism, interpretivism, critical theory, and feminist poststructuralism) could and should be relied on together to most effectively address "educational administration in a pluralistic society" (p. 27). I no longer believe that structural functional and interpretivist epistemologies can be joined with critically oriented epistemologies to view or analyze organizations or to guide leadership practice. These epistemologies are ultimately incommensurable because, as we will see in the forthcoming chapters, these epistemologies all have fundamentally different histories, worldviews, and goals.

More explicitly, to date, structural functional and interpretive epistemologies have been presented as ideologically neutral epistemologies. However, I argue in this book that these two epistemologies not only do not advance social justice, but are also strategic instruments of oppression and as such these epistemologies are racist, classist, sexist, homophobic, transphobic, and nativist all under the guise of neutrality (Scheurich & Young, 1998).

Can or should critically oriented epistemologies be relied on in tandem to address organizational theory and educational inequities? That question has been answered with contemporary scholars unearthing intersectional marginalization by combining, for example, Disability Studies in Education with Critical Race Theory for a theory of DisCrit (Annamma, Connor, & Ferri, 2013), or Queer Theory and Critical Race Theory in Queer of Color Theory (Ferguson, 2004), all discussed in Chapter 12 on organizational theories and theories of intersectionality.

SUMMARY

The history of organizational theory itself and within educational leadership has privileged particular worldviews and marginalized others. This book conveys the importance of our identities and the identities of others along race, class, gender, ability, language, sexual identity, gender identity and expression, and their intersections in relation to organizational theory. In Chapter 12, I discuss the relationship between individual identity development along dimensions of difference, the social justice leadership identity development and practices of social justice leaders, and educational settings as organizations as they evolve toward social justice ends. First, we turn to Chapter 2 to explore the importance of understanding organizational theories and critical epistemologies for leading equitable schools, and to examine the history of organizational theory and equity in the field.

REFERENCES

Anderson, G. (1990). Toward a critical constructivist approach to school administration: Invisibility, legitimation, and the study of non-events. *Educational Administrative Quarterly, 26*(1), 38–59.

Annamma, S.A., Connor, D., & Ferri, B. (2013). Dis/ability Critical Race Studies (DisCrit): Theorizing at the intersections of race and dis/ability. *Race Ethnicity and Education, 16*(1), 1–31.

Anzaldúa, G. (1990). *Making face, making soul/hacienda caras: Creative and critical perspectives by feminists of color*. San Francisco, CA: Aunt Lute Books.

Banks, J.A. (1993). The canon debate, knowledge construction, and multicultural education. *Educational Researcher, 22*(5), 4–14.

Bensimon, E.M. (1989). A feminist reinterpretation of presidents' definitions of leadership. *Peabody Journal of Education, 66*(3), 143–156.

Best, S. & Kellner, D. (1991). *Postmodern theory; Critical interrogations*. New York: Guilford Press.

Bolman, L. & Deal, T. (2017). *Reframing organizations: Artistry, choice, and leadership* (6th edn). San Francisco, CA: Jossey-Bass.

Brayboy, B.M.J. (2005). Toward a Tribal Critical Race Theory in education. *The Urban Review, 37*(5), 425–446.

Bryk, A., Gomez, L.M., Grunow, A., & LeMahieu, P.G. (2015). *Learning to improve: How America's schools can get better at betting better*. Cambridge, MA: Harvard University Press.

Burrell, G. & Morgan, G. (1982). *Sociological paradigms and organizational analysis.* London: Heinemann.

Burrell, G. & Morgan, G. (2003). *Sociological paradigms and organisational analysis: Elements of the sociology of corporate life.* Burlington, VT: Ashgate.

Capper, C.A. (1992). A feminist, poststructural critique and analysis of non-traditional theory and research in educational administration. *Educational Administration Quarterly, 28*(1), 103–124.

Capper, C.A. (Ed.). (1993). *Educational administration in a pluralistic society.* Albany, NY: State University of New York Press.

Capper, C.A. (1994a). "We're not housed in an institution, we're housed in the community:" Possibilities and consequences of neighborhood-based interagency collaboration. *Educational Administration Quarterly, 30*(3), 237–277.

Capper, C.A. (1994b). "… And justice for all": Critical perspectives on outcomes-based education in the context of secondary school restructuring. *Journal of School Leadership, 4*(2), 132–155.

Capper, C. A. (1995). An otherist poststructural perspective of the knowledge base in educational administration. In R. Donmoyer and J. J. Scheurich (Eds.), *The knowledge base in educational administration: Multiple perspectives* (pp. 287–301). Albany, NY: State University of New York Press.

Capper, C.A. (1998). Critically oriented and postmodern perspectives: Sorting out the differences and applications for practice. *Educational Administration Quarterly, 34*(3), 354–379.

Capper, C.A. (2005). Moving beyond the spiritual Jacuzzi in education leadership: Spiritualities, epistemologies, and social justice. *Journal of Curriculum and Pedagogy, 2*(2), 96–99.

Capper, C.A. (2015). The 20th-year anniversary of Critical Race Theory in education: Implications for leading to eliminate racism. *Educational Administration Quarterly, 51*(5), 791–833.

Capper, C.A. & Jamison, M.T. (1993a). Outcomes-based education re-examined: From structural functionalism to poststructuralism. *Educational Policy, 7*(4), 427–446.

Capper, C. A. & Jamison, M.T. (1993b). Let the buyer beware! Total quality management and educational research and practice. *Educational Researcher, 22*(8), 25–30.

Capper, C.A., Hafner, M.M., & Keyes, M.W. (2001). Moving beyond good/bad accountability measures: Multiple perspectives of accountability. *Journal of School Leadership, 11*(3), 204–216.

Capper, C.A., Keyes, M.W., & Hafner, M.M. (2002). The role of community in spiritually centered leadership for justice. In G. Furman (Ed.), *School as community: From promise to practice* (pp. 77–94). Albany, NY: State University of New York Press.

Capper, C.A., Keyes, M.W., & Theoharis, G.T. (2000). Spirituality in leadership: Implications for inclusive schooling. In J. Thousand and R. Villa (Eds), *Restructuring for caring and effective education: Piecing the puzzle together* (pp. 513–530). Baltimore, MD: Brookes.

Capper, C.A., Ropers Huilman, B., & Hanson, S. (1994). Community-based interagency collaboration: A poststructural interruption of critical practices. *Journal of Educational Policy, 9*(4), 335–351.

Cherryholmes, C.H. (1988). *Power and criticism: Poststructural investigations in education.* New York: Teachers College Press.

Cherryholmes, C.H. (1993). Reading research. *Journal of Curriculum Studies, 25*(1), 1–32.

Crenshaw, K.W. (1991). Mapping the margins: Intersectionality, identity politics, and violence against women of color. *Stanford Law Review, 43*(6), 1241–1299.

Delgado Bernal, D. (2002). Critical race theory, Latino critical theory, and critical raced-gendered epistemologies: Recognizing students of color as holders and creators of knowledge. *Qualitative Inquiry, 8*, 103–124.

Donnor, J.K. & Ladson-Billings, G. (2018). Critical race theory and the postracial imaginary. In N.K. Denzin and Y.S. Lincoln (Eds), *The Sage handbook of qualitative research* (pp. 195–213). Thousand Oaks, CA: Sage.

Dumas, M. J., & ross, k. m. (2016). "Be real Black for me": Imagining BlackCrit in education. *Urban Education, 51*(4), 415–442.

English, F. (1993). *Discourse and theory in educational administration.* New York: Harper/Collins.

English, F.W. (1998). The postmodern turn in educational administration: Apostrophic or catastrophic development? *Journal of School Leadership, 8*(5), 426–447.

Evers, C.E. & Lakomski, G. (1991). *Knowing educational Administration: Contemporary methodological controversies in educational administration research.* Elmsford, New York: Pergamon Press.

Ferguson, R.A. (2004). *Aberrations in Black: Toward a queer of color critique* (Critical American studies series). Minneapolis, MN: University of Minnesota Press.

Foster, W.P. (1980). Administration and the crisis in legitimacy: A review of Habermasian thought. *Harvard Educational Review, 50*(4), 496–505.

Foster, W.P. (1986a). *Paradigms and promises: New approaches to educational administration.* Buffalo, NY: Prometheus Books.

Foster, W.P. (1986b). Toward a critical theory of educational administration. In T.J. Serqiovanni and J.E. Corbally (Eds), *Leadership and organizational culture.* Urbana, IL: University of Illinois Press.

Frattura, E. & Capper, C.A. (2007). *Leading for social justice: Transforming schools for all learners.* Thousand Oaks, CA: Corwin Press.

Gioia, D.A. & Pitre, E. (1990). Multiparadigm perspectives on theory building. *Academy of management review, 15*(4), 584–602.

Hafner, M. & Capper, C.A. (2005). Defining spirituality: Critical implications for the practice and research of educational leadership. *Journal of School Leadership, 15*(6), 624–638.

Hassard, J. (1991). Multiple paradigms and organizational analysis: A case study. *Organization Studies, 12*(2), 275–299.

Huber, L.P. (2010). Using Latina/o Critical Race Theory (LatCrit) and Racist Nativism to explore intersectionality in the educational experiences of undocumented Chicana college students. *Educational Foundations, 24*(1), 77–96.

Jackson, N. & Carter, P. (1991). In defense of paradigm incommensurability. *Organization Studies, 12*(1), 109–127.

Keyes, M.W., Capper, C.A., Jamison, M., Martin, J., & Opsal, C. (1999). Tradition and alternative in educational practice: Three stories of epistemological conflict. *Journal for a Just and Caring Education, 5*(4), 502–519.

Ladson-Billings, G. (1998). Just what is critical race theory and what's it doing in a nice field like education? *Qualitative Studies in Education, 11*(1), 7–24.

Ladson-Billings, G., & Tate, W.F., IV. (1995). Toward a critical race theory of education. *Teachers College Record, 97*(1), 47–68.

Lather, P. (1991). *Getting smart: Feminist research and pedagogy with/in the postmodern.* New York: Routledge.

López, G.R. (2003). The (racially neutral) politics of education: A critical race theory perspective. *Educational Administration Quarterly, 39*(1), 68–94.

Palincsar, A.S. & Brown, A.L. (1984). Reciprocal teaching of comprehension-fostering and comprehension-monitoring activities. *Cognition and instruction*, *1*(2), 117–175.

Parker, L. & Lynn, M. (2002). What's race got to do with it? Critical Race Theory's conflicts with and connections to qualitative research methodology and epistemology. *Qualitative Inquiry*, *8*(1), 7–22.

Parker, M. & McHugh, G. (1991). Five texts in search of an author: A response to John Hassard's "Multiple paradigms and organizational analysis". *Organization Studies*, *12*(3), 451–456.

Popkewitz, T.S. (1984). *Paradigm and ideology in educational research: The social functions of the intellectual*. London and New York: The Falmer Press.

Poplin, M.S. & Stone, S. (1992). *Paradigm shifts in instructional strategies: From reductionism to holistic/constructivism*. In W. Stainback & S. Stainback (Eds), *Controversial issues confronting special education: Divergent perspectives* (pp. 153–179). Needham Heights, MA: Allyn and Bacon.

Rawls, J. (1986). *A theory of justice*. Cambridge, MA: Belknap Press of Harvard University Press.

Reitzug, R. & Capper, C.A. (1996). Deconstructing site-based management: Possibilities for emancipation and alternative means of control. *Journal of Educational Administration, 5*(1), 56–59.

Scanlan, M. & Theoharis, G. (2015). *Leadership for increasingly diverse schools*. New York: Routledge.

Scheurich, J.J. & Young, M.D. (1998). Coloring epistemologies: Are our research epistemologies racially biased? *Educational Researcher, 26*(4), 4–16.

Sirotnik, K.A. & Oakes, J. (1986). *Critical perspectives on the organization and improvement of schooling*. Boston, MA: Kluwer-Nijhoff.

Solórzano, D. & Yosso, T. (2001). Critical race and LatCrit theory and method: Counterstorytelling. *International Journal of Qualitative Studies in Education, 14*(4), 471–495.

Theoharis, G. (2007). Social justice educational leaders and resistance: Toward a theory of social justice leadership. *Educational Administration Quarterly, 43*(2), 221–258.

CHAPTER 2

History of Organizational Theory and Equity in the Field[1]

Some may question why it is important for current and prospective educational leaders committed to equity to learn about organizational theories. This question may be asked especially when, as I discuss in a later section, current organizational theory texts in education and educational leadership are grounded primarily in structural functionalism and do not address the range of epistemologies and theories. Put another way, how are theories that are typically written by "White guys who are now dead based on studies of White guys who are also now dead" relevant to the complexity of leading integrated, socially just educational settings with demographically diverse students, staff, families, and community members?

In addition, current or prospective educational leaders committed to equity are well aware of the sense of urgency needed to overcome the persistent and pervasive inequities in education; that indeed, students are struggling in K-12 schools, and the entire rest of these students' existence is being determined by the decisions and non-decisions of educational leaders. Leaders need proactive strategies and practices they can implement now in their educational settings. Young students who are struggling cannot wait. Given this dire sense of urgency, is it time well invested or wasted in understanding organizational theories?

Hatch and Cunliffe (2006) in their text that addresses organizational theories across three epistemologies argue that students of organizational theory cannot expect a simple list of "how-tos" to immediately emerge from their study of theory.

> I believe a great deal of the frustration with organization theory that many students and practitioners report feeling is the result of not recognizing that the application of theory is a creative act. A belief that abstract theory can generate

> instant solutions to specific problems is naïve. It is equally naïve to reject theory as having little value simply because you have not yet learned how to use it. Theory is better suited to raising important questions at critical moments and reminding you what relevant knowledge is available, than it is to providing ready-made answers to your problems. Use theory as a tool to help you reason through complex situations; do not expect it to guarantee your success. (Hatch & Cunliffe, 2006, p. 10)

As such, Hatch and Cunliffe (2006) admonish that students of organizational theory cannot expect to be "spoon-fed" organizational theories and to sit back and let the instructor identify a bulleted list of leadership practices extracted from the theories. Instead, the study of organizational theories and their associated epistemologies demands a "creative act" from the student, to intellectually dig deep in the direct study of the theories and in the critical reflection about the theories as it relates to their practice.

Given this "creative act" expected of prospective and current educational leaders, these leaders should be introduced to the wide range of epistemologies and their associated theories as discussed in this book. I identified seven benefits in response to the question: How can understanding organizational theories develop leader capacity for integrated, socially just educational settings?

BENEFITS OF ORGANIZATIONAL THEORY FOR SOCIAL JUSTICE LEADERSHIP

First, studying organizational theories that extend beyond structural functionalism and interpretivism pushes students' intellectual thinking or "stretches the mind." In the introduction to their organizational theory text, Hatch and Cunliffe (2006) note, "Organization theory draws on the sciences, the humanities and the arts, and so presents the intellectual challenge of thinking in interdisciplinary ways" (p. 3). Educators expect staff to routinely challenge students with a rigorous, intellectually rich curriculum. Yet, educational leaders in the midst of their day-to-day work may intellectually drift, their leadership informed by a bland intellectual diet consisting of practitioner publications that most often align with status quo thinking. Because of their epistemological unconsciousness (described later in the chapter), practitioners often fail to realize that what is touted as "new" or "innovative" in education often emanates from status quo (i.e., structural functional) epistemologies. Thus, the interdisciplinary basis of organizational theories can expand equity leaders' intellectual capacity beyond the field of education.

This critically oriented intellectual challenge and continual learning about these theories can sustain leaders in the long haul and can alleviate burnout. In some ways, continued learning about organizational theories can be an intellectual break that is a relief from the rigors of daily equity leadership. At the same time, what leaders learn during the intellectual respite from their day-to-day work can inform their practice in new ways. As such, the study of organizational theories does not necessarily require leaders step out of their practice. In contrast, studying organizational theories can engage leaders in their leadership practice more deeply, and in so doing facilitate leaders' critical mindfulness about their life and work.

(2) Second, studying organizational theory can teach prospective educational leaders to examine the larger context, or "bigger picture" within which their work is taking place. Being able to step back from day-to-day leading can help leaders not take personally the inevitable resistance to their social justice efforts (Theoharis, 2007). Being able to step back from day-to-day leading and examine the larger context of the educational setting can also help leaders see their educational setting as a complex system of interrelated aspects. In so doing, taking a larger perspective on their educational setting as an organization can help leaders see how the different aspects of the organization do and should work together. Understanding differing epistemologies and their associated theories can help leaders mentally organize aspects of the educational setting into coherent groups. For example, when considering moving toward more equitable outcomes, leaders may consider power, politics, culture, and structure among other organizational aspects.

Relatedly, possessing an understanding of organizational theories and their originating epistemologies can help leaders see the epistemological similarities across seemingly differing phenomena within their educational setting, and, in so doing can be made aware of and do something about contradictions in practice. For example, some principals include students with disabilities, but exclude or segregate students who are bilingual and, even while doing so, claim they are an inclusive school. Likewise, some educational leaders claim they are an inclusive school while including some students with disabilities and segregating students with significant intellectual disabilities. A third example in public school settings is applying strict punishment to students who make a racially offensive comment, but ignoring students who make comments such as "that's so gay." One explanation for these contradictions in leadership practice is the inability of leaders to see the conceptual and philosophical similarities in practice across student differences, or to see the ways in which their practice contradicts their equity beliefs.

(3) Third, having an understanding of organizational theories and their associated epistemologies can provide leaders who care about equity and excellence with intellectual and analytical tools to be able to dissect and make sense of the complexities of their work. Hatch and Cunliffe (2006) agree with this benefit, and testify that "Organization theory has helped me time and again to analyze complicated situations in the organizations with which I have worked, and to discover or invent effective and creative means for dealing with them" (p. 3).

(4) Fourth, understanding organizational theories from a range of different epistemologies can provide a new set of introspective lenses for educational leaders. Indeed, educational leaders can learn that the act of introspection itself is conducted differently and demands a different set of questions of the self, depending on which epistemological lens the leader is using. As such, organizational theories can serve as a means for equity leaders to engage in their work, not as distant administrators,

but to recognize their leadership as autobiographical; that how leaders lead is deeply reflective of their own life and identity development.

Fifth, understanding organizational theories across epistemologies can help leaders become conscious of the epistemologies that guide their values and leadership practices. This epistemological consciousness can help leaders realize that they have been living and working from particular epistemological perspectives, or have evolved through perspectives, and that those perspectives have a distinct name. This epistemological consciousness also helps leaders identify and gain support from others who lead or live from similar perspectives.

At the same time, this epistemological self-consciousness helps leaders begin to understand the epistemologies that inform the values and actions of others. Hence, for example, when leaders experience resistance to their equity efforts, rather than viewing the resistance as personal either to the leader or from the individuals who resist, and rather than viewing the resistance from others as monolithic and immutable, leaders can understand the epistemological similarities and differences in the resistance to help guide their decisions in how to respond and how to be proactive. Relatedly, having an understanding of epistemological orientations that may differ from one's own preferred orientations can help equity leaders be less fearful of and be able to find avenues of collaboration with individuals who may have epistemological perspectives different from their own perspectives.

Sixth, learning about varying epistemologies and their associated theories can help leaders realize that there are commonalities across all organizations, regardless of purpose or structure (e.g., from the Epic medical record corporation based in Verona, Wisconsin to an Alcoholics Anonymous group that meets once a week in a church basement). The formation and function of nearly all organizations, regardless of moral purpose, requires consideration of human resources, a structure, a decision-making process, roles and responsibilities, and a culture among others. Having an understanding of these similarities and differences can motivate equity leaders to learn from others about their organizations, how they work, how people are rewarded or motivated, the unique culture of that organization, how people are trained, hired, supported, how diversity and difference are addressed or not, whether the organization has a goal to make society better or not, how leadership is addressed and cultivated, and how all these aspects vary by country or geographic location in the United States. Educational leaders for social justice can benefit from learning about these different organizations – profit and nonprofit, loosely structured, and not – lessons that can inform the leading of integrated, socially just educational settings.

Finally, knowing critically oriented epistemologies can help equity leaders understand that there are common experiences across leaders working toward equity and excellence. These shared experiences can be generalized across equity leaders and contribute to theories about this experience; that what the equity leader is doing or experiencing is not an isolated situation. This shared understanding can move leaders beyond the sense of being an "N of 1" individual, isolated as a social justice leader making this particular equity decision. Instead, a web of epistemological and theoretical interconnectedness can be woven among equity-oriented leaders. In this way, for example, equity leaders can know that how the change process unfolds in their settings may not be a random happening of events, but is somewhat predictable based on others' experiences.

In sum, understanding organizational theories and their associated epistemologies can significantly contribute to developing leader capacity for integrated, socially just schools. Given this relevancy context, I will next discuss the status of organizational theory in the past and present.

Summary

ORGANIZATIONAL THEORIES THAT INFORMED THE FIELD IN THE PAST

HISTORY

More than two decades ago, Nicolaides and Gaynor (1992) examined "the knowledge base of administrative and organizational theory that currently informs doctoral administrator preparation programs in the member universities of the University Council for Educational Administration (UCEA)" (p. 240), After soliciting syllabi from faculty who teach organizational theory in the 50 universities that were UCEA members at the time, the authors narrowed their review to 36 syllabi (11 of these syllabi were courses taught by white women). They concluded that:

> [T]he course content [of these syllabi] subscribes to a perspective that socializes graduates intellectually and theoretically to mainstream interpretations of educational administration. … [T]eaching in these courses is limited to topics and themes shaped by traditional perspectives. … Alternative perspectives … were neither systematically or consistently incorporated into the courses examined. Issues such as those dealing with race, gender, ethnicity, and social class were underrepresented. (Nicolaides & Gaynor, 1992, pp. 262–263)

More specifically, Nicolaides and Gaynor (1992) found that "Only 5 of the 36 syllabi" addressed gender. Only a few of the syllabi cited authors who wrote from perspectives other than structural functionalism (e.g., interpretive or critical theories) (we will learn the details of all the epistemological perspectives named here in the forthcoming chapters), and only one syllabus addressed leaders of color (p. 256). The authors also noticed that a trend toward critical theory was more apparent in the readings, course objectives, and topical outlines prepared by the 11 female professors than in the majority of those developed by the 55 male professors. All 11 female professors participating in the study included topics, subtopics, and required readings on women as educators, though these readings were only of white women (e.g., Gilligan, 1982; Lincoln, 1985; Shakeshaft, 1987; Silver, 1978), and only a few women addressed individuals of color. In sum, Nicolaides and Gaynor agreed with Griffiths (1988) in stating that "one finds the same kind of theory being espoused as 24 years ago – positivism" (cited in Nicolaides & Gaynor, 1992, p. 238). Now fast forward to 2018, nearly three decades after Nicolaides and Gaynor's study, and over a half century (54 years) after the time span of Griffiths' 1988 review of the literature since 1964: have the organizational theories that inform the field today moved beyond positivism?

ORGANIZATIONAL THEORIES THAT CURRENTLY INFORM THE FIELD

I reviewed the most recent book lists of publishers of organizational theory texts (e.g., Sage, Open University, Charles C. Thomas, Temple University Press, Prentice-Hall, Allyn and Bacon, Scott Foreseman, Jossey-Bass, Routledge, State University of New York Press, Lawrence Erlbaum, Oxford University Press, Falmer, Wadsworth, and Pearson) and talked informally with colleagues in the field about the organizational theory texts used in their programs. Texts generally adopted for the teaching of organizational theory and behavior in educational leader preparation draw from literature on (1) organizations in general (Bolman & Deal, 2017; Morgan, 2006; Perrow, 1986; Pfeffer, 1997); (2) education (Earle & Kruse, 1999; Owens & Valesky, 2014), and (3) educational administration (Hanson, 2003; Hoy & Miskel, 2012). Other related texts focus on one set of theories, such as those associated with leadership (Northouse, 2015), new institutionalism (Greenwood, Oliver, Sahlin, & Suddaby, 2008; Meyer & Rowan, 2012), or organizations and their environments (Lawrence & Lorsch, 1986). Several texts provide a compendium of previously published theories on organizational theory, called "classics" (Ott, Parkcs, & Simpson, 2007; Shafritz, Ott, & Jang, 2015).

All of these texts are grounded primarily in structural functional and interpretivist epistemologies. For example, Northouse's (2015) examination of leadership includes traits, skills, behavioral approaches, path–goal theory, leader–member exchange theory, transformational leadership, authentic leadership, team leadership, psychodynamic leadership, gender and leadership (not authored by Northouse), culture and leadership, leadership ethics, servant leadership, and adaptive leadership. Northouse does not make explicit the epistemological perspectives addressed in the book and why some epistemologies are considered and others are not; when the text addresses theories or perspectives beyond those based on studies of white, heterosexually assumed males (Shakeshaft, 1987) (e.g., a chapter on white females and a chapter that addresses global culture), these chapters are simply added to the volume – a literal "add-on" to the other chapters grounded in structural functionalism and interpretivism, and these two chapters are themselves epistemologically structural functional and interpretive. The author does not draw upon critically oriented theories and epistemologies that could inform the gender and culture chapters, nor do these theories or epistemologies disrupt the structural functionalism in the rest of the text.

Owens and Valesky (2014) open their text with a chapter on organizational and critical theory where they devote two paragraphs to critical theory, a section on Critical Race Theory, and a few paragraphs on social justice. The remainder of the book includes chapters on mainstream organizational thought, bureaucratic and human resource development views, systems approaches, motivation, the human dimensions of organization, organizational culture and climate, organizational change, leadership, decision-making, conflict in organizations, and school reform. Thus, even though the authors briefly address critically oriented epistemologies, the remainder of the book is grounded in structural functionalism or interpretivism.

As these examples illustrate, the use of such texts in educational leadership programs perpetuates structural functionalist and interpretivist perspectives of organizational theory. Even Morgan's (2006) iconic use of multiple metaphors to portray organizations excludes any metaphors associated with power and privilege beyond position within the structural hierarchy of the organization; that is, issues of race, class, gender, sexual/gender identity, ability, and their intersections are not addressed at all.

Somewhat surprisingly, the literature on the preparation of school leaders (Young & Crow, 2017) does not explicitly address the role of organizational theory in leadership preparation. In their comprehensive text *Handbook of research on the education of school leaders*, the phrases "organizational theory," "theory," or "epistemology" do not appear in the index. In the chapter devoted to reconceptualizing a curriculum for leadership preparation, the authors' opening sentence recognizes the groundbreaking scholarship of William Foster:

> Almost 30 years ago, the educational leadership field initiated a major paradigm shift in scholarly focus through the influence of William Foster (1986) and others, shifting from an emphasis on organizational theory, management, and logical positivism toward a conception of leadership informed by theories from other fields and disciplines. (Ylimaki & Henderson, 2016, p. 148)

Critiquing both structural functionalism and social justice perspectives, the authors do not consider the role of epistemology or organizational theory in their reconceptualized curriculum for leadership preparation; nor do they recognize the underlying epistemological assumptions of their recommendations.

In sum, the status of organizational theory in the past and present as reflected in syllabi and texts used in the preparation of educational leaders continues to be grounded in structural functionalism with little attention to critically oriented perspectives – over 50 years after Griffiths concluded the same in his 1988 review of the status of theory in the preparation of educational leadership since 1964. Yet, in spite of the persistent structural functional status of organizational theory in the field, the number of empirical studies focused on equity questions has grown over the past decade, offering hope for the future. I turned to these equity studies in educational leadership to identify the theoretical frameworks that ground these studies and the equity theories developed as a result of these studies.

THEORIES THAT INFORM EMPIRICAL STUDIES ON SOCIAL JUSTICE LEADERSHIP

As illustrated in the previous sections, the movement of organizational theories in educational leadership preparation beyond structural functionalist and interpretivist perspectives to critically oriented perspectives has hardly advanced at all. To date, that work has failed to build on the scholarship of Foster, who more than 30 years ago published *Paradigms and promises: New approaches to educational administration*

(1986) – the first text to apply critical theories to organizational theory in educational leadership. Smyth (1989) contributed to this critical theory literature with an edited book on critical perspectives on educational leadership. This text includes chapters on critical perspectives on organizational theory, organizational change, and leadership. Years later, several scholars published texts examining educational leadership from a feminist perspective, including Blackmore (1999), though in this example the text does not specifically apply feminist perspectives to organizations. Some equity-oriented texts adopt a conceptual approach toward leadership and equity (e.g., Marshall & Oliva, 2009), and one text addresses issues associated with inclusive leadership practices and identifies some limitations of current leadership theory (Lumby & Coleman, 2007). However, Lumby and Coleman limit inclusive leadership to race and gender and do not propose alternatives to traditional leadership theories for the field.

To further assess the status of organizational theories in the field of educational leadership, we reviewed the empirical and theoretical articles on social justice leadership and equitable leadership practices published in the *Educational Administration Quarterly* (*EAQ*) from 2000 to 2018. We selected this journal for this analysis because it is regarded as the most prestigious in the field of educational leadership, confirmed by its impact factor relative to other related journals in the field based on the *Journal of Citation Reports*.

The 18 years of *EAQ* included 67 volumes and 317 articles. We did not include in the article count book reviews, editor notes, announcements of award winners, or a short article that included several scholars each writing separate paragraphs regarding their reflections on William Foster. We did include the introductions to special issues, as some of these were substantive in content.

We conducted a qualitative content analysis of each of the 317 articles. First, we coded each article into an Excel spreadsheet as to whether or not the article directly addressed equity. We defined the article as addressing equity if equity or social justice, addressing opportunity gaps between students, or if race, gender, social class, ability, sexual orientation/gender identity, language, or other differences and their intersections were directly addressed. Those that focused on general school improvement with no attention to achievement differences among typically privileged and marginalized students, or articles focused on technical aspects of schooling without equity considerations, were not identified as equity articles. We included all articles in the coding – empirical and theoretical. This coding scheme resulted in identifying 77 articles (or 24 percent of all articles) that were oriented toward equity or social justice.

We then read all 77 equity articles to determine whether each article drew upon a theoretical or conceptual framework to ground the article and wrote the specific theoretical framework(s) into the spreadsheet. We also noted whether or not the article promulgated a new theoretical framework and the name of that theory.

Of the 77 equity articles, 56 were guided by a clearly identified conceptual framework (6 of these articles also contributed a new theory to the field). We identified four articles that did not begin with a clearly identified conceptual framework, but put forth a new theory. Thus, a total of 60 articles were either grounded in a clear theory (or theories) or put forth a new theory, or both. These 60 articles formed our dataset for a deeper analysis of the status of theory in the subfield of educational administration that focuses specifically on equity, diversity, and social justice.

With this dataset of 60 equity-oriented articles that addressed theory in some aspect, we identified the number of studies that drew from a single conceptual framework to guide the article and how many drew from multiple theories. To that end, 32 of the 60 articles were framed by a single theoretical framework. Of the 60 articles, scholars chose critical theory to frame the article more times than any other theory – either alone or in combination with other theories. That is, critical theory served as the primary framework for three of the articles (Brown, 2004; Hoffman & Burrello, 2004; Murtadha & Watts, 2005). Seven articles were conceptually grounded with critical theories paired with other theories: critical theory, pragmatic thinking, and postmodernism (Dantley, 2005); critical theory and postmodernism (Foster, 2004; Grogan, 2004); critical theory and feminist poststructuralism (Sherman, 2005); critical perspectives and a positioned subject approach (Theoharis, 2007); adult learning theory, transformative learning theory, critical social theory (Brown, 2006); and multiple critical and feminist perspectives (Rusch, 2004). Thus, these seven articles combined with the three articles in which critical theory singularly anchored the piece result in critical theory being the most frequent theoretical orientation selected to frame studies focused on leadership and equity across these eighteen years of scholarship. 18 yrs.

Critical Theory and Critical Race Theory

While critical theory was the most frequently cited theory in this equity research, Critical Race Theory (CRT) was a close second with just one less article citing Critical Race Theory than critical theory. Four scholars selected CRT as the single framework for their articles (Horsford, 2010a; López, 2003; Smith, Yosso, & Solórzano, 2007; VanDeventer Iverson, 2007). Another set of five authors conceptually framed their work by combining Critical Race Theory with other theories. For example, Marx and Larson (2012) grounded their study in CRT and critical studies in whiteness; Alemán (2007) paired CRT with Latina/o Critical (LatCrit) theory; Evans (2007) joined CRT with sense-making; André-Bechely (2005) viewed her study through the lens of Critical Race Theory combined with "feminist critical policy studies (Marshall, 1997), feminist standpoint theory (Harding, 1991), and feminist sociology (Smith, 1987, 1999)" (cited in André-Bechely, 2005, p. 269), and Bloom and Erlandson (2003) drew from Black feminist standpoint theory to study African American women principals. Thus, four articles were grounded primarily in Critical Race Theory while five additional articles combined CRT with other theoretical perspectives to guide their research – the second most frequent theoretical perspective (nine articles in total across these eighteen years of equity research).

Critically Oriented Theoretical Intersections

Other scholars wrote at theoretical intersections that were derivatives of critical, critical race, and feminist theories, and among these articles feminist theories were most prominent. For example, Cooper (2009) drew from three theories to ground her study: transformative leadership for social justice, Cornel West's critical philosophies, and a cultural politics of difference. Alston (2005) advanced the field by studying black female superintendents through the lenses of tempered radicalism and servant leadership. Brunner (2002) turned to discourse analysis and feminist postmodernism to reconceptualize the superintendency, Grogan (2000) relied on feminist postmodernism, and Mahitivanichcha and Rorrer (2006) combined feminist economic theory and feminist organizational theory to guide their data collection and analysis related to women's access to and participation in the superintendency.

Two related articles drew from a combination of theoretical perspectives to address students who are linguistically and culturally diverse. Scanlan and Lopez (2012) relied on the framework of Integrated Comprehensive Services (ICS) (Frattura & Capper, 2007) and a tripartite theoretical model that emphasizes cultivating language proficiency, providing access to high-quality curricula, and promoting sociocultural integration. To guide their research, Theoharis and O'Toole (2011) developed a conceptual framework from the literature on leadership, social justice, and students who are linguistically and culturally diverse that centers on the principal, assets-based perspectives, collaboration, and inclusive practices.

Single Critically Oriented Frameworks

Aside from the seven articles that were solely grounded in critical theory or Critical Race Theory, 13 articles relied on a single critically oriented framework – and these 13 were different from each other, including Lin's (1999) theory of social capital as applied to individuals of nondominant backgrounds (Miller, 2011), equity theory (Michener, DeLamater, & Myers, 2004, cited in Young, Reimer, & Young, 2010), poststructuralist perspectives (Tooms, Lugg, & Bogotch, 2010), organizational cultural competence and proficiency theories (Bustamante, Nelson, & Onwuegbuzie, 2009), resiliency theory (Christman & McClellan, 2008), critical mentoring theory (Tillman, 2005), similarity/attraction perspectives (Addi-Raccah, 2006), sex stratification theory (Tallerico & Blount, 2004), transformative leadership (Anderson, 2004), job attraction model (Newton, Giesen, Freeman, Bishop, & Zeitoun, 2003), Coleman's social capital theory (Kahne, O'Brien, Brown, & Quinn, 2001), evolutionary stages of a paradigmatic shift (Bjork, 2000), and Swindler's (1986) theoretical discussion of "unsettled" and "settled" cultural periods in social life (Brunner, 2000).

Equity Studies without a Critically Oriented Framework

Another set of authors selected singular or combined theories to guide their studies that are typically considered outside of critically oriented theories, but applied these theories to questions of equity. For example, Newton (2006) drew from role theory, recruitment models, and job attraction theory to analyze superintendent recruitment that normalizes the superintendency as male, and Goddard and Skrla (2006) relied on social cognitive theory and perceived collective efficacy to study the influence of school social composition on teachers' collective efficacy beliefs. Gooden (2005) grounded his study on the role of an African American principal in bureaucratic administration and ethno-humanist theory and research, while Eckman (2004) compared male and female high school principals via the framework of role conflict, role commitment, and job satisfaction. Other similar studies that applied theories not typically considered critically oriented to equity research questions included theories such as interpretive interactionism (Anderson & Larson, 2009), definitions of trust (Goddard, Salloum, & Berebitsky (2009), trust development (Owens & Johnson, 2009), districts as institutional actors (Rorrer, Skrla, & Scheurich, 2008), theories of absenteeism (Rosenblatt & Shirom, 2006), life-course theory (Loder, 2005), interpersonal and institutional caring (Foster, 2005), legal impact studies (Stefkovich & Torres, 2003), social distance theory (Young & Fox, 2002), new institutional theory (Sunderman, 2001), and gatekeeping theory (Tallerico, 2000).

Ten of the equity articles offered a new critically oriented theory to advance the field. These new theories included a conceptual framework of social justice leadership as praxis to inform leadership preparation (Furman, 2012), theories of transformative leadership (Shields, 2010), racial literacy (Horsford, 2010), cultural work as transformative leadership (Cooper, 2009), a theoretical framework for social justice leadership preparation (McKenzie et al., 2008), a theory of social justice leadership (Theoharis, 2007), progressive transformative leadership in urban schools (Dantley, 2005), equity traps (McKenzie & Scheurich, 2004), a critical leadership of place (Furman & Gruenewald, 2004), and a transformative pedagogical framework (Brown, 2004). Importantly, none of the 77 articles oriented toward equity and social justice was informed by, nor resulted in further expansion of Disability Studies theories, Queer Theory (with just one study drawing from Queer Legal Theory; Lugg, 2003), or theories of intersectionality (Crenshaw, 1991; Hancock, 2007) that address the intersection of multiple identities.

Given this status of organizational theory in educational leadership – in the preparation of educational leaders and in the equity research – are organizational theories in the organizational sciences more promising in the way they address power and privilege associated with gender, race, class, ability, language, sexuality, gender identity and their intersections? We turn to this field next.

CRITICAL AND POSTMODERN THEORIES: LESSONS FROM THE ORGANIZATIONAL SCIENCES

Sociologists Zey-Ferrell and Aiken (1981) led an effort to consider perspectives beyond interpretivism and structural functionalism in the organizational sciences.

Their edited book offered a critical perspective of complex organizations. In describing the impetus for their text, they noted becoming:

> keenly aware of the limitations of [structural perspectives]; yet these popular conceptions of organizations so dominated the thinking of most organizational researchers that we deemed it necessary to go outside what is traditionally defined as organization analysis to find fresh, insightful approaches. ... We were discouraged however, by the limited number of well-developed, thoughtful alternatives approaches. As in any field, <u>critiquing existing work is easier</u> than developing well-conceived, fresh exciting alternatives. (Zey-Ferrell & Aiken, 1981, p. ii)

In the mid- to late 1980s, other scholars offered non-traditional approaches to the organization sciences. Kathy Ferguson's seminal work *The feminist case against bureaucracy* (1984) was the first book-length work that applied feminist theories to bureaucratic discourse. In addition, in the late 1980s and early 1990s, several books were published that applied critical (Alvesson & Willmott, 1992), postmodern (Clegg, 1990), gender (Mills & Tancred, 1992), and sexuality perspectives to organizations (Hearn, Sheppard, Tancred-Sheriff, & Burrell, 1990). Mills and Tancred's volume includes a critique of organizational analysis and feminist perspectives on varying aspects of organizations. Hassard and Parker (1993) published the edited volume *Postmodernism and organizations*, a collection of essays applying postmodern thought to the study of organizations.

The *Oxford handbook of organization theory* (Tsoukas & Knudsen, 2005) offers a meta-theoretical approach to the study of organizations, including the history, current status, and future prospects for the field of organizational theory from some of the most radical scholars in the organizational studies field. Disappointingly, the volume completely excludes theories such as Disability Studies theories, Queer Theory, and Critical Race Theory as applied to organizations.

Scholars of organizational theory have noted the lack of gender, race, social class, sexuality, and nationality, and their intersections in organizational theory (Holvino, 2010). Holvino summarizes the situation:

> Few scholars, in particular in the USA, advocate the inclusion of race in mainstream organization theorizing ... even though the inclusion of more sophisticated perspectives on gender has gained ground. ... Fewer scholars still address the intersections of race and gender ... race, ethnicity and gender ... or race, class and gender. ... In the field of organization development and change, the silence on these intersections is outstanding, even within the discourse of managing diversity.

What is even more disturbing about Holvino's (2010) summary of the literature gaps in the organizational studies is the fact that she fails to mention that Disability Studies theory, Queer Theory, and race through the lens of Critical Race Theory are not addressed at all.

SUMMARY OF THE HISTORY AND FUTURE OF ORGANIZATIONAL THEORY FOR EQUITY AND DIVERSITY

In sum, organizational theory gaps lie within the field of organizational studies as they do in the field of educational leadership – in similar and different ways. In educational leadership, of all the critically oriented perspectives, critical theories and Critical Race Theory have received the most attention. Like educational leadership, organizational studies have been influenced by critical theories. However, unlike educational leadership, organizational studies has benefitted from a significant volume of literature in gender studies. Scholars in both fields have addressed race; however, while Critical Race Theory is nearly absent in the organizational studies literature, educational leadership has benefitted from many scholars applying Critical Race Theory to the field. Both fields are woefully inadequate in their attention to disability theories and Queer Theory, and theories of intersectionality.

The history and current status of organizational theories in the field of educational leadership contribute to a vicious and dangerous intellectual and practical cycle. Students enter into educational leadership programs and typically find that equity and diversity are addressed directly within one particular course (Hawley & James, 2010). Although the "diversity course" in educational leadership programs may address an array of differences related to social class, race, language, gender, ability, sexual/gender identity, and their intersections, it is highly likely that such a course does not address or under-addresses theories associated with difference, such as critical theories, Critical Race Theory, Queer Theory, Disability Studies theories, feminist theories, postmodern theories, and their intersections. Given that diversity is typically not deeply addressed in the other courses a student takes (Hawley & James, 2010), then we can assume, as attested to in this chapter, that theories associated with difference are typically also not addressed or under-addressed in educational leadership.

In these same programs, in the one course where organizational theory is specifically addressed and in other courses where organizational theories are tangentially addressed, the texts and readings used in these courses tend to be grounded in structural functionalism and interpretivism. Thus, when students develop their dissertation research for their doctoral program, they have been repeatedly exposed to a narrow view of organizational theories. The continued promulgation of these theories throughout their program limits students' thinking about what research questions are worth asking, may be asked, and should be asked, in their own dissertation studies and in their leadership practice. Given this preparation context, most students approach their research and leadership practice from a place of epistemological unconsciousness. That is, they have not been made aware of the epistemological orientation of their program or coursework and how this orientation has been operating on them throughout their program.

When these leadership students decide what conceptual framework will guide their dissertation research, they can turn to nearly any organizational theory book in the field of organizations, education, or education leadership, where they will find lists of literally dozens of theories, nearly all originating out of structural functionalism or interpretivism from which to select. These students complete their degree, and those who join the faculty ranks are highly likely to teach and conduct research in ways that they have been taught – devoid of deep engagement with critically oriented theories. Students enroll in their classes and the cycle continues.

To be sure, the literature on equity and social justice as applied to the educational leadership field has increased over the past 18 years. Thus, even though most programs may prepare scholars to draw upon traditional theoretical orientations, some scholars do emerge from some programs with the theoretical tools to engage in critically oriented scholarship. However, while much of this scholarship has made an important contribution to the field, as we found in our review, this scholarship has had a limited influence on theory development and expansion in the field as exemplified in leadership preparation texts. This may be due to a conceptually weak theoretical framework or weak application of theory that guided the study, and/or the failure of the studies to purposefully draw out the implications of their work for theory development. Likewise, to date, scholars who produce organizational theory texts – in organizational studies, educational leadership, or education – simply ignore this work.

The lack of critically oriented theories in the teaching of organizational theory in the field also limits the insightful practice of leaders in the field toiling to erase achievement differences in inclusive ways. This lack of critically oriented theories in educational leadership programs and the continued proliferation of structural functionalism and interpretivism in organizational theory is a primary limiter of educational leader and scholar preparation. Until this changes, we will continue to graduate epistemologically unconscious scholars and practitioners and we, as a field, will continue to be complicit in the underachievement of typically marginalized youth. Likewise, given the status of organizational theory in the field, it is no wonder that one colleague proclaimed that the teaching and understanding of organizational theory is irrelevant to leading and sustaining high-achieving, integrated schools and districts. I argue, however, that critically oriented organizational theory can be a powerful lever for preparing equity leaders to lead for equity.

IMPLICATIONS

From our study and analysis of organizational theory in the field of educational leadership, we identified three implications for future research. First, the field could benefit from texts, such as this one, that clearly identify, define, describe, and apply critically oriented theories to organizational theory. Scholars whose work is grounded in structural functionalist and interpretivism have access to many organizational theory books with tables of contents that list dozens of theories from which to choose to inform their research. However, critically oriented scholars have no such resource, other than Foster's (1986) text, as previously mentioned, that applies critical theory to organizational theory, leadership, and change in educational leadership.

In this sense, then, the field could benefit from applying critically oriented perspectives to classic topics in the field such as leadership, decision-making, and change as this book aims to do. In so doing, this book sorts out the convergences and divergences among sociological identity theories (e.g., Queer Theory, feminist theories, Critical Race Theory) and organizational theories.

The field could benefit from researchers who apply critically oriented perspectives to equity-related research as reviewed in this chapter and consider how their findings could inform or be informed by organizational theory. For example, how can the findings related to studies of African American female principals inform new concepts of leadership in the field? How can the empirical research on leaders who have co-created inclusive schools and reduced opportunity gaps inform alternative views of organizational change or decision-making?

Third, all scholars in the field whose research focuses on equity bear a responsibility to ensure that their research is grounded in a well-explicated and thoroughly developed theoretical framework, or that the research generates a robust new theory to the field and that the implications of each study include clear and well-developed implications for theory. To this end, to date, no studies have been published that are informed by Disability Studies or theories of intersectionality, and few studies are informed by Queer Theory. The field could greatly benefit from studies that are grounded in these epistemologies. These implications taken together, along with the analyses laid out in this chapter, lead forward to the ways in which organizational theories can leverage the development of leadership capacity for integrated, socially just schools. In Chapter 3, we begin our journey with the structural functional epistemology, organizational theory, and educational leadership.

LEADERSHIP DEVELOPMENT ACTIVITY: THE PERSONAL CASE STUDY

Throughout this book, I share suggestions and insights about the course "Organizational Theory and Critical Epistemologies" which I teach. As one of the first assignments for students, I ask them to write a personal case study about a troublesome situation in their leadership/professional life that they feel remains unresolved. As one way to apply their understandings of the various epistemologies, students will analyze their case throughout the course from each epistemology, details of which I will provide throughout the book. I provide details for the assignment below.

PERSONAL CASE STUDY

For the first class, students should bring with them a two-page, double-spaced case study of a situation they have experienced in an educational setting that was troubling or may feel unresolved. See below for how to write a case study. Students will use their cases throughout the course to analyze and apply the ideas we are discussing. Please note that your case study will be confidential so far as the instructors will not share any information about your case study. You will be sharing your case study in a one-to-one discussion with several peers in the class. These conversations about your case are also confidential.

How to Write the Case Study (Limit to two pages, double-spaced)

I Purpose

Your personal case study should describe an organizational/professional event or experience that was significant or challenging for you. You should pick an event or situation that you found particularly troublesome or that has bothered you over a period of time or on some level feels unresolved.

The personal case *should be a description*, not an analysis or interpretation of the event.

You should write it as a story in the first person. That is, describe what happened as you saw it, including your thoughts and feelings.

II Focus

It is usually best to focus the case around a particular experience or set of experiences, rather than trying to cover many months of your participation in the setting. A single critical event (e.g., an important meeting, the early stages of a difficult project, a significant accomplishment, a difficult conflict) is usually the best focal point for the study.

III Organization of the Case Study

1. Set the stage with a relatively brief description of the organizational context and your role in it. Provide the information that you think is most important to enable a reader unfamiliar with the situation to understand the most important elements. (This inevitably requires selectivity; part of the art of case writing is separating the significant facts from the mass of information that might be included.)
2. Wherever possible, include a direct description of events. For example, if there was a significant meeting, try to include a direct description of what different people actually said in the meeting. (A script representing part of the conversation is very helpful in such cases.)
3. Think about the following as possible elements: (a) organization structure, (b) who were the significant individuals or groups and what were their relationships to one another, (c) was there conflict and, if so, over what, (d) were there power differentials among the persons involved in terms of organizational hierarchy or race, class, gender, language, ability, sexuality, gender identity, and their intersections?

4. A good case often ends with a question, unsolved problem, or dilemma (e.g., what decision should I make at this point? How could I solve this problem?) Don't solve the case. Leave it hanging.

5. You should disguise the identity of the organization and individuals. Use fictitious names wherever you feel it is appropriate.

This case description is adapted from work by Professor Terry Deal, formerly of Vanderbilt University.

NOTE

1   This chapter is adapted from Capper, C.A. & Green, T.L. (2013). Organizational theories and the development of leadership capacity for integrated, socially just schools. In L. Tillman, J.J. Scheurich and Associates, *Handbook of educational leadership for equity and diversity* (pp. 186–197). New York: Routledge. Used by permission.

REFERENCES

Addi-Raccah, A. (2006). Accessing internal leadership positions at school: Testing the similarity-attraction approach regarding gender in three educational systems in Israel. *Educational Administration Quarterly, 42*(3), 291–323.

Alemán, E., Jr. (2007). Situating Texas school finance policy in a CRT framework: How "substantially equal" yields racial inequity. *Educational Administration Quarterly, 43*(5), 525–558.

Alston, J.A. (2005). Tempered radicals and servant leaders: Black females persevering in the superintendency. *Educational Administration Quarterly, 41*(4), 675–688.

Alvesson, M. & Willmott, H. (Eds). (1992). *Critical management studies.* London: Sage.

Anderson, G.L. (2004). William Foster's legacy: Learning from the past and reconstructing the future. *Educational Administration Quarterly, 40*(2), 240–258.

Anderson, N.S. & Larson, C.L. (2009). "Sinking like quicksand": Expanding educational opportunity for young men of color. *Educational Administration Quarterly, 45*(1), 71–114.

André-Bechely, L. (2005). Public school choice at the intersection of voluntary integration and not-so-good neighborhood schools: Lessons from parents' experiences. *Educational Administration Quarterly, 41*(2), 267–305.

Bjork, L.G. (2000). Introduction: Women in the superintendency – Advances in research and theory. *Educational Administration Quarterly, 36*(1), 5–17.

Blackmore, J. (1999). *Troubling women: Feminism, leadership, and educational change.* Buckingham: Open University Press.

Bloom, C.M. & Erlandson, D.A. (2003). African American women principals in urban schools: Realities, (re)constructions, and resolutions. *Educational Administration Quarterly, 39*(3), 339–369.

Bolman, L. & Deal, T. (2017). *Reframing organizations: Artistry, choice, and leadership* (6th edn). San Francisco, CA: Jossey-Bass.

Brown, K.M. (2004). Leadership for social justice and equity: Weaving a transformative framework and pedagogy. *Educational Administration Quarterly, 40*(1), 77–108.

Brown, K.M. (2006). Leadership for social justice and equity: Evaluating a transformative framework and andragogy. *Educational Administration Quarterly, 42*(5), 700–745.

Brunner, C.C. (2000). Unsettled moments in settled discourse: Women superintendents' experiences of inequality. *Educational Administration Quarterly, 36*(1), 76–116.

Brunner, C.C. (2002). A proposition for the reconception of the superintendency: Reconsidering traditional and nontraditional discourse. *Educational Administration Quarterly, 38*(3), 402–431.

Bustamante, R.M., Nelson, J.A., & Onwuegbuzie, A.J. (2009). Assessing schoolwide cultural competence: Implications for school leadership preparation. *Educational Administration Quarterly, 45*(5), 793–827.

Christman, D. & McClellan, R. (2008). "Living on barbed wire": Resilient women administrators in educational leadership programs. *Educational Administration Quarterly, 44*(1), 13–29.

Clegg, S.R. (1990). *Modern organizations: Organization studies in the postmodern world.* London: Sage.

Cooper, C.W. (2009). Performing cultural work in demographically changing schools: Implications for expanding transformative leadership frameworks. *Educational Administration Quarterly, 45*(5), 694–724.

Crenshaw, K. (1991). Mapping the margins: Intersectionality, identity politics, and violence against women of color. *Stanford Law Review, 43*(6), 1241–1299.

Dantley, M.E. (2005). African American spirituality and Cornel West's notions of prophetic pragmatism: Restructuring educational leadership in American urban schools. *Educational Administration Quarterly, 41*(4), 651–674.

Earle, J. & Kruse, S. (1999). *Organizational literacy for educators.* Mahwah, NJ: Lawrence Erlbaum.

Eckman, E.W. (2004). Similarities and differences in role conflict, role commitment, and job satisfaction for female and male high school principals. *Educational Administration Quarterly, 40*(3), 366–387.

Evans, A.E. (2007). School leaders and their sensemaking about race and demographic change. *Educational Administration Quarterly, 43*(2), 159–188.

Ferguson, K.E. (1984). *The feminist case against bureaucracy.* Philadelphia, PA: Temple University Press.

Foster, L. (2005). The practice of educational leadership in African American communities of learning: Context, scope, and meaning. *Educational Administration Quarterly, 41*(4), 689–700.

Foster, W. (1986). *Paradigms and promises: New approaches to educational administration.* Amherst, NY: Prometheus Books.

Foster, W.P. (2004). The decline of the local: A challenge to educational leadership. *Educational Administration Quarterly, 40*(2), 176–191.

Frattura, E. & Capper, C.A. (2007). *Leading for social justice: Transforming schools for all learners.* Thousand Oaks, CA: Corwin Press.

Furman, G. (2012). Social justice leadership as praxis developing capacities through preparation programs. *Educational Administration Quarterly, 48*(2), 191–229.

Furman, G.C. & Gruenewald, D.A. (2004). Expanding the landscape of social justice: A critical ecological analysis. *Educational Administration Quarterly, 40*(1), 47–76.

Gilligan, C. (1982). *In a different voice.* Cambridge, MA: Harvard University Press.

Goddard, R.D. & Skrla, L. (2006). The influence of school social composition on teachers' collective efficacy beliefs. *Educational Administration Quarterly, 42*(2), 216–235.

Goddard, R.D., Salloum, S.J., & Berebitsky, D. (2009). Trust as a mediator of the relationships between poverty, racial composition, and academic achievement: Evidence from Michigan's public elementary schools. *Educational Administration Quarterly, 45*(2), 292–311.

Gooden, M.A. (2005). The role of an African American principal in an urban information technology high school. *Educational Administration Quarterly, 41*(4), 630–650.

Greenwood, R., Oliver, C., Sahlin, K., & Suddaby, R. (2008). *The Sage handbook of organizational institutionalism.* Thousand Oaks, CA: Sage.

Griffiths, D. E. (1988). Administrative theory. In N. J. Boyan (Ed.), *Handbook of research on educational administration* (pp. 27–52). New York: Longman.

Grogan, M. (2000). Laying the groundwork for a reconception of the superintendency from feminist postmodern perspectives. *Educational Administration Quarterly, 36*(1), 117–142.

Grogan, M. (2004). Keeping a critical, postmodern eye on educational leadership in the United States: In appreciation of Bill Foster. *Educational Administration Quarterly, 40*(2), 222–239.

Hancock, A.M. (2007). When multiplication doesn't equal quick addition: Examining intersectionality as a research paradigm. *American Political Science Association, 5*(1), 63–79.

Hanson, E.M. (2003). *Educational administration and organizational behavior* (5th edn). Boston, MA: Allyn and Bacon.

Harding, S. (1991). *Whose science? Whose knowledge? Thinking from women's lives.* Ithaca, NY: Cornell University Press.

Hassard, J. & Parker, M. (Eds). (1993). *Postmodernisms and organizations.* London: Sage.

Hatch, M.J. & Cunliffe, A.L. (2006). *Organization theory: Modern, symbolic, and postmodern perspectives* (2nd edn). New York: Oxford University Press.

Hawley, W. & James, R. (2010). Diversity responsive school leadership. *UCEA Review, 51*(3), 1–5.

Hearn, J., Sheppard, D.L., Tancred-Sheriff, P., & Burrell, G. (1990). *The sexuality of organization.* London: Sage.

Hoffman, L.P. & Burrello, L.C. (2004). A case study illustration of how a critical theorist and a consummate practitioner meet on common ground. *Educational Administration Quarterly, 40*(2), 268–289.

Holvino, E. (2010). Intersections: The simultaneity of race, gender and class in organization studies. *Gender, Work and Organization, 17*(3), 248–277.

Horsford, S.D. (2010). Mixed feelings about mixed schools: Superintendents on the complex legacy of school desegregation. *Educational Administration Quarterly, 46*(3), 287–321.

Hoy, W. & Miskel, C. (2012). *Education administration: Theory, research, and practice* (9th edn). New York: McGraw-Hill.

Kahne, J., O'Brien, J., Brown, A., & Quinn, T. (2001). Leveraging social capital and school improvement: The case of a school network and a comprehensive community initiative in Chicago. *Educational Administration Quarterly, 37*(4), 429–461.

Lawrence, P.R. & Lorsch, J.W. (1986). *Organization and environment: Managing differentiation and integration.* Boston, MA: Harvard Business Press.

Lin, N. (1999). Building a network theory of social capital. *Connections, 22,* 28–51.

Lincoln, Y.S. (1985). *Organizational theory and inquiry: The paradigm revolution.* Beverly Hills, CA: Sage.

Loder, T.L. (2005). Women administrators negotiate work–family conflicts in changing times: An intergenerational perspective. *Educational Administration Quarterly, 41*(5), 741–776.

López, G.R. (2003). The (racially neutral) politics of education: A critical race theory perspective. *Educational Administration Quarterly, 39*(1), 68–94.

Lugg, C. (2003). Sissies, faggots, lezzies, and dykes: Gender, sexual orientation, and a new politics of education? *Educational Administration Quarterly. 39*(1), 95–134.

Lumby, J. & Coleman, M. (2007). *Leadership and diversity: Challenging theory and practice in education.* London: Sage.

Mahitivanichcha, K. & Rorrer, A. (2006). Women's choices within market constraints: Re-visioning access to and participation in the superintendency. *Educational Administration Quarterly, 42*(4), 483–517.

Marshall, C. (1997). *Feminist critical policy analysis II: A perspective from post-secondary education.* New York: RoutledgeFalmer.

Marshall, C. & Oliva, M. (2009). *Leadership for social justice: Making revolutions in education* (2nd edn). Upper Saddle River, NJ: Prentice Hall.

Marx, S., & Larson, L.L. (2012). Taking off the color-blind glasses: Recognizing and supporting Latina/o students in a predominantly white school. *Educational Administration Quarterly, 48*(2), 259–303.

McKenzie, K.B. & Scheurich, J.J. (2004). Equity traps: A useful construct for preparing principals to lead schools that are successful with racially diverse students. *Educational Administration Quarterly, 40*(5), 601–632.

McKenzie, K.B., Christman, D. E., Hernandez, F., Fierro, E., Capper, C.A., Dantley, M., Gonzalez, M.L., Cambron-McCabe, N., & Scheurich, J.J. (2008). From the field: A proposal for educating leaders for social justice. *Educational Administration Quarterly, 44*(1), 111–138.

Meyer, H. & Rowan, B. (2012). *The new institutionalism in education.* Albany, NY: New York Press.

Michener, H.A., DeLamater, J.D., & Myers, D.J. (2004). *Social psychology* (5th edn). Belmont, CA: Wadsworth.

Miller, P.M. (2011). Homeless families' education networks: An examination of access and mobilization. *Educational Administration Quarterly, 47*(4), 543–581.

Mills, A.J. & Tancred, P. (1992). *Gendering organizational analysis.* Newbury Park, CA: Sage.

Morgan, G. (2006). *Images of organizations.* Thousand Oaks, CA: Sage.

Murtadha, K. & Watts, D.K. (2005). Linking the struggle for education and social justice: Historical perspectives of African American leadership in schools. *Educational Administration Quarterly, 41*(4), 591–608.

Newton, R.M. (2006). Does recruitment message content normalize the superintendency as male? *Educational Administration Quarterly, 42*(4), 551–577.

Newton, R.M., Giesen, J., Freeman, J., Bishop, H., & Zeitoun, P. (2003). Assessing the reactions of males and females to attributes of the principalship. *Educational Administration Quarterly, 39*(4), 504–532.

Nicolaides, N. & Gaynor, A.K. (1992). The knowledge base informing the teaching of administration and organizational theory in UCEA universities: A descriptive and interpretive survey. *Educational Administration Quarterly, 28*(2), 237–265.

Northouse, P.G. (2015). *Leadership: Theory and practice* (7th edn). Thousand Oaks, CA: Sage.

Ott, J.S., Parkes, S.J., & Simpson, R.B. (2007). *Classic readings in organizational behavior* (4th edn). Independence, KY: Wadsworth.

Owens, M.A. & Johnson, B.L., Jr. (2009). From calculation through courtship to contribution: Cultivating trust among urban youth in an academic intervention program. *Educational Administration Quarterly, 45*(2), 312–347.

Owens, R.G. & Valesky, T.C. (2014). *Organizational behavior in education: Leadership and school reform* (11th edn). Boston, MA: Prentice Hall.

Perrow, C. (1986). *Complex organizations a critical essay* (3rd edn). Las Vegas, NV: Scott Foresman.

Pfeffer, J. (1997). *New directions for organization theory: Problems and prospects.* New York: Oxford University Press.

Rorrer, A.K., Skrla, L., & Scheurich, J.J. (2008). Districts as institutional actors in educational reform. *Educational Administration Quarterly, 44*(3), 307–357.

Rosenblatt, Z. & Shirom, S. (2006). School ethnicity and governance influences on work absence of teachers and school administrators. *Educational Administration Quarterly, 42*(3), 361–384.

Rusch, E. (2004). Gender and race in leadership preparation: A constrained discourse. *Educational Administration Quarterly, 40*(1), 14–46.

Scanlan, M. & Lopez, F. (2012). Vamos! How school leaders promote equity and excellence for bilingual students. *Educational Administration Quarterly, 48*(4), 583–625.

Shafritz, J.M., Ott, J.S., & Jang, Y.S. (2015). *Classics of organization theory* (8th edn). Belmont, CA: Wadsworth Publishing.

Shakeshaft, C. (1987). *Women in educational administration.* Newbury Park, CA: Sage.

Sherman, W.H. (2005). Preserving the status quo or renegotiating leadership: Women's experiences with a district-based aspiring leaders program. *Educational Administration Quarterly, 41*(5), 707–740.

Shields, C. (2010). Transformative leadership: Working for equity in diverse contexts. *Education Administration Quarterly, 46*(4), 558–589.

Silver, P.F. (1978). *Educational administration: Theoretical perspectives on practice and research.* New York: Harper & Row.

Smith, D.E. (1987). *The everyday world as problematic: A feminist sociology.* Boston, MA: Northeastern University Press.

Smith, D.E. (1999). *Writing the social: Critique, theory, and investigations.* Toronto, Canada: University of Toronto Press.

Smith, W.A., Yosso, T.A., & Solórzano, D.G. (2007). Racial primes and Black misandry on historically White campuses: Toward critical race accountability in educational administration. *Educational Administration Quarterly, 43*(5), 559–585.

Smyth, J. (Ed.). (1989). *Critical perspectives on educational leadership.* London: Falmer Press.

Stefkovich, J.A. & Torres Jr., M.S. (2003). The demographics of justice: Student searches, student rights, and administrator practices. *Educational Administration Quarterly, 39*(2), 259–282.

Sunderman, G. (2001). Accountability mandates and the implementation of Title I schoolwide programs: A comparison of three urban districts. *Educational Administration Quarterly, 37*(4), 503–532.

Swindler, A. (1986). Culture in action: Symbols and strategies. *American Sociological Review, 51*, 273–286.

Tallerico, M. (2000). Gaining access to the superintendency: Headhunting, gender, and color. *Educational Administration Quarterly, 36*(1), 18–43.

Tallerico, M. & Blount, J.M. (2004). Women and the superintendency: Insights from theory and history. *Educational Administration Quarterly, 40*(5), 633–662.

Theoharis, G. (2007). Social justice educational leaders and resistance: Toward a theory of social justice leadership. *Educational Administration Quarterly, 43*(2), 221–258.

Theoharis, G. & O'Toole, J. (2011). Leading inclusive ELL social justice leadership for English language learners. *Educational Administration Quarterly, 47*(4), 646–688.

Tillman, L.C. (2005). Mentoring new teachers: Implications for leadership practice in an urban school. *Educational Administrational Quarterly, 41*(4), 609–629.

Tooms, A., Lugg, C.A., & Bogotch, I. (2010). The politics of fit. *Educational Administration Quarterly, 46*(1), 96–131.

Tsoukas, H. & Knudsen, C. (2005). *The Oxford handbook of organizational theory: Meta-theoretical perspectives.* Oxford: Oxford University Press.

VanDeventer Iverson, S. (2007). Camouflaging power and privilege: A critical race analysis of university diversity policies. *Educational Administration Quarterly, 43*(5), 586–611.

Ylimaki, R.M. & Henderson, J.G. (2016). Reconceptualizing curriculum in leadership preparation. In *Handbook of research on the education of school leaders* (pp. 148–172). Abingdon, Oxon: Taylor & Francis.

Young, I.P. & Fox, J.A. (2002). Asian, Hispanic, and Native American job candidates: Pre-screened or screened within the selection process. *Educational Administration Quarterly, 38*(4), 530–554.

Young, M.D. & Crow, M. (Eds). (2017). *Handbook of research on the education of school leaders.* New York: Routledge, Taylor & Francis

Young, P., Reimer, D., & Young, K.H. (2010). Effects of organizational characteristics and human capital endowments on pay of female and male middle school principals. *Educational Administration Quarterly, 46* (4), 590–616.

Zey-Ferrell, M. & Aiken, M. (1981). *Complex organizations: Critical perspectives.* Glenview, IL: Scott Foresman.

CHAPTER 3

Structural Functional Epistemology

As described in Chapter 2, historically, organizational theories have remained rooted in structural functionalism. On the epistemology framework, a structural functional epistemology emanates from the nature of knowledge axis (horizontal) oriented toward the objective end and the nature of change axis (vertical) toward regulation (see Figure 3.1). Educators taking structural functional epistemologies strive toward efficiency and effectiveness via regulation, and directly apply the principles of natural science to social science (Foster, 1986a; Ritzer, 1980; Skrtic, 1991). Burrell and Morgan (2003) explain: "The functionalist approach to social science tends to assume that the social world is composed of relatively concrete empirical artifacts and relationships which can be identified, studied, and measured through approaches derived from the natural sciences" (p. 26, cited in Capper, 1993, p. 11). These educators believe the world to be measurable, quantifiable, and predictable, as their unitary view of reality posits a steady baseline against which behavior may be compared (Capper & Jamison, 1993a; Popkewitz, 1984).

Foster (1986) described the key organizational theories associated with the structural functional epistemology to include Weber's (1987) bureaucracy. Weber viewed bureaucracy as progress compared to the preceding feudal period. Clear rules, procedures, governance structure, division of labor, policies and documents, hiring, rewards and sanctions all advance technical efficiency. Foster identified the positive effects of bureaucracy (again from a structural functional epistemology assumed to be neutral), including "bureaucracy's positive effects on worker rights, fair treatment, and equal opportunities for appointment and advancement" (p. 125).

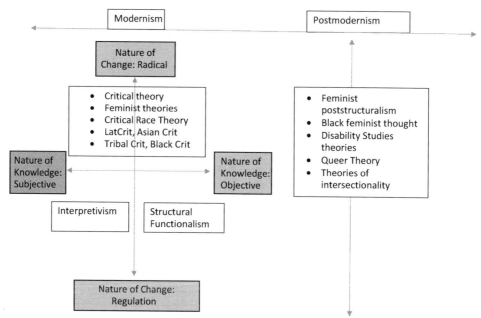

Figure 3.1 An Epistemology Framework

Educators from structural functional epistemologies tend to view the existing social order and its institutions as legitimate and desirable (Capper, 1993, p. 11). They hope to make progress via change that is step-by-step, linear, and evolutionary (Foster, 1986a, 1986b). While often seeking to make changes in the operation of the educational "machine," educators taking structural functional epistemologies accept its basic structures and roles (Gioia & Pitre, 1990; Sleeter, 1991). These educators:

> are interested in understanding how institutions work and how the educational bureaucracy might be made more efficient assuming that change can happen while maintaining existing systems intact. ... Language to describe this epistemology includes the terms rational, efficient, concrete, real, standardized, systematic, traditional. (Capper, 1993, p. 11)

From this epistemology power is earned, based on merit and on the strength of individualism, autonomy, and independence (Foster, 1986a, 1986b; Gibson, Ivancevich, & Konopaske, 1984). Power tends to be top down with decisions made either by majority vote or anarchistically (Sirotnik & Oakes, 1986). Nearly all education reforms and processes are grounded in structural functional epistemologies, and nearly all the heralded foundations of education emanate from this epistemology, including behavioral learning theories, Bloom's taxonomy of learning, Hunter's teaching methods, evaluation and assessment, direct instruction, improvement science, the standards movement, and strategic planning.

STRUCTURAL FUNCTIONAL EPISTEMOLOGY AND THE STRUCTURAL FRAME

As I explain further in this book, all four frames of Bolman and Deal's (2017a) approach to organizational theory are grounded in structural functionalism, interpretivism, or a combination of both; none of the frames are oriented toward equity or social justice. The structural frame of Bolman and Deal's four frames provides another way to illustrate the structural functional epistemology. The assumptions of Bolman and Deal's structural frame include the following:

- Organizations exist to achieve established goals and objectives.
- Organizations increase efficiency and enhance performance through specialization and the appropriate division of labor.
- Suitable forms of coordination and control ensure that diverse efforts of individuals and units mesh.
- Organizations work best when rationality prevails over personal agendas and extraneous pressures.
- Effective structures fit an organization's current circumstances (including its goals, technology, workforce, and environment).
- Troubles arise and performance suffers from structural deficits, remedied through problem solving and restructuring (Bolman & Deal, 2017a, p. 48).

Bolman and Deal contend that two key aspects of considering structure in an organization are how to divide up the work ("differentiation," p. 53), and then how to coordinate the work of different people and units once it is divided ("coordination," p. 60). Organizational theory suggests two ways to coordinate the work: vertically through authority, supervision, rules and policies, planning and control systems; or laterally through meetings, task forces, or standing committees.

Bolman and Deal (2017a) suggest that the way an organization should be structured depends on its mission and goals (unclear or conflicting), the process and procedures to accomplish those goals, and the environment. These structural considerations include levels of authority, communication systems (formal and informal), and procedures (laws, rules, and policies).

Within educational organizations, considerations of structure may include the following:

1. How much autonomy should individual schools have in a district and how much control should emanate from the district office?
2. How should decision-making be structured at the school? Should there be a building leadership team? Who should be on this team and how should that be decided? What decisions does this team make? Should these teams be advisory to the principal who makes the final decisions or should the majority rule?
3. What additional teams or committees are needed at the school and for what purpose? How will membership be decided? Who leads these committees? Who coordinates the work among the committees?

4. How should the school be organized and where should classrooms be placed? Should a larger high school be divided into smaller schools? Should a middle school be organized into houses? Should an elementary school be structured into multi-age grades? Should the upper level elementary classrooms be placed next to or apart from the lower elementary classrooms?

Bolman and Deal (2017a) identified structural issues and dilemmas as follows:

1. "Differentiation vs. Integration" (p. 73): The need to divide the work and the difficulty of coordinating work after it has been divided.
2. "Gaps vs. Overlaps": Key responsibilities must be carried out by individuals or groups. But roles and activities can overlap, creating unwanted redundancies, wasted effort, and conflict (p. 73).
3. "Underuse vs. Overload" (p. 73): Some people or resources are vastly underused or misused. Others are way overworked.
4. "Lack of clarity vs. Lack of creativity" (p. 73): Some people do not fully understand what it is they are supposed to be doing. Others get stuck in a role, which undermines creativity.
5. "Excessive autonomy vs. Excessive interdependence" (p. 74): Individuals may feel they have too much autonomy and not enough guidance, or believe they spend too much time interacting with individuals in teams or groups, making it difficult to accomplish goals.
6. "Too loose vs. Too tight" (p. 74): Individuals may believe the structure is too loose with little sense of who is in charge, lack understanding of organizational goals, and lack clarity about what others are doing. Individuals may believe the structure is too tight and overwhelmed with bureaucratic requirements, which stifles creativity, or spend time plotting how to subvert it.
7. "Diffuse authority vs. Over-centralization" (p. 55): Individuals can perceive the situation as confusion over who has authority and over what decisions. In contrast, final decision-making authority may be far removed from the source, which can make the decision slow or inaccurate.
8. "Goal-less vs. Goal-bound" (p. 75): This structural dilemma considers the lack of goals or lack of clarity about goals, purpose, or mission, compared to structural dilemmas where the specific goals may not be relevant and constraining to action.
9. "Irresponsible vs. Overly responsive" (p. 75): Individuals may be unclear about their responsibilities, or uncommitted or adhering too closely to job responsibilities.

In sum, the structural frame of Bolman and Deal's (2017a) four-frame conceptualization of organizational theory clearly reflects the structural functionalist epistemology. The structural frame considers the structure of an organization, how tasks and people are allocated and integrated, and can lead to a host of structural issues and dilemmas.

STRUCTURAL FUNCTIONALISM REACTION TO DIVERSITY, DIFFERENCE, AND EQUITY IN EDUCATION

In this section, I consider how educators grounded in a structural functionalist epistemology react to diversity, difference, and equity. To begin, the goal of structural functionalism remains efficiency, not equity. Thus, from a structural functional epistemology, equity or social justice are not considered – implicitly or explicitly. As explained in Chapter 2, nearly all organizational theory emanates from the structural functional epistemology and nearly all leadership books and education books emanate from the structural functional epistemology (Capper & Green, 2013). Educators and educational leaders spend considerable time and resources on "educational reform" efforts without any mention of social justice or equity as the goal of those efforts. Thus, as we will learn in later chapters related to critically oriented epistemologies, because structural functionalism does not consider equity or social justice, then the structural functionalist epistemology and education practices that emanate from structural functionalism perpetuate inequities and social injustice.

Frattura and Capper (2015) detail the history of marginalization in education which illustrates a structural functionalist reaction to diversity and difference in schools (see Figure 3.2).

In this figure, Frattura and Capper (2015) illustrate that public schools in the United States were initially developed for white, upper class males. Following that, school systems were historically designed to "promote the Americanization of immigrants, and public schools carried out societal expectations by encouraging immigrants to abandon their heritage and conform to American ways" (Pai & Adler, 1997, p. 57). Compulsory attendance, which began in 1852 (Tyack, 1976), ensured that all children were present for instruction. Over the years, class action lawsuits

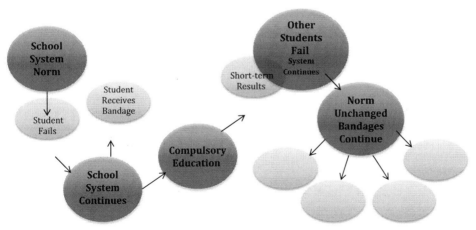

Figure 3.2 History of Marginalization in Education

related to students with disabilities and students who are English-language learners were filed to ensure an equal education for students with these labels, and federal policy allowed for additional resources to schools with higher numbers of low-income students (i.e., Title 1). As a result, legislation was developed for these groups of students in public schools, reinforcing educational tracks by categories (e.g., special education, Title 1, ELL). Within this system, when students struggle, rather than address the white, male, upper class norm upon which public schools were founded, educational "bandages" are applied where, most often, students are pulled out of the system and educated separately – in separate rooms, programs, tracks, or schools.

As Figure 3.3 depicts, as time moves on and more and more students do not fit the upper class, white, male norm, these students become labeled for these educational "bandages". From an educator perspective it is much easier to blame the child, the child's family, or society for the child's struggles and try to fix the child outside of the system, than attend to changing the white normative core of the system itself.

Most recently, Response to Intervention (RtI) practices have become part of this reactionary, deficit-based system. Although RtI policy was designed to require interventions before a child could be labeled with a disability, most educators view RtI policy through a structural functional lens and thus have implemented the policy in structural functional ways. That is, educators place a great emphasis on

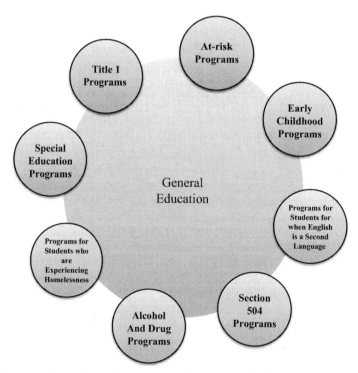

Figure 3.3 Structural Functional Response to Diversity and Difference

establishing a complex system of evaluating and labeling a student to determine if a student needs a Level 2 or Level 3 intervention. In so doing, they do not consider transforming core instructional process in proactive ways to meet the learning needs of all students to prevent student struggle in the first place. Thus, RtI has become another separate, reactionary practice (see Figure 3.4).

All these separate programs perpetuate teaching to an illusory average (Rose, 2015) and expect all students to assimilate to this white, middle/upper class core. Students who cannot assimilate are labeled and referred to these separate remedial programs, all of which research and school data show to perpetuate inequities (Frattura & Capper, 2015).

In summary, structural functionalism is about separateness, segregation, and maintaining historic systems and structures of oppression. As such, I identify ten characteristics of a structural functional epistemological reaction to student difference that have perpetuated the segregation of students into separate programs such as special education, bilingual education, Tier 2 or 3 interventions, schools within schools, alternative schools, typical charter schools, tracking and other ability groupings established for students considered "at risk."

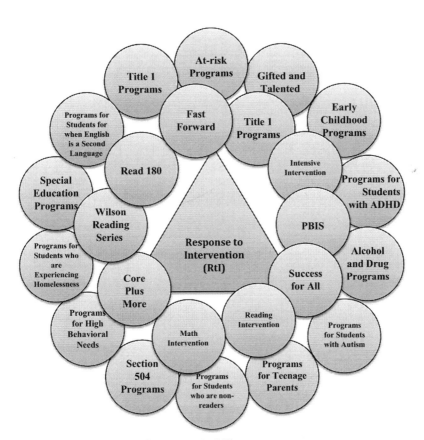

Figure 3.4 Structural Functional Response to Difference

First, within a structural functional epistemology, rather than focusing on assets, students, families, communities, neighborhoods, and student identities across gender, race, class, gender identity, language, sexual identities, abilities and their intersections are viewed from a deficit ideology (Valencia, 2010). With a deficit ideology, we focus on what these entities do not have or come up short as always compared to white, middle/upper class identities. Educators blame student struggle on factors outside the school (such as societal poverty, lack of resources, and families) and claim that, until these aspects can be fixed, educators are not responsible for student struggle.

Second, from this deficit view, a structural functionalist epistemology response to diversity and difference systematically marginalizes difference by language, ability, class, race, sexual orientation/gender identity, and their intersections. A structural functionalist epistemology does so by creating a system based on white, middle-class culture, and then, when students do not assimilate to this culture, students are negatively labeled and segregated into separate programs. Thus, in all these separate programs (e.g., special education, RtI, Title 1, etc.), students of color (especially African American students) and students from low-income homes are over-represented.

Third, rather than being proactive and addressing student needs from an assets-based perspective to prevent student struggle in the first place, educators wait to respond until after a student struggles, spending time and resources on reactionary practices that perpetuate inequities.

Fourth, within structural functionalism, educators view the student as the problem who needs to be fixed rather than addressing how the system created and perpetuated the student's struggle in the first place. Fifth, the system of marginalization within structural functionalism is masked under the guise of helping and perpetuating inequities while doing so.

Sixth, the separate programs operate as silos apart from the white system all with their own assessment requirements to be labeled and placed in the program, separate teachers, separate materials, and separate spaces, all requiring additional resources and finances. Thus, these separate programs are the most expensive and least effective way to address student differences.

Seventh, from a structural functionalist epistemology reaction to diversity and difference, student days are fragmented. These students must leave the general education classroom throughout the day to attend the program for their label, losing valuable instructional time in the process. The students who often need the most structure, routine, consistency, and predictability in their day are often the students who must leave in the middle of a class to attend a special program. Thus, the student removed is receiving the least comprehensive education, while students who are more capable of synthesizing information from a range of adults and environments receive the most cohesive educational opportunity.

Eighth, from a structural functional epistemology, at the middle school or high school levels students attend courses that are lower tracked with lower expectations coupled with a less rigorous curriculum. Sometimes, students are required to take additional remedial courses, missing opportunities for electives such as languages, music, or art that are vital to student learning.

Ninth, within structural functionalism, student remediation is provided in discrete units for short periods of time separate from the core curriculum, rather than integrated and addressed throughout the day. For example, students are removed from the general education environment for thirty minutes of reading instruction, three time a week, instead of having their reading needs addressed across the curriculum throughout the seven-hour instructional day, five days a week.

Finally, with a structural functional systemic response to diversity and difference, professionals work in isolation which spawns practices where some professionals take responsibility for some students and other professionals take responsibility for other students, otherwise known as "my kids" and "your kids." Thus, professionals are physically isolated in their separate programs, limiting opportunity to share expertise. Some of the most promising teaching strategies derive from specialists in special education, gifted education, multicultural education, bilingual education, and reading who have discovered that their expertise can be used to the benefit of all students, not just a select few.

STRUCTURAL FUNCTIONALIST EPISTEMOLOGY: THE CASE OF STUDENTS WITH DISABILITIES

These aspects of structural functional reactions to difference and diversity may be applied to the specific example of students labeled with disabilities. For educational leaders who come from a structural functional epistemology, whether at the district or school level, students labeled with disabilities are viewed as someone else's responsibility – that someone else is responsible for "those kids." These leaders "rely on a distant district-level administrator to manage special education services rather than take direct responsibility for the education of all students in their building" or district (Capper, Keyes, & Theoharis, 2000, p. 519). Special education and the divide between special and general education is viewed as necessary.

Most often, the district-level department of special education and student services operates as a separate entity from the department of curriculum and instruction, with, at times, a separate department maintained for multicultural/diversity work. The superintendent's leadership team sometimes excludes the department of special education. Special education and associated remedial programs, including response to intervention, are often the constructors and maintainers of structural and systemic oppression in schools. Districts that maintain this district-level separation between curriculum and instruction, special education, and multicultural/diversity efforts experience little to no progress toward eliminating inequities.

When students are referred to and labeled for special education, leaders from a structural functionalist epistemology view the problem as within the student, and the entire system of referral, testing, and placement in special education reinforces this view. A structural functionalist epistemology supports the development of "expert" teams, and the usual function of these teams includes identifying students who are struggling and what can be done with or for these students. Rather than focus on student problems, rarely, if ever, do these teams consider the history of that student's failure in the school, how educator practices may have failed these students over time, and what can be done within the school practices, policies, and systems to prevent student failure. These leaders advocate support services and special programs, as they believe that this is the only way students will receive the support and help that they need. They do so without considering how the current core instruction in the school is perpetuating a system of student failure.

Further, within a structural epistemology of disability, educators do not collect equity data which would illustrate that students from low-income homes are nearly universally over-identified for special education. Race data are rarely disaggregated related to students identified for special education, and if students of color are over-represented, most educators do not know how to eliminate this disparity. Further, the research is clear that students of color are placed in more segregated settings and included with their peers without disability labels less than white students (Baglieri, Valle, Connor, & Gallagher, 2011).

STRUCTURAL FUNCTIONAL RESPONSE TO DIVERSITY, EQUITY, AND DIFFERENCE: THE CASE OF POVERTY

Related to social class, from a structural functional epistemology, poverty is viewed as the problem of the person in poverty. From this perspective, myths and assumptions and a deficit view of poverty prevail, such as that the parents of students of lower social class do not care about education, and societal poverty must be eradicated before students can be successful in school. Educators taking structural functional perspectives do not see how schools themselves perpetuate the cycle of poverty through the way they respond to students from lower social class homes or who are experiencing poverty (see Figure 3.5).

Importantly, a structural functional epistemology does not mean that structure is to be avoided when working toward social justice. As may be seen from the structural functionalist response to diversity and difference in the previous paragraphs, transforming the structures of schooling at the state, regional, district, and school levels is a critical aspect of social justice leadership. Given the limitations of structural functional epistemology and organizational theory, many scholars have called for and developed an antidote to these limitations, namely the interpretivist epistemology, discussed next in Chapter 4.

LEADERSHIP DEVELOPMENT ACTIVITIES

After reading the chapter, educator development activities that I describe next for structural functional epistemology include (1) playdough sculpture; (2) questions for whole-class discussion; (3) critical analysis of the educator's own leadership, and (4) case study analysis. It is best to work through all the activities in the order they are presented here. I also provide time estimates for each activity.

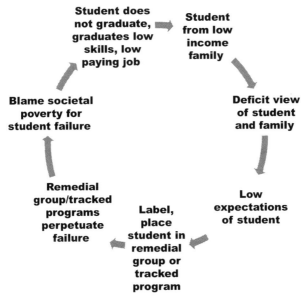

Figure 3.5 Structural Functional Response to Poverty Perpetuates Poverty

---

ACTIVITY 1: **Playdough Constructions**

1. Using playdough and with a partner, construct a symbolic representation of the structural functional epistemology (10 minutes).
2. Large group check-in: One person in each dyad presents their construction. Ask students to take notes, and the instructor takes notes for all to see, writing down the keywords for each construction so that by the end, educators have used their own language and words to describe structural functionalism (depending on group size 15 to 20 minutes).

ACTIVITY 2: **Discussion Questions for Structural Functional Epistemology (Large group about 20 minutes)**

From structural functionalist epistemology:

1. What are the organizational goals?
2. What does leadership look like?
3. How is the organization structured?
4. What does decision-making look like?
5. What does change look like?
6. What aspects of education emanate from this epistemology?

(Continued)

7. What is the goal of education?
8. What does the curriculum look like?
9. What does instruction look like?
10. What does assessment look like?
11. What does evaluation/supervision look like?
12. When a student struggles academically, how does the school respond?
13. How does this epistemology respond to differences and diversity?
14. What are the strengths and limitations of this epistemology?

ACTIVITY 3: **Critical Reflection on Your Own Leadership from the Structural Functionalist Epistemology (5 minutes of self-reflection, 10-minute share with partner, each taking 5 minutes, large group ask, "What is one point of your discussion you want to share out?")**

1. Identify two or three examples of how your leadership practices reflect structural functional epistemologies.
2. Describe two or three examples of how your educational setting responds to difference/diversity and in what ways these responses reflect the structural functional epistemology.

ACTIVITY 4: **Case Analysis from the Structural Functional Epistemology (About 35 minutes)**

1. First, each educator reviews the structural functional case analysis handout below (5 minutes).
2. Individual case analysis: What are the issues in your case from a structural functional epistemology? What are the possible solutions in your case from a structural functional epistemology? (Write down notes to these questions, 7 to 10 minutes).
3. With a partner, exchange and read each other's case (5 minutes).
4. With the same partner, share the issues and possible solutions to your case from structural functional epistemology. The partner can add additional ideas they saw that you may have missed; then the other partner takes a turn (7 minutes each, 14 minutes total).
5. Due the following week, educators then write up the structural functional case analysis – the issues and possible solutions – supported by the literature and limited to about two pages.

STRUCTURAL FUNCTIONAL EPISTEMOLOGY
ANALYSIS OF CASE SITUATION

Using *italics* I include questions to help analyze (1) the possible issues from a structural functional epistemology, and (2) possible *solutions* to the issue from a structural functional epistemology.

"Structural Forms" (Bolman & Deal, 2017a, p. 51)

1. Goals: *To what extent is your case an issue of unclear or conflicting goals?*
2. Levels of authority: *To what extent is your case an issue of too many or too few levels of authority?*
3. Communication systems: *To what extent is your situation a problem with communication systems in place (formal and informal)?*
4. Coordinating mechanisms: *To what extent is your situation a problem with coordinating work, either "vertically or laterally" (p. 60)?*
5. Procedures: *To what extent is your situation a problem with laws, policies, rules, or procedures?*

"Key Structural" (Bolman & Deal, 2017a, p. 62) Aspects to Consider in the Case

1. "Size of the organization" (p. 62): *To what extent is your situation a problem of organization size?*
2. "Core Technology" (p. 65), what an organization does, its central purpose, mission: *To what extent is your situation a problem with confusion or lack of agreement over the central purpose or mission?*
3. "Environment" (p. 64): *To what extent is your situation or problem related to coordinating or communicating with the "environment" (e.g., the community, parents, business)?*
4. "Strategy and goals" (p. 64): *To what extent is your situation a problem with strategy or goals (e.g., too many, too few, unclear, disagreement over)?*
5. "Information technology" (p. 64): *To what extent is your situation a problem with lack of information, too much information, or the wrong kind of information?*
6. People, "the nature of the workforce" (p. 64): *To what extent is your situation a problem with people not suited or prepared for the work?*

Key Structural Issues and Dilemmas (Bolman & Deal, 2017a)

1. "Differentiation vs. Integration" (p. 73): *To what extent is your situation a problem of work not divided appropriately? To what extent is your situation a problem of work not coordinated effectively?*
2. "Gaps vs. Overlaps" (p. 73): *To what extent is your situation a problem of gaps in who is supposed to be doing what? To what extent is your situation a problem of people assigned to do similar work and people are stepping on each other's toes?*

3. "Underuse vs. Overload" (p. 73): *To what extent is your situation a problem of underused or misused people or resources? To what extent is your situation a problem of people being overworked, making it impossible to get everything done?*
4. "Lack of clarity vs. Lack of creativity" (p. 73): *To what extent is your situation a problem of people not fully understanding their tasks? To what extent is your situation a problem of people overly subscribing to their role, stifling their own and others' creativity?*
5. "Excessive autonomy vs. Excessive interdependence" (p. 74): *To what extent is your situation a problem that people feel they have so much autonomy that they feel abandoned, unsupported, or isolated? To what extent is your situation a problem that people spend so much time working with each other in meetings and· committees that they cannot get their own work done?*
6. "Too loose vs. Too tight" (p. 74): *To what extent is your situation a problem that the problem is so loose that "no one knows what it is, and people go their own way with little sense of what others are doing?" (p. 72). To what extent is your situation a problem that people feel so constrained by the structure that they spend lots of time figuring out how to subvert it, or constrained in their creativity?*
7. "Diffuse authority vs. Over-centralization" (p. 55): *To what extent is your situation a problem that no one really knows who has authority over what? To what extent is your situation a problem that people must go through layers and layers of formal authority which removes decisions so far from their source that decision-making is excessively slow or inaccurate?*
8. "Goal-less vs. Goal-bound" (p. 75): *To what extent is your situation a problem that people are unclear about the goals, purpose, and mission? To what extent is your situation that people are clinging to goals that are no longer relevant or that do not work?*
9. "Irresponsible vs. Unresponsive" (p. 75): *To what extent is your situation a problem that people are unclear about their responsibilities or uncommitted to them, or are too accommodating? To what extent is your situation a problem that people are adhering too closely to their job description and not attending to the needs of the situation?*

Structural Functionalism and Diversity/Difference

1. *To what extent is the issue in your case a result of your situation reacting to diversity/difference from the structural functional epistemology?*

REFERENCES

Baglieri, S., Valle, J.W., Connor, D.J., & Gallagher, D.J. (2011). Disability Studies in education: The need for a plurality of perspectives on disability. *Remedial and Special Education, 32*(4), 267–278.

Bolman, L. & Deal, T. (2017a). Getting organized. In L.G. Bolman & T.E. Deal, *Reframing organizations: Artistry, choice, and leadership* (pp. 43–79). San Francisco, CA: Jossey-Bass.

Bolman, L. & Deal, T. (2017b). Structuring and restructuring. In L.G. Bolman & T.E. Deal, *Reframing organizations: Artistry, choice, and leadership* (pp. 79–100). San Francisco, CA: Jossey-Bass.

Burrell, G. & Morgan, G. (2003). *Sociological paradigms and organisational analysis: Elements of the sociology of corporate life*. Burlington, VT: Ashgate.

Capper, C.A. (1993). *Educational administration in a pluralistic society*. Albany, NY: State University of New York Press.

Capper, C.A. & Green, T.L. (2013). Organizational theories and the development of leadership capacity for integrated, socially just schools. In L. Tillman & J.J. Scheurich and Associates, *Handbook of educational leadership for equity and diversity* (pp. 62–82). New York: Routledge.

Capper, C.A. & Jamison, M.T. (1993a). Outcomes-based education re-examined: From structural functionalism to poststructuralism. *Educational Policy, 7*(4), 427–446.

Capper, C.A., Keyes, M., & Theoharis, G. (2000). Spirituality in leadership: Implications for inclusive schooling. In R.A. Villa & J.S. Thousand (Eds), *Restructuring for caring and effective education: Piecing the puzzle together* (pp. 513–530). Baltimore, MD: Brookes.

Foster, W.P. (1986a). *Paradigms and promises: New approaches to educational administration*. Buffalo, NY: Prometheus Books.

Foster, W.P. (1986b). *Toward a critical theory of educational administration*. In T.J. Serqiovanni and J.E. Corbally (Eds), *Leadership and organizational culture*. Urbana, IL: University of Illinois Press.

Frattura, E. & Capper, C.A. (2015). *Integrated comprehensive systems*. Retrieved from www.icsequity.org.

Gibson, J., Ivancevich, J., & Konopaske, R. (1984). *Organizations: Behavior, structure. processes*. New York: McGraw Hill.

Gioia, D.A. & Pitre, E. (1990). Multiparadigm perspectives on theory building. *Academy of Management Review, 15*(4), 584–602.

Pai, Y. & Adler, S. (1997). *Cultural foundations of education*. New York: Pearson/Merrill/Prentice Hall.

Popkewitz, T.S. (1984). *Paradigm and ideology in educational research: The social functions of the intellectual*. London and New York: The Falmer Press.

Ritzer, G. (1980). *Sociology: A multiple paradigm shift*. Boston, MA: Allyn & Bacon.

Rose, T. (2015). *The end of average: How we succeed in a world of sameness*. New York: HarperCollins.

Sirotnik, K.A. & Oakes, J. (1986). *Critical perspectives on the organization and improvement of schooling*. Boston, MA: Kluwer-Nijhoff.

Skrtic, T. (1991). *Behind special education: A critical analysis of professional culture and school organization*. Denver, CO: Love.

Sleeter, C. (1991). *Empowerment through multicultural education*. Albany, NY: State University of New York Press.

Tyack, D. (1976). Ways of seeing: An essay on the history of compulsory schooling. *Harvard Educational Review, 46*(3), 355–389.

Valencia, R. (2010). *Dismantling contemporary deficit thinking: Educational thought and practice*. New York: Routledge.

Suggested Key Readings on Organizational Theories and Structural Functionalism

Mintzberg, H. (1987). The five basic parts of the organization. In J.M. Shafritz & J.S. Ott, *Classics of organization theory* (2nd ed) (pp. 219–233). Chicago, IL: Dorsey.

Taylor, F.W (1987). The principles of scientific management. In J.M. Shafritz & J.S. Ott, *Classics of organization theory* (2nd ed) (pp. 66–81). Chicago, IL: Dorsey.

Weber, M. (1987). Bureaucracy. In J.M. Shafritz & J.S. Ott (Eds), *Classics of organization theory* (2nd ed) (pp. 81–86). Chicago, IL: Dorsey.

CHAPTER 4

Interpretivist Epistemology

On the epistemological framework described in Figure 4.1, interpretivism is premised on the subjective nature of knowledge (horizontal axis) and nature of change oriented toward regulation (vertical axis). An interpretivist epistemology of organizations focuses on social life interactions and the meaning of these interactions as perceived by individuals, rather than so-called objective reality (Sirotnik & Oakes, 1986). Because this epistemology is rooted in the sociology of regulation, "the problems of conflict, domination, contradiction ... and change play no part ... in this epistemology" (Burrell & Morgan, 1982, p. 31, cited in Capper, 1993, p. 11). While the structural functional epistemology focuses on how organizations operate with a goal of efficiency, interpretivists are concerned mainly with how people experience the organization with a goal of understanding.

As I wrote in 1993, "An interpretivist epistemology shares structural functionalists' assumption that the existing social order and its institutions are legitimate, necessary, and not problematic" (Capper, 1993, p. 12; Burrell & Morgan, 1982). Educators who adopt the interpretivist epistemology posit that schools as "organizations are socially constructed and exist only in the perceptions of people" (Capper, 1993, p. 11) Individuals are viewed as interdependent, dependent on others (Gibson, Ivancevich, & Konopaske, 1984). Interpretivist epistemologies and research methodologies focus on participant meaning and understanding, patterns of behavior, and feelings of persons which undergird qualitative research methodologies (Sirotnik & Oakes, 1986). Using interviews and observations of events and interactions in this interpretive mode can uncover the similar and different perceptions of what is happening in the setting.

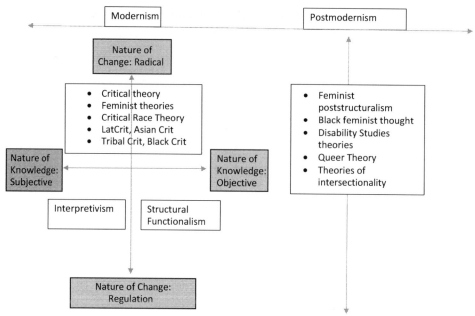

Figure 4.1 An Epistemology Framework

Sometimes interpretivist understandings and analyses may point to the necessity of change, but this change is oriented toward regulation (Gioia & Pitre, 1990; Sirotnik & Oakes, 1986). Even though multiple perspectives are solicited on proposed changes, interpretivism is like structural functionalism in that change is believed to be evolutionary, step-by-step and maintains the status quo (Burrell & Morgan, 1982; Fullan, 2016). Similarly, a leader may ensure that stakeholder perspectives are included, but maintains the leader's own perspective, and in the end the leader makes the final decision and the goal of stability remains the same. As such, a collaborative effort among teachers, students, community members, and agencies does not necessarily mean that equity will be prioritized unless this is the goal of the collaboration.

THE HUMAN RESOURCE FRAME

Many organizational theories emanate from and span structural functional and interpretive perspectives, including human relations and systems theories (Burrell & Morgan, 1982; Foster, 1986). For example, systems theories were espoused beginning in the late 1940s. They suggested, in part, that schools as organizations are dependent on their environments, and information sustaining the organization is gained via communication and systems feedback loops. Dating back to the 1950s, human relations theories suggested that educational organizations exist to serve human needs. Human relations theories include participatory management, job enrichment, self-managing work teams, and organizational development.

Two frames of Bolman and Deal's (2017) four-frames approach can be aligned to the interpretivist epistemology: the human resource frame and the symbolic frame. With the human resource frame, Bolman and Deal offer the following assumptions based on the organizational theory literature:

1. Organizations exist to serve human needs rather than the converse.
2. People and organizations need each other. Organizations need ideas, energy, and talent; people need careers, salaries, and opportunities.
3. When the fit between individual and system is poor, one or both suffer. Individuals are exploited or exploit the organization – or both become victims.
4. A good fit benefits both. Individuals find meaningful and satisfying work, and organizations get the talent and energy they need to succeed (p. 118).

From Bolman and Deal's (2017) human resources frame, the metaphor for organizations is family; central concepts are needs, skills, and relationships; and the basic leadership challenge is aligning the organization to human needs. The human resources frame suggests, "Build and implement an HR strategy. Hire the right people. Keep them. Invest in them. Empower them. Promote diversity" (p. 138).

With "promoting diversity" (p. 138), Bolman and Deal (2017) discuss the importance of welcoming and hiring individuals across race, gender, and sexual identity. They cite several high-profile discrimination cases from Denny and Coke as reasons to "promote diversity" because, in their words, "in the end, it makes good business sense for companies to promote diversity. If a company devalues certain groups, word tends to get out and customers become alienated" (2017, p. 152). Thus, from the human resources perspective, organizations should "promote" diversity in hiring as a means to avoid alienating customers.

Motivation theory resides within the human resource frame as discussed by Bolman and Deal (2017). They refer to Maslow's Hierarchy of Needs Theory for leaders to consider when leading an organization and working with individuals within the organization, even though, as they explain, little empirical evidence exists for the effectiveness of this theory in practice. Further, as Shakeshaft (1989) discusses in her ground-breaking book on women in educational leadership, Maslow's theory is steeped in androcentric bias. Shakeshaft explains how theories, like Maslow's, are "formulated using a male lens but applied to both males and female" (p. 159), and that, according to Maslow, "Excellence in humanity is, therefore, excellence in masculinity" (p. 158).

Additional theories from a human resource frame include the literature on organizational development. Bolman and Deal (2017) cite Lewin's work in the 1940s on sensitivity training, known as "T-groups"(p. 154),) as one example of organizational development work. Interestingly, Lewin was one of the first organizational theory scholars to address race (Burnes, 2004), and sought to understand how racial conflict and intergroup relations related to race could be addressed. Bolman and Deal report that one criticism of his work was that this sensitivity training was "better at changing individuals than organizations" (p. 154).

The human resource frame also includes theories by Argyris and Schon (1978), who explored the contradictions between "espoused theory" (i.e., what people say they believe) and "theory in use" (cited in Bolman & Deal, 2017, p. 161) (i.e., what people actually do or theory of action). Often, educators are encouraged to articulate a "theory in action" for their practice – to be explicit about the theory guiding their practice. At the same time, just because an educator is clear about the theory guiding their action, the theory or action may not be equity focused. Similarly, ensuring that an espoused theory aligns with one's actions does not necessarily mean that the actions advance equitable ends.

Argyris and Schon (1978) also described two models for human behavior. Model I is based on:

> the core assumption that an organization is a dangerous place where you have to look out for yourself or someone else may do you in. This assumption leads individuals to follow a predictable set of steps in their attempts to influence others. (Bolman & Deal, 2017, p. 162)

These steps include the following:

1. Assume that the problem is caused by the other person(s).
2. Develop a private, unilateral diagnosis and solution.
3. Since the other person is the cause of the problem, get him or her to change, using one or more of three basic strategies: facts, logic, and rational persuasion (argue the merits of your point of view or your solution); indirect influence (ease in, ask leading questions, manipulate the other person); and direct critique (tell the other person directly what he or she is doing wrong and how he or she should change).
4. If the other person resists or becomes defensive, this confirms the original diagnosis (that the other person caused the problem).
5. Respond to resistance through some combination of intensifying pressure, protecting the other person, or rejecting the other person.
6. If your efforts are unsuccessful, or less successful than hoped, it is the other's fault. You need feel no personal responsibility (pp. 162–163).

In contrast, Argyris and Schon's Model II of human behavior suggests the following:

1. Emphasize common goals and mutual influence.
2. Communicate openly; publicly test assumptions and beliefs.
3. Combine advocacy with inquiry (cited in Bolman & Deal, 2017, p. 163).

Neither Model I and Model II considers how individuals from traditionally marginalized identities may experience typical organizations as repressive and oppressive, which in turn informs their response to these oppressive environments and situations.

Argyris and Schon (1978) suggest that when people are frustrated in an organization, they resist or adapt to the frustration in the following ways (cited in Bolman & Deal, 2017, p. 125):

1. Withdraw from the organization via absenteeism or simply by quitting.
2. Stay on the job, but withdraw psychologically, becoming indifferent, passive, apathetic.
3. Resist the organization by restricting productivity, deception, and sabotage.
4. Climb the hierarchy to better jobs.
5. Create groups/coalitions to address the power imbalance.

In sum, Bolman and Deal's human resource frame and the theories that comprise the frame all emanate from the interpretivist epistemology. While the assumptions and theories within the frame move beyond structural functional approaches, they stop short of considerations of power, privilege, and equity.

THE SYMBOLIC FRAME

In addition to the human resource frame, Bolman and Deal's (2017) symbolic frame of organizational theory also emanates from interpretivist epistemology. According to Bolman and Deal, "The symbolic frame forms an umbrella for ideas from several disciplines, including organization theory and sociology (Selznick, 1957; Blumer, 1969; Schutz, 1967; Clark, 1972; Corwin, 1976; March & Olsen, 1976; Meyer & Rowan, 1978; Weick, 1976; Davis and others, 1976; Hofstede, 1984)" (p. 241). The assumptions of the symbolic frame include the following:

1. What is most important about an event is not what happened, but what it means.
2. Events and meanings are loosely coupled: the same events can have very different meanings for different people because of differences in the schema they use to interpret their experience.
3. Many organizational events and processes are important more for what they express than for what they produce.
4. Facing uncertainty and ambiguity, people create symbols to resolve confusion, find direction, and anchor hope and faith.
5. These events and processes weave a tapestry of secular myths, heroes and heroines, rituals, ceremonies, and stories to help people find purpose and passion (p. 241).

Throughout their text, nearly all the leaders and associated heroes and heroines portrayed are white males adhering to traditional notions of masculinity.

In their discussion of the symbolic frame, Bolman and Deal (2017) reference Collins' (2001) book *Good to great,* a study of corporations and an often-used text in educational leadership programs. Representative of the interpretivist epistemology, the book does not ask readers to consider "Good for whom?" If educators assume that their schools are already "good," then good for whom? Our public schools have always been decently good for white, middle-upper class students who are heterosexual, cisgender, whose home language is English, and without a disability label. However, for students who do not fit that category – students from low-income families, of color, for whom English is not their home language, labeled with a disability; lesbian, gay, bisexual; or transgender and their intersections – most schools have been anything but good. To declare our schools as "good" schools reflects our denial about the inequities in those schools. Thus, educators could become deeply enamored with Collins' concepts and ideas, but in so doing remain distracted from addressing inequities.

Out of Bolman and Deal's (2017) symbolic frame emerged their popular definition of culture as "the way we do things around here" (p. 258). Yet, as one would predict of a concept grounded in the interpretivist epistemology, "the way we do things around here" reflects systems of privilege and power. That is, "the way we do things around here" most often reflects white and other privileged assumptions with the expectation that all will fit into this culture of simultaneous privilege and oppression.

Bolman and Deal (2017) also identify "Diversity as a competitive advantage" (p. 269) as an important tenet of the symbolic frame, taken from a review of a computer company more than 30 years ago. Bolman and Deal defined diversity among the all-male engineers in the company as diversity of "specialty and personality" (p. 269) – yet none of their other intersecting identities was mentioned. The only woman to appear in their case example was a woman they described who functioned as the "mother superior" (p. 269) or "den mother" (p. 275) to the all male group.

Bolman and Deal (2017) again mention diversity when discussing the symbolism of structure. They refer to an example of hiring a diversity officer, establishing diversity committees and task forces, and developing diversity plans which symbolize that something is being done, even if nothing changes. They explain:

> New structures reflect legal and social expectations and represent a bid for legitimacy and support from the attending audience. An organization without an affirmative action program, for example, is suspiciously out of step with prevailing concerns for diversity and equity. Nonconformity invites questions, criticism, and inspection. It is easier to appoint a diversity officer than to change hiring practices deeply embedded in both individual and institutional beliefs and practices. Because the presence of a diversity officer is more visible than revisions in hiring priorities, the addition of a new role may signal to external constituencies that there has been a new development in the drama even if the appointment is "window dressing" and no real change has occurred. (Bolman & Deal, 2017, p. 286)

In sum, the symbolic frame, like the human resources frame, is grounded in interpretivist epistemology. Although a leader or educator may believe they are shifting among frames when viewing a situation from the human resources frame versus the symbolic frame, both frames are grounded in the interpretivist epistemology and thus both frames can perpetuate oppression and inequities. Does this mean that considerations of human relations and of symbolism and culture are not relevant to social justice leadership? In the chapter on critical theory (Chapter 5), I will explore in more detail whether and how theories associated with the human resource and symbolic frame could be recast toward social justice ends.

LEADERSHIP AND THE INTERPRETIVIST EPISTEMOLOGY

Leaders leading from an interpretivist epistemology emphasize personal awareness, the significance of relationships, and having a purpose or mission. From the interpretivist epistemology, the education leader serves as a facilitator and collaborator. Although it appears that these interpretivist themes move beyond a structural functional perspective, they stop short of equity goals.

Other leadership practices aligned with the interpretive epistemology include the work on emotional intelligence, leadership styles, the Myers-Briggs inventory, distributed leadership, spirituality and leadership, the reflective practitioner, leading for learning, and the learning organization. All these aspects of leadership move beyond structural functionalism, but equity and social justice are not the explicit goals of these practices. Thus, these practices can mask and distract from equity work, and in so doing perpetuate inequities.

The differences between the interpretivist epistemology and critically oriented epistemologies which I discuss later in the book may be summed up by the phrase "Charity, not justice." For example, from an interpretivist epistemology, educators may feel sorry for students from low-income homes, hold a deficit view of these students and their families, and thus hold lower expectations of these students. As such, educators with an interpretivist epistemology focus on charity and sympathy but not on changing the systems and practices to prevent poverty in the first place, as discussed in Chapter 3.

"Caring" leadership has emerged again recently in the educational leadership literature (Louis, Murphy, & Smylie, 2016). Yet, as Reitzug (1994) noted: "even such notable notions as caring can result in inequity" (p. 213). I wrote in 1993 that the problem with the "caring" literature:

> is because parents "cared" for the welfare of their white children that they established segregated schools in the south. It is because people "care" about the educational achievement of their own children and believe that students with special needs deserve "special help" away from "typical students" that administrators … and parents promote the continued segregation of students without disability labels away from students with those labels. (Capper, 1993, p. 295)

Leadership from an interpretivist epistemology shifts from structural functionalism. Nearly all of the leadership literature in business and education advocates an emphasis on relationships, collaboration, professional learning communities, constructivist learning, and caring. Yet it stops short of considering power, privilege, or equity.

THE INTERPRETIVIST EPISTEMOLOGY, ORGANIZATIONAL THEORY, AND RESPONSE TO DIVERSITY

Many educational practices emanate from the interpretivist epistemology, including constructivist learning theory, multiple intelligences (Gardner, 2011), cooperative learning, whole language, some forms of multicultural education, professional learning communities, adaptive schools, differentiated instruction, Universal Design for Learning, learner-centered classrooms, multi-age classrooms, project-based learning, co-teaching, and personalized learning. While all these educational practices shift beyond structural functional epistemologies, none addresses equity or makes eliminating inequities the explicit goal. That is, none of these educational practices identifies "to what ends" these practices are directed and the goal of eliminating inequities is not identified as the goal for this work. As previously discussed, when the goal is not equity or social justice explicitly, then these practices can perpetuate inequities by educators being deeply engaged in these practices but not addressing inequities in doing so. Thus, the outcomes of these practices do not change the inequities in the school, even though educators believe they are fundamentally changing what is happening in the classroom.

Most of these practices rely on the language of "all students," "all learners," similar to most school districts in their mission statements; yet the practices are not specific to eliminating inequities among learners. These instructional practices are laid on top of the broken structural functional education system reviewed in the chapter on structural functional epistemology (Chapter 3), and ignore the assimilationist culture and oppressive system of schooling.

Like most leadership or educational practices grounded in an interpretivist epistemology, many of these educational practices claim to be about systems change, changing the system, or transforming education. For example, in their book on personalized learning, Bray and McCleskey (2014) argue: "Our system is broken, and it's time to really look at personalizing learning as a way to transform education" (p. 205), and "Consider personalized learning as a culture shift and transformational revolution shaking up teaching and learning" (p. 7). Yet, the transformation called for in most education practices is speaking about transformation from structural functional to interpretivist epistemology, as is the case with Bray and McCleskey's articulation of personalized learning – which is no small shift. At the same time, this epistemological shift falls short of shifting toward equitable outcomes for all students, as I will discuss in the chapters on critically oriented epistemology.

This does not mean that an educational practice grounded in an interpretivist epistemology cannot be utilized toward equitable ends. However, because equity is not the explicit purpose of the practice, nor are all the associated professional development, materials, and examples oriented toward these ends, then the practice is highly unlikely to be leveraged for, or result in equitable outcomes. Personalized learning that is not focused on equity can distract from the equity work and, as a result, inequities may increase. Further, "personalizing" learning could mean ascribing lower expectations for students from low-income families, students of color, students labeled with disabilities, and students who are linguistically diverse. These students are routed into lower level "personalized" learning experiences.

Given the plethora of educational practices that emanate from the interpretivist epistemology, this epistemology along with structural functionalism guides much of educators' responses to diversity and difference. I characterize interpretivist response to diversity or difference as a "it's a small world" response where educators are seeking harmony and "celebrating diversity," informed by school curricula of studying cultures around the world, ethnic nights at school, or when extra-curricular clubs develop service projects to "help the under-privileged." While these practices shift beyond completely ignoring race, culture, and class, at the same time these practices do not address the historic, systemic, structural oppression across these differences.

For example, the popular Tribes program aptly represents the interpretivist epistemology with its focus on building community in schools. Tribes defines its work as follows (Tribes Learning Community, 2016): "Every school should be a model home, a complete community actively developing future compassionate citizens capable of creating, leading and contributing to the kind of democratic communities – in which we all long to live." Yet, the Tribes program suggests implementing these practices with no mention of addressing segregated, tracked, pull-out programs that perpetuate student hierarchy and inequities. Thus, in practice, educators have shared that teachers in their schools have been implementing a Tribes community-building activity while, during that activity, students labeled with disabilities have been pulled out of the classroom for instruction. Thus, Tribes activities are occurring in classrooms that are not a "model home" or "complete community" and are not representative of "democratic communities – in which we all long to live."

With the specific case example of disability, like the structural functional epistemology, when educators address disability from an interpretivist epistemology they continue to defer to the experts who deliver student services, maintaining the divide between general and special education. These educators will most often claim that their schools are "inclusive" as long as some students with disabilities are educated in general education for part of the time. Students with disabilities are included because of the importance of social relationships for these students, with less attention given to academic needs. Students labeled with disabilities are viewed as needing support and as objects of pity among other students. Programs in schools such as "disability buddies" or other similar artificial friendship systems emanate from the interpretivist epistemology. If students labeled with disabilities were truly thought of as peers and equals in the school and integrated throughout the school

H. nature?
?

in natural proportions learning alongside students without disability labels, natural friendships would form and there would be no need for contrived friendship groups based on charity.

Educators addressing diversity and difference from an interpretivist epistemology perhaps unknowingly favor charity over justice. Students outside the norm, as previously described, may be felt sorry for or may be objects of pity based on deficit assumptions about students and families outside of the norm. Students labeled with disabilities may be included in ways that do not disrupt the status quo of schooling, in particular courses or classes. Students experiencing poverty are viewed as deficit, and that they have a "culture of poverty" (Donnor & Ladson-Billings, 2018), that all experience "trauma" while ignoring the daily trauma of oppressive structures and cultures that schools inflict upon students. Students of color and their families are also viewed as deficient – that difference equals deficient, that intrinsic student learning and life potential remains limited.

Nearly all "diversity" trainings and workshops emanate out of the interpretivist epistemology (Evans, 2007; Stovall, 2004; Sue, 2015). While educators may at best be challenged to disrupt their notions of, in particular race, this possible increase in racial consciousness often does not extend to other identities and their intersections to disrupting the structures and systems of schooling that oppress and marginalize. Critically oriented epistemologies push beyond charity and arise from and center justice. Historically, critical theory emerged as the first critically oriented epistemology that I take up next in Chapter 5.

LEADERSHIP DEVELOPMENT ACTIVITIES

After reading the chapter, educator development activities I describe next for the interpretivist epistemology include (1) playdough sculpture, (2) discussion questions for whole class discussion, (3) critical analysis of the educator's own leadership, and (4) case study analysis. It is best to work through all the activities in the order they are presented here. I also provide time estimates.

ACTIVITY 1: Playdough Constructions

1. Using playdough and with a partner, construct a symbolic representation of the interpretivist epistemology (10 minutes).
2. Large group check-in: One person in each dyad presents their construction. Ask students to take notes, and the instructor takes notes so that all can see, writing down the keywords for each construction such that by the end, educators have used their own language and words to describe interpretivism (depending on group size 15 to 20 minutes).

ACTIVITY 2:   **Discussion Questions for the Interpretivist Epistemology (Large group about 20 minutes)**

From the interpretivist epistemology:

1. What are the organizational goals?
2. What does leadership look like?
3. How is the organization structured?
4. What does decision-making look like?
5. What aspects of education emanate from this epistemology?
6. What is the goal of education?
7. What does the curriculum look like?
8. What does instruction look like?
9. What does assessment look like?
10. What does evaluation/supervision look like?
11. How does this epistemology respond to power, privilege, and difference?
12. What are the strengths and limitations of this epistemology?

ACTIVITY 3:   **Critical Reflection on Your Own Leadership from the Interpretivist Epistemology (5 minutes of self-reflection, 10-minute share with partner with each taking 5 minutes, large group asks, "What is one point of your discussion you want to share out?")**

1. Identify two or three specific examples of your leadership practices that reflect the interpretivist epistemology.
2. How have these interpretivist practices identified in number 1 prevented more equitable practices from happening?

ACTIVITY 4:   **Case Analysis from the Interpretivist Epistemology (About 35 minutes)**

1. First, each educator reviews the interpretivist epistemology case analysis handout below (5 minutes).
2. Individual case analysis: What are the issues in your case from an interpretivist epistemology? What are the possible solutions in your case from an interpretivist epistemology? (Write down notes to these questions, 7 to 10 minutes.)
3. With a partner, exchange and read each other's cases (5 minutes).

(Continued)

4. With the same partner, share the issues and possible solutions to your case from the interpretivist epistemology. Your partner may add additional ideas they saw that you may have missed. Next, switch partners and repeat (7 minutes each, 14 minutes in total).

5. Due the following week, educators will then write up the interpretivist epistemology case analysis – the issues and possible solutions – supported by the literature, and limited to about two pages.

INTERPRETIVIST EPISTEMOLOGY ANALYSIS OF CASE SITUATION (ADAPTED IN PART FROM BOLMAN AND DEAL, 2017)

1. Concept: Espoused theories vs. theory in use/action (Argyris & Schon, 1978). *To what extent is your situation a problem between espoused theories (what you believe) and theories in action of yourself, or the people involved in the case? Are your espoused beliefs lining up with your actions? Are the espoused beliefs of individuals in the case lining up with their actions?*

2. Review the Model I that Argyris and Schon (1978) propose above. To what extent is this going on in your case?

3. To solve what is going on in the case, how helpful would Argyris and Schon's (1978) Model II be?

4. To what extent does your case address collaboration without a goal of equity?

5. To what extent does your case seek stakeholder perspectives, yet, in the end, the leader makes the final decision; that the case illustrates an illusion of democratic decision-making?

6. What role does Bolman and Deal's (2017) symbolic frame play in your case? Are policies or practices in place in your case that are symbolic of addressing equity on the surface, but in the end are not addressing the historical, cultural, and structural inequities of the system?

REFERENCES

Argyris, C. & Schon, D. (1978). *Organizational learning: A theory of action perspective.* Reading, MA: Addison Wesley.

Blumer, H. (1969). *Symbolic interaction: Perspective and method.* Upper Saddle River, NJ: Prentice Hall.

Bolman, L.G. & Deal, T.E. (2017). *Reframing organizations: Artistry, choice, and leadership.* Hoboken, NJ: Jossey-Bass.

Bray, B A. & McCleskey, K.A. (2014). *Make learning personal: The what, who, WOW, where, and why.* New York: Sage. Kindle Edition.

Burnes, B. (2004). Kurt Lewin and the planned approach to change: A re-appraisal. *Journal of Management Studies, 41*(6), 997–1002.

Burrell, G. & Morgan, G. (1982). *Sociological paradigms and organisational analysis: Elements of the sociology of corporate life.* Burlington, VT: Ashgate.

Capper, C.A. (1993). Educational administration in a pluralistic society: A multiple paradigm approach. In C.A. Capper (Ed.), *Educational administration in a pluralistic society* (pp. 7–35). Albany, NY: State University of New York Press.

Capper, C.A., Keyes, M., & Theoharis, G. (2000). Spirituality in leadership: Implications for inclusive schooling. In R.A. Villa & J.S. Thousand (Eds), *Restructuring for caring and effective education: Piecing the puzzle together* (pp. 513–530). Baltimore, MD: Brookes.

Clark, B. (1972). The organizational saga in higher education. *Administrative Science Quarterly, 17*(2), 178–184.

Collins, J.C. (2001). *Good to great. Why some companies make the leap and others don't.* New York: HarperCollins.

Corwin, R. (1976). *Organizations as loosely coupled systems: Evolution of a perspective.* Paper presented at the Conference on Schools as Loosely Coupled Organizations, Stanford University, November.

Davis, M. & others. (1976). *The structure of the educational systems.* Paper presented at the conference on schools loosely coupled organizations, Stanford University, November.

Donnor, J. J. & Ladson-Billings, G. (2018). Critical race theory and the postracial imaginary. In N. K. Denzin & Y.S. Lincoln (Eds) *The Sage handbook of qualitative research* (5th edn) pp. 195–213, Thousand Oaks, CA: Sage.

Evans, A.E. (2007). School leaders and their sensemaking about race and demographic change. *Educational Administration Quarterly, 43*(2), 159–188.

Foster, W.P. (1986). *Paradigms and promise: New approaches to educational administration.* Buffalo, NY: Prometheus Books.

Fullan, M. (2016). *The new meaning of educational change* (5th edn). New York: Routledge.

Gardner, H. (2011). *Frames of mind.* New York: Basic Books.

Gibson, J., Ivancevich, J., & Konopaske, R. (1984). *Organizations: Behavior, structure, processes.* New York: McGraw Hill.

Gioia, D.A. & Pitre, E. (1990). Multiparadigm perspectives on theory building. *Academy of Management Review, 15*(4), 584–602.

Hofstede, G. (1984). *Culture's consequences: International differences in work-related values.* Thousand Oaks, CA: Sage.

Louis, K., Murphy, J., & Smylie, M. (2016). Caring leadership in schools. *Educational Administration Quarterly, 52*(2), 310–348.

March, J.G. & Olsen, J. (Eds). (1976). *Ambiguity and choice in organizations.* Bergen, Norway: Universitetsforlaget.

Meyer, J.W. & Rowan, B. (1978). The structure of educational organizations. In Meyer and associates, *Environments and organizations: Theoretical and empirical perspectives.* San Francisco, CA: Jossey-Bass

Reitzug, U.C. (1994). A case study of empowering principal behavior. *American Educational Research Journal, 31*(2), 283–307.

Schutz, A. (1967). *The phenomenology of the social world.* Evanston, IL: Northwestern University Press.

Selznick, P. (1957). *Leadership and administration.* New York: HarperCollins.

Shakeshaft, C. (1989). *Women in educational administration.* Newbury Park, CA: Corwin.

Sirotnik, K.A. & Oakes, J. (1986). *Critical perspectives on the organization and improvement of schooling.* Boston, MA: Kluwer-Nijhoff.

Stovall, D. (2004). School leader as negotiator: Critical theory praxis and the creation of productive space. *Multicultural Education, 12*(2), 8–12.

Sue, D. W. (2015). *Race talk and the conspiracy of silence: Understanding and facilitatingdifficult dialogues on race.* Hoboken, NJ: John Wiley & Sons.

Tribes Learning Community. (2016). *A new way of learning and growing together.* Retrieved from http://tribes.com (accessed October 14, 2016).

SUGGESTED READINGS

Sergiovanni, T.J. (1994). Organizations or communities: Changing the metaphor changes the theory. *Educational Administration Quarterly, 30*(2), 214–226.

Weick, K.E. (1981). Educational organizations as loosely coupled systems. In M. Zey-Ferrell & M. Aiken (Eds), *Complex organizations: Critical perspectives* (pp. 217–226). Glenview, IL: Scott Foresman.

CHAPTER 5

Critical Theory Epistemology

Referring to the epistemological framework that guides this book, the critical theory epistemology emerged as the first historic critically oriented epistemology that lies on the radical change end of the change continuum (vertical axis) (see Figure 5.1) with the nature of knowledge for critical theory oriented along the subjective/objective continuum (horizontal axis). Though Burrell and Morgan (1985) parse out the differences between the subjective (radical humanism) and objective (radical structuralism) ends of the nature of knowledge continuum, the epistemological framework for this book examines radical social change along both dimensions of knowledge.

Critical theory originated in the 1930s within the Frankfurt School of Thought in Germany that comprised a group of intellectual elite white men (sexuality unknown), including Habermas, Marcuse, Adorno, and Horkheimer (Foster, 1980, 1986a, 1986b). William Foster introduced critical theory to the field of educational leadership in his *Harvard Education Review* publication on critical theory scholar Habermas (1980), followed by his ground-breaking book *Paradigms and promises* that featured critical theory applications to educational administration (1986a). Though Foster reviews the organizational theory literature across time, he stops short of articulating how critical theory could inform organizational theory. He ends his organizational theory review by advocating a dialectical view of organizations, moving beyond organizations such as schools as static, to recognizing "organizations as human constructs that become concretized over time but still remain open to change by human intervention" (p. 146).

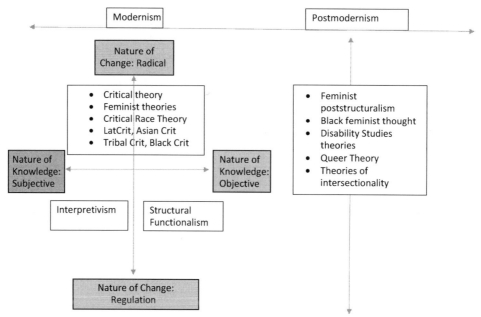

Figure 5.1 An Epistemology Framework

As mentioned in Chapter 2, at about the same time as Foster's (1980) scholarship, Zey-Ferrell and Aiken (1981) contributed to the initiation of critical theory approaches to management in Europe with their volume on critical perspectives of complex organizations. The European critical management theory scholarship remains robust today, recognized as Critical Management Studies (see criticalmanagement.org) applied largely to businesses and organizations other than education. The Critical Management Studies website description reflects some of the tenets of critical theory:

> Critical Management Studies (CMS) is a largely left-wing and theoretically informed approach to management and organisation studies. It challenges the prevailing conventional understanding of management and organisations. CMS provides a platform for debating radical alternatives whilst interrogating the established relations of power, control, domination and ideology as well as the relations among organisations, society and people. (criticalmanagement.org retrieved January 1, 2018)

The explicit focus on power, inequities, oppression, and marginalization distinguishes critical theory from the structural functionalist epistemology (Chapter 3) and the interpretivist epistemology (Chapter 4). Further, structural functional and interpretivist renderings of organizational theory clearly demarcate between theories associated with leadership, change, and decision-making. We will discover that within critically oriented epistemologies – including critical theory – leadership, change, and decision-making are inextricably intertwined.

CRITICAL THEORY TENETS

I identify key principles and assumptions of critical theory, and all these principles and assumptions inform leadership, change, and decision-making. Critical theory tenets include a concern for suffering and oppression, a critical view of education, reuniting facts and values with a goal of social justice, an emphasis on power between the oppressor and the oppressed, disrupting power via communication and dialogue, praxis, and leadership as a political act (Capper, Keyes, Theoharis, 2000; Foster, 1986b; Sirotnik & Oakes, 1986).

Acknowledge and relieve suffering and oppression. Critical theory pivots upon relationships of power—who has power, who does not—and assumes the presence of suffering and oppression in organizations. According to Gioia and Pitre (1990), "The goal of [leaders informed by critical theory] is to free organization members from sources of domination, alienation, exploitation, and repression" (p. 588). Because of its foundation in Marxian thought, critical theory originally focused on social class as "first and foremost ... a critical analysis of the capitalistic system" (Foster, 1986a, p. 67). According to Smyth (1989), within the organizational theory literature, oppression meant the "inability to participate in capitalistic society in economic terms" (Capper, 1993, p. 12, Foster, 1986a). Freire's tome *Pedagogy of the Oppressed* (2000) remains one of the most significant scholarly contributions of critical theory to education, spawning critical pedagogy. Contemporary scholars who rely on critical theory may also include gender, race, and class in their work (Apple, 1988) as reviewed in the equity research in educational leadership detailed in Chapter 2.

Critique education's perpetuation and disruption of power. Within education, critical theorists explicitly link education "to its historical, political, economic, and societal contexts" (Capper, 1993, p. 13), and leaders critique policy and practice to determine the degree to which they address or perpetuate oppression (Apple, 2014; Sirotnik & Oakes, 1986). According to Foster (1986a), educational leaders "must critically examine taken for granted assumptions and what is considered common sense" and determine "to what degree ... this administrative practice contribute[s] to the development of truth, freedom, or justice, and offer[s] options for change" (p. 255). When educational leaders engage in a critique of their school's practices based on critical theory, they uncover "how some individuals and groups have access to resources and others do not, why some groups are underrepresented and others are not, why certain influences prevail and others do not" (Yeakey, Johnston, & Adkinson, 1986, p. 115).

Reunite facts with values with a goal of social justice praxis. Rather than based on one objective "truth" devoid of values within a structural functionalist epistemology, critical theory reunites facts with values (Foster, 1986b), and the educational leader must practice morally and ethically. Beyond critique, educational leaders practicing within the critical theory epistemology aim for social change and their hallmark is an unwavering drive to emancipate the oppressed and disenfranchised (Gioia & Pitre, 1990). From this epistemology, leaders critically analyze situations and align moral concerns with their actions, and as a result, persons along the axis of oppression are empowered (Foster, 1986a; Sirotnik & Oakes, 1986). Thus, according to Foster, effective leaders are not determined from a community and school popularity contest; rather, "it is the ends of schooling that really must be at the heart of the dialogue on what constitutes effective administrative behavior" (Foster, 1980, p. 504). Foster then advocates practice informed by theory informed by practice or critical praxis.

Power between the oppressor and oppressed. As featured in Freire's scholarship on the pedagogy of the oppressed (2000), the critical theory epistemology centers on "empowerment" and sharing power to disrupt oppression. Educators engaged in critical theory epistemology then work to "give voice to the voiceless" in their work with oppressed persons (Tierney & Foster, 1991, p. 3). For educators grounded in a critical theory epistemology, "the nature of power is an 'all or nothing' phenomenon. That is, a person either possesses power or does not; a person is either an oppressor or a member of an oppressed group" (Capper, 1998, p. 356). Critical theory-based educators typically view power as a "seamless entity with the power elite holding all the power within the upper hierarchical echelons of organizations and institutions; marginalized individuals have the potential for power, but those in power hold opportunities beyond their reach" (Capper, 1998, pp. 356–357; Gioia &. Pitre, 1990). This power is exercised through "unobtrusive forms of control" primarily through knowledge and communication (Foster, 1986a, p. 44).

Power disrupted via communication from equal participation. Although educators engaged in critical theory recognize ubiquitous societal oppression, that recognition is not without hope for change. As Foster (1986a) explains, "One aspect of leadership is communicating to others that the particular situation, the particular organizational form, is made by us and can be changed by us" (p. 184). Strongly influenced by the work of Habermas (1984), a critical theory epistemology suggests that educators accomplish social justice by engaging in dialogue about problems of practice, with an explicit focus on power relationships (Apple, 1988; Popkewitz, 1984; Sirotnik & Oakes, 1986). Accordingly, when Sirotnik and Oakes (1986) discuss critical theory in action, they pay considerable attention to competent communication and consensus in group decision-making about the "truth" of what exists. They argue that the essential ingredient for this critical process is "unlimited opportunity for discussion, free of constraints from any source" (p. 37). They suggest that educators strive for "free exploration, honest exchange, and non-manipulative discussion ... in light of critical questions like: What goes on in this school? Who benefits from the way things are?" (p. 39). Accordingly, as I wrote in Capper (1998):

> These educators rely on the deliberate involvement of typically marginalized individuals in dialogue to identify problems, causes, and solutions based on the individual's personal experiences with inequity. In turn, this involvement helps typically disempowered people recognize, understand, and act against the objects of their oppression. (p. 356)

For Foster (1986a), characteristics of critical change require the following:

1. Develop truly representative systems of participation in the school and democratic ways of realizing organization.
2. Develop a *process* [emphasis in the original] wherein individuals can rationally attempt to communicate wants and needs without distortion and be instrumental in the participatory development of an educational institution.
3. Rais[e] the consciousness about possibilities by penetrating the dominating ideas or total ideologies and analyzing the possible forms of life.
4. Cut through the "natural," taken-for-granted status quo to explore new arrangements.
5. Question the given structures and divisions: those between teachers and administrators and students.
6. Suspend our heritage and history, particularly as they have determined our structures. (p. 167).

Foster's (1986a) definition of critical inquiry and its role in change reflects his previous work on Habermas and the emphasis on competent communication:

> [T]he heart of critical inquiry involves developing an organization populated by a *community of scholars* [italics in the original] who can engage in continuing and unrepressed communication about existent school conditions and possibilities for change. *Such a community does not look at change efforts as additive, adding to the structure that is already there, but as transformative, changing and transforming the basic structures that have been established* (emphasis added). (p. 167)

Leadership is political. Leading via critical praxis requires leadership that is not neutral but political (Anderson, 2009; Foster, 1986a). According to Foster (1986a),

> Organizational change requires political action (p. 168). ... At its heart, leadership – the search for democratic and rational participation in social events – is political. It is a political act to educate people, it is a political act to demystify structures and penetrate "normal" conditions; it is a political act to argue for participation in decision making. (p. 187)

Although Bolman and Deal (2017) identify the political frame as one of their four frames of organizations, their political frame is positioned within structural functional and interpretive epistemologies. That is, their description of politics represents maneuvering for scarce resources within a system without questioning the larger systemic, societal marginalization context. Within Bolman and Deal's political frame, regardless of who "wins" or "loses" in the conceptualization of politics, the existing system remains intact. To be sure, to lead for social justice requires the leader to be politically astute in the way that Bolman and Deal describe. In that sense, Bolman and Deal's political frame can and probably should be appropriated toward social justice ends. I discuss why and how to leverage considerations of politics further in Chapter 7 on Critical Race Theory. One of the political examples in their most recent text describes the work of a community organizer. Yet, without a critical theory epistemology understanding of the unique ways politics plays out when leading toward social justice ends, understanding and deploying the political frame as Bolman and Deal describe ignores and thus perpetuates inequities.

CRITICAL THEORY, DIVERSITY, AND DIFFERENCE

From critical theory, the goal of education focuses on social justice and equity. Curriculum and instruction emphasizes learning about the history of oppression and continued oppression globally and in the United States to develop students' critical consciousness, knowledge, and skills to work against oppression for the rest of their lives (McKenzie et al., 2008). Attempting to level the hierarchy through interpretivist epistemology practices (discussed in Chapter 4), such as professional learning communities, distributed leadership, or meeting students' needs via personalized learning, is not enough. Educators grounded in critical theory ask the question: professional learning communities to what end? Personalized learning to what end? Distributed leadership to what end? For critical theorists the end centers on social justice and equity. By not explicitly addressing inequities, these practices uphold and perpetuate the status quo, existing power structures, and their associated inequities.

Several publications on education practice emanate from the critical theory epistemology, including *Rethinking Schools,* the journal *Democracy and Education, Teaching Tolerance,* and *Engaging Schools* (formerly Educators for Social Responsibility) (Capper, 1998). Scholars have relied on the critical theory epistemology to frame particular approaches to multicultural education such as multicultural education for social reconstruction (Sleeter, 1991), to analyze the hegemonic role of textbooks in schools (Apple, 1988), to discuss the hegemonic use of knowledge in school administration (Bates, 1980), to frame action research in teacher education (Liston & Zeichner, 1991), and as the basis for the entire democracy in education movement that continues today (Apple & Beane, 2007; Dewey, 2015).

THE EDUCATIONAL LEADERSHIP FOR SOCIAL JUSTICE MOVEMENT

Critical theory in educational leadership forms the theoretical and epistemological basis for the social justice movement in educational leadership. McKenzie et al. (2008) acknowledged this basis when describing a framework for the preparation of social justice leaders, and in so doing acknowledged the relationship between critical theory and social justice:

> [we] suggest ... four differences between critical theory and the newer orientation toward social justice. First, the latter sees the social world as less

totalized or monolithic in terms of injustice and inequity. Second, there are, instead, multiple, dynamic, shifting discourses and activities within all contexts, from schools and universities to corporations and churches, and some of these discourses favor social justice and equity, whereas others favor injustice and inequity. Third, as a result, institutions or organizations, such as schools, are loosely coupled to the dominant norms of injustice and inequity, which means that it may be possible to have social justice as a dominant norm within one school or district while the larger society has a dominant norm of injustice and inequity. Fourth, many of the newer advocates of social justice are more willing to involve themselves within institutions and organizations and appropriate various complex discourses, such as school accountability, with the goal of moving social justice forward. All of these four, though, are arguable and certainly would not apply to every case for the advocates of critical theory or for the advocates of the more recent focus on social justice. (p. 115)

In a previous review, I outlined limitations of critical theory (Capper, 1998), which included the limitations of rationality in dialogue and the impossibility of an "ideal speech situation" promulgated by Habermas and those who interpret his work (Foster, 1980). As Ellsworth (1989) explained, "rational argument has operated in ways that set up as its opposite an irrational Other which has been understood historically as the province of women and other exotic Others" (p. 301, cited in Capper, 1993, p. 16). The origination of critical theory in Marxism and the emphasis on social class even with subsequent acknowledgement of racial and gender power inequities constituted a second limitation.

More recently, I identified five ironies and limitations of the educational leadership for social justice literature (Capper & Young, 2014). One irony and limitation addressed integration/inclusion. Although the concept and practice of inclusion/integration anchored the civil rights movement, integration that dismantles segregation via tracking, ability, grouping, and pull-out programs "tends not to be central in the educational leadership for social justice discourse; rather, it remains marginalized, ill defined, and undebated" (p. 159).

Second, the educational leadership for social justice literature also struggles with identity in a number of different ways. The literature tends to generically address "all students" or includes a list of some identities, though often excluding sexuality and disability (Capper, Theoharis, & Sebastian, 2006). Related, then, the literature does not typically substantively address disability, sexuality (O'Malley & Capper, 2013), poverty, race (Khalifa, Gooden, & Davis, 2016), language, or the intersections thereof. From its inception in educational leadership, the social justice movement has been rightfully severely criticized for the way it glosses over racial inequities, explained by Knaus (2014): "it is in the interest of White educators to adopt social justice language instead of integrating anti-racism into the foundation of academic programs" (p. 422).

Third, the educational leadership for social justice literature remains unclear on the role and measure of student learning and achievement in social justice work. Further, district and school leaders must contend with state policies that send mixed messages about inclusive/integrative practices and the role of student achievement in those policies. The lack of policy and practice coherence to address inequities at the federal, state, and local levels and the lack of an equity framework or process at the district and school levels to filter the conflicting federal and state policy messages significantly dilutes the social justice leadership impact.

Finally, social justice leadership requires both super-hero and collaborative leadership – one without the other is not enough. In our social justice critique, we called upon educational leaders for social justice to engage the following:

1. An agreed upon understanding of what inclusion/integration means should be the central, visible, unambiguous anchoring feature of all scholarship, policies, and practices aimed toward eliminating educational inequities.
2. Make increased student learning and achievement the primary goal of their work.
3. Attune themselves to, and become experts on, the range of student differences and their intersections.
4. Suggestions for creating more socially just schools must be understood as the responsibilities of a principal for social justice along with leadership teams and community members rather than the domain of single individuals (Capper & Young, 2014, pp. 162–163).

Although the critical theory epistemology addresses oppressed groups and individuals in general with some allusions to social class, race, and gender, other critically oriented epistemologies are rooted in and centered from a range of marginalized identities that I discuss in each of the following chapters. Many of these critically oriented epistemologies emerged in response to the limitations of critical theory and others emerged unto themselves. These critically oriented epistemologies' only point of convergence with critical theory lies in an examination of power inequities. Beyond that, however, all differ in significant ways. Next, in Chapter 6, we learn about the feminist and poststructural critique of critical theory, and the feminist poststructural critique of feminism and poststructuralism in relation to organizational theory.

LEADERSHIP DEVELOPMENT ACTIVITIES

After reading the chapter, educator development activities that I describe next for the critical theory epistemology include (1) playdough sculpture, (2) discussion questions for whole class discussion, (3) critical analysis of the educator's own leadership, and (4) case study analysis. It is best to work through all the activities in the order they are presented here. I also provide time estimates.

ACTIVITY 1: Playdough Constructions

1. Using playdough and with the assistance of a partner, construct a symbolic representation of the critical theory epistemology (10 minutes).
2. Large group check-in: One person in each dyad presents their construction. Ask students to take notes, and someone takes notes for all to see, writing down the keywords for each construction. By the end of the activity, educators have used their own language and words to describe critical theory (depending on group size 15 to 20 minutes).

ACTIVITY 2:   Discussion Questions for the Critical Theory Epistemology (Large group about 20 minutes)

1. What are the organizational goals?
2. What does leadership look like?
3. How is the organization structured?
4. What does organizational culture look like?
5. What does decision-making look like?
6. What does change look like?
7. What aspects of education emanate from this epistemology?
8. What is the goal of education?
9. What does the curriculum look like?
10. What does instruction look like?
11. What does assessment look like?
12. What does evaluation/supervision look like?
13. When a student struggles academically, how does the school respond?
14. How does this epistemology respond to difference and diversity?
15. What are the strengths and limitations of this epistemology?

ACTIVITY 3:   Critical Reflection on Your Own Leadership from the Critical Theory Epistemology (5 minutes of self-reflection, 10-minute share with partner, with each taking 5 minutes. Large group discussion, "What is one point of your discussion you want to share out?")

1. Identify one or two specific positive examples of how your leadership for social justice reflects the critical theory epistemology.
2. Identify two or three aspects of your social justice leadership which you need to develop further to reflect the critical theory epistemology, and how you will do so.

ACTIVITY 4:   Case Analysis from the Critical Theory Epistemology (About 35 minutes)

1.   First, each educator reviews the critical theory epistemology case analysis handout below (5 minutes).
2.   Individual case analysis: What are the issues in your case from the epistemology? What are the possible solutions in your case from the critical theory epistemology? (Write down notes to these questions, 7 to 10 minutes.)
3.   With a partner, exchange and read each other's case (5 minutes).
4.   With the same partner, share the issues and possible solutions to your case from critical theory epistemology. The partner can add additional ideas they saw that you may have missed; next, switch partners and repeat (7 minutes each, 14 minutes in total).
5.   Due the following week, educators then write up a critical epistemology case analysis – the issues and possible solutions – supported by the literature, and limited to about two pages.

CRITICAL THEORY EPISTEMOLOGY ANALYSIS OF CASE SITUATION (ADAPTED FROM CAPPER, 1998)

1.   Are the experiences, attitudes, values, and behaviors of persons from different identities considered?
2.   How is the situation perpetuating unequal relations among people?
3.   Are there any indications of questioning related to "how some individuals and groups have access to resources and others do not; why some groups are underrepresented and others are not; why certain influences prevail and others do not" (Yeakey et al., 1986)?
4.   Who is benefitting from the way things are? Whose interests are being served (and are not) by the way things are? Whose knowledge or point of view is privileged?
5.   To what extent do the persons in the situation seek the input of others with identities different from themselves?
6.   To what extent is the situation perpetuating stereotypes, unequal power?
7.   To what extent can the "solution" take into account individual differences (race, gender, etc.)?
8.   To what extent is your situation a "dodge" or "crisis point" which serves to distract the people in the setting from working on issues of equity and justice?
9.   What are the unquestioned assumptions/givens of the situation?
10. How would people with identities different from yours view the situation? (i.e., in terms of gender/race, etc.)?

REFERENCES

Anderson, Gary L. (2009). *Advocacy leadership: Toward a post-reform agenda in education (Critical social thought)*. New York: Routledge.

Apple. M. (1988). *Teachers and texts: A political economy of class and gender relations in education*. New York: Routledge.

Apple, M. (2014). *Official knowledge: Democratic education in a conservative age* (3rd edn). New York: Routledge.

Apple, M. & Beane, J. (2007). *Democratic schools, second edition: Lessons in powerful education*. Portsmouth, NH: Heinemann.

Bates, R.J. (1980). Educational administration, the sociology of science, and the management of knowledge. *Educational Administrative Quarterly, 16*(2). 1–20.

Bolman, L.G. & Deal, T.E. (2017). *Reframing organizations: Artistry, choice, and leadership*. Hoboken, NJ: Jossey-Bass.

Burrell, G. & Morgan, G. (1985). *Sociological paradigms and organisational analysis: Elements of the sociology of corporate life*. Florence: Taylor and Francis.

Capper, C.A. (1993). *Educational administration in a pluralistic society*. Albany, NY: State University of New York Press.

Capper, C.A. (1998). Critically oriented and postmodern perspectives: Sorting out the differences and applications for practice. *Educational Administration Quarterly, 34*(3), 354–379.

Capper, C.A. & Young, M. (2014). Ironies and limitations of educational leadership for social justice: A call to social justice educators. *Theory Into Practice, 53*(2), 158–164.

Capper, C.A., Keyes, M., & Theoharis, G. (2000). Spirituality in leadership: Implications for inclusive schooling. In R.A. Villa & J.S. Thousand (Eds), *Restructuring for caring and effective education: Piecing the puzzle together* (pp. 513–530). Baltimore, MD: Brookes.

Capper, C.A., Theoharis, G., & Sebastian, J. (2006). Toward a framework for preparing leaders for social justice. *Journal of Educational Administration, 44*(3), 209–224.

Critical Management. (2018). Critical management studies. Retrieved January 1, 2018, from http://criticalmanagement.org.

Dewey, J. (2015). *Democracy and education*. New York: Simon & Schuster.

Ellsworth, E. (1989). Why doesn't this feel empowering? Working through the repressive myths of critical pedagogy. *Harvard Educational Review, (59)*3, 297–374.

Foster, W. (1980). Administration and the crisis in legitimacy: A review of Habermasian thought. *Harvard Educational Review, 50*(4), 496–505.

Foster, W.P. (1986a). *Paradigms and promises: New approaches to educational administration*. Buffalo, NY: Prometheus Books.

Foster, W.P. (1986b). Toward a critical theory of educational administration. In T.J. Serqiovanni and J.E. Corbally (Eds), *Leadership and organizational culture*. Urbana, IL: University of Illinois Press.

Freire, P. (2000). *Pedagogy of the oppressed*. New York: Continuum.

Gioia, D.A. & Pitre, E. (1990). Multiparadigm perspectives on theory building. *Academy of Management Review, 15*(4), 584–602.

Habermas, J. (1984). *The theory of communicative action: Reason and the rationalization of society. Vol 1*. Translated by T. McCarthy. Boston, MA: Beacon Press.

Khalifa, M., Gooden, M., & Davis, J. (2016). Culturally responsive school leadership. *Review of Educational Research, 86*(4), 1272–1311.

Knaus, C.B. (2014). Seeing what they want to see: Racism and leadership development in urban schools. *Urban Review, 46*(3), 420–444.

Liston, D. & Zeichner, K. (1991). *Teacher education and the social conditions of schooling.* New York: Routledge.

McKenzie, K., Christman, D., Hernandez, F., Fierro, E., Capper, C., Dantley, M., & Scheurich, J. (2008). From the field: A proposal for educating leaders for social justice. *Educational Administration Quarterly, 44*(1), 111–138.

O'Malley, M. & Capper, C. (2015). A measure of the quality of educational leadership programs for social justice: Integrating LGBTIQ identities into principal preparation. *Educational Administration Quarterly, 51*(2), 290–330.

Popkewitz, T.S. (1984). *Paradigm and ideology in educational research: The social functions of the intellectual.* London and New York: Falmer Press.

Sirotnik, K.A. & Oakes, J. (1986). *Critical perspectives on the organization and improvement of schooling.* Boston, MA: Kluwer-Nijhoff.

Sleeter, C. (1991). *Empowerment through multicultural education.* Albany, NY: State University of New York Press.

Smyth, J. (Ed.). (1989). *Critical perspectives on educational leadership.* London: Falmer Press.

Tierney, W.G. & Foster, W. (1991). Editor's introduction. *Peabody Journal of Education, 66*(3), 1–4.

Yeakey, C., Johnston, G., & Adkinson, J. (1986). In pursuit of equity: A review of research on minorities and women in educational administration. *Educational Administration Quarterly, 22*(3), 110–149.

Zey-Ferrell, M. & Aiken, M. (1981). *Complex organizations: Critical perspectives.* Glenview, IL: Scott Foresman.

CHAPTER 6

Feminist, Poststructural, and Feminist Poststructural Epistemologies[1]

Nearly all the scholarship related to feminist, poststructural, and feminist post-structural epistemologies in educational leadership to date remains unconsciously white, straight, "abled," and not intersectional with other identities. I address all three epistemologies in this chapter primarily because doing so renders the central tenets of each epistemology visible and, in the comparison of each, the tenets distinct to each epistemology clearer. I devote the chapter that follows this one to Black feminist epistemologies.

In the epistemology framework (see Figure 6.1), historically, feminism followed the development of critical theory, followed by poststructuralism, then feminist poststructuralism, then Black feminism – all a critique of the preceding epistemology. As mentioned, I briefly discuss feminist and poststructural epistemologies, then spend the bulk of the chapter discussing feminist poststructural epistemologies. I consider how each of these epistemologies can inform organizational theory and what they can contribute to educational leadership for social justice.

FEMINIST EPISTEMOLOGIES

Kenway and Modra (1992) offer the following definition of feminism and its relationship to education:

> Feminism is premised on the recognition that gender is a phenomenon which helps to shape our society. Feminists believe that women are located unequally in the social formation, often devalued, exploited and oppressed. Education systems, the knowledge which they offer and the practices which constitute them,

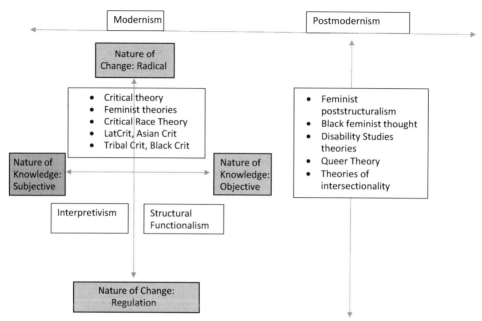

Figure 6.1 An Epistemology Framework

are seen to be complicit in this. Feminists share a commitment to a form of politics directed towards ending the social arrangements which lead to women to be "other than," less than, put down, and put upon. (p. 139)

Feminist scholars have offered considerable critique of critical theory – that despite occasional nods to feminist work, critical theorists historically tended to ignore feminist perspectives/scholarship, including the feminist perspective on the private/public sphere, citizenship, democracy, emancipation, the individualist ethic, and critique and action (Luke & Gore, 1992). Referring to the limitations of critical theory, Luke and Gore (1992) argued for "a serious skepticism of and critical attention to those contemporary educational narratives that claim to be emancipatory, ideologically critical, self-reflexive, and politically conscientious, and yet remain theoretically entrenched in gender- and color-blind patriarchal liberalism" (p. 49). Kenway and Modra (1992) concurred and argued that for educators relying on the critical theory epistemology,

[I]t is uncommon for them to either examine the gendered assumptions embodied deeply and subtly in their theoretical premises or to grasp the full significance of the presence and power of gender in educational settings. Such theorists seem to believe that gentle genuflections alone demonstrate their gender sensitivity and make respectable their politics, while at the same time relieving full range and complexity of feminist literature on and for education. As critical pedagogy theorists claim that they are quintessentially engaged in democratization in the education process, this failure to engage with feminism casts considerable doubt on their authenticity. (p. 138)

As with critical theorists, educators who adopt feminist epistemologies value dialogue and consensus. Unlike critical theorists, educators who adopt feminist epistemologies do not cling so tightly to rationality and the intellect, but value intuition, emotion, experience, and the relational over abstract moral reasoning. For example, Ellsworth (1989) asserts that "rational argument has operated in ways that set up as its opposite an irrational Other, which has been understood historically as the province of women and other exotic Others" (p. 301). Educators who adopt feminist epistemologies maintain a closer connection to practice and context rather than perseverating on theoretical abstractions (Lather, 1991; Luke & Gore, 1992).

Scholars who have examined women in educational leadership include Blackmore (1999, 2007, 2013, 2014), Brunner (1999, 2000; Brunner & Grogan, 2007), Grogan (1996, 2000; Grogan & Shakeshaft, 2011; Grogan & Smith, 1998), Mansfield (2014; Mansfield, Welton, & Grogan, 2014), Marshall (1997; Marshall & Young, 2013), Shakeshaft (1987, 2011), and Sherman Newcomb (2005, 2014; Sherman Newcomb & Niemeyer, 2015; Sherman & Beatty, 2010; Sherman & Wrushen, 2009; Newcomb & Mansfield, 2014). Although these scholars examine women and educational leadership, they do not necessarily rely on feminist epistemologies. For example, gender research in educational leadership includes a study related to legal issues and single-sex schools (Eckes & McCall, 2014); how identities including gender impact leadership practice (Santamaría, 2014); the importance of listening to student voice in social justice research with a focus on Latina girls who attended a Latina female academy (Mansfield, 2014); and a meta-analysis of gender differences in instructional leadership which suggest that female principals are more actively involved in instructional leadership than male principals (Hallinger, Dongyu, & Wang, 2016). Newton (2006) also examined how superintendent recruitment normalizes the superintendent as male, and Eckman (2004) compared the work of male and female high school principals and how they manage their roles.

In this chapter, I only address educational leadership research anchored in feminist epistemologies. A special issue of *Educational Administration Quarterly* focused exclusively on women and the superintendency (2000, 36(1)), and all studies in the special issue were conceptualized with feminist or feminist poststructural epistemologies (Grogan, 2000). Blount's ground-breaking scholarship on the history of women in the superintendency (1998) forms the backdrop to this work. None of these studies examined race, ability, sexual/gender identity, and their intersections with gender.

As mentioned in Chapter 2, Capper and Green's (2013) analysis of equity research in the *Educational Administration Quarterly* found that when scholars conceptually framed their work from combinations of critical, critical race, and feminist theories, feminist theories were relied on more centrally and frequently than the other two. For example, André-Bechely (2005) examined parent choice in schools through the perspectives of low-income and middle-income white females and an upper income female relying on a combination of Critical Race Theory and "feminist critical policy studies (Marshall, 1997); feminist standpoint theory (Harding, 1991), and feminist sociology (D. Smith, 1987, 1999)" (cited in André-Bechely, 2005, p. 269).

Mahitivanichcha and Rorrer (2006) combined feminist economic theory and feminist organizational theory to guide their data collection and analysis related to women's access to and participation in the superintendency.

Jackson et al. (2013) co-authored the first publication in educational leadership that specifically addressed gender across all races and all sexual identities. Jackson et al. explain the status of the educational leadership literature related to gender:

> Within [this literature], issues of gender, race and ethnicity, and sexual iden-tity are typically addressed separately. Yet every individual is positioned along a gender, race, and sexual identity continuum. An emerging literature base in school leadership seeks to illuminate the intersection of (typically) two identity components, either gender and race or gender and sexual orientation, but rarely race and sexual orientation or gender and sexual orientation, let alone all three together. … This chapter argues that an important next step in our inquiry is to avoid uncritically narrowing the focus of our research in such a way that one or more aspects of identity are assumed away, and therefore silenced. (p. 327–328)

I agree with Jackson and co-authors' (2013) definition and delimitation of the liter-ature on women in educational leadership:

> Research on women that does not explicitly address the intersection of gender and race is presumed to refer to White women; research on women and race that does not explicitly reference sexual identity is presumed to refer to hetero-sexual women. (p. 328)

Jackson et al.'s chapter reviews the educational leadership of women of all races and sexualities, including women who are African American, Asian, Native American, Latino, and women educational leaders on the sexuality spectrum. Jackson et al. point out that, to date, not a single study in educational leadership has addressed the sexual-ity spectrum within women. Thus, in their review, Jackson et al. relied on "the current state of scholarship on gays and lesbians in educational leadership (with no specific ref-erences in that literature to bisexual women or transgender women)" (p. 349). Jackson et al. conclude their review and recommendations for future research by reinforcing:

> The intersection of gender, race, and sexual identity in school remains a fruitful and under-researched nexus of identity, position, and privilege. The literature base in school leadership that explores the intersection of two of these aspects of individual identity has grown in recent years. In addition to encouraging the continuation on these avenues of scholarship, this chapter highlights the importance of expanding our inquiry to include the intersection of all three of the identity components simultaneously. This step is vital to ensure that inquiry designed as emancipatory does not itself inadvertently silence or marginalize individual or group voices and perspectives. (p. 349)

Within organizational studies, as mentioned in Chapter 2, Kathy Ferguson's ground-breaking text *The Feminist Case Against Bureaucracy* (1984) was the first book-length work to apply feminist theories to bureaucratic discourse. Mills and Tancred (1992) examined gender, including a critique of organizational analysis and feminist perspectives on varying aspects of organizations. Holvino (2010) analyzed organizational theories to date and noted that "though the inclusion of more sophisticated perspectives on gender has gained ground" (p. 248), fewer scholars address the intersections of gender with race, ethnicity, and social class.

POSTSTRUCTURALISM, ORGANIZATIONS, AND ORGANIZATIONAL THEORY

Thus far, all the epistemologies we have reviewed are positioned on the modernism end of the modernism/postmodernism continuum (see Figure 6.1). Thus, whether the epistemologies addressed thus far in this book are oriented toward radical social change (e.g., feminism, critical theory), all these epistemologies share common assumptions from being grounded in modernism. According to Cherryholmes (1988), the structural aspects of modernism "operate prescriptively in education when preferred structural procedures, interpretations, and organizations are promoted with a promise of order and rationality" (p. 16). Within modernism, decision-making can proceed from the top down (structural functionalism), initiated through teams of people representing differing perspectives (interpretive epistemologies), or agreement arrived at through dialogue and consensus (critical theory). Although change may be initiated top down (structural functionalism), as a result of considering multiple perspectives (interpretive), or through a democratic process (critical theory) within modernism, change moves step-by-step, is evolutionary, and is clearly linked to ideas of cause and effect. Epistemologies within modernism consider knowledge to be along a continuum from objective to socially constructed. Educators who adopt modernist approaches believe that power is all or nothing; that is, "you either have it, or you do not" (Capper, 1998, p. 362). Power is considered at the top and to be hoarded at all costs (structural functionalism), to provide the appearance of power sharing, though the power continues to be contained at the top of the organization (interpretivism), or power needs to move from oppressive to empowering (critical theory). Within modernist epistemologies, individuals have an essential nature that remains stable, fully aware, or in need of others to bring forth this awareness.

The poststructural epistemology influence on educational leadership followed the typical trajectory of social philosophy and theory, first in the social sciences, then within the field of organizations while somewhat simultaneously in the field of education, then in the field of educational leadership in the early 1990s (Anderson, 1990; English, 1998). Given the unequivocal focus of this book on leadership for social justice, I spend less time on poststructural epistemologies compared to critically oriented epistemologies given that poststructural epistemologies are more about analysis than about practice (see Capper (1998), where I detail the differences between critically oriented epistemologies and poststructuralism). However, I find some aspects of poststructural thought useful in social justice work that I explain in this chapter. Although nuanced differences exist between the terms postmodern and poststructural, I use the terms interchangeably.

Poststructural scholars include Derrida (1981), Lacan (1977), Althusser (1969), Foucault (1980, 1988), and Lyotard (1984). Poststructural epistemologies offer critiques of structural functionalism, interpretivism, and critically oriented epistemologies. Poststructuralists view a person as part of "an observer-community which constructs interpretations of the world," with interpretations that are neither wrong nor right (Cooper & Burrell, 1988, p. 94). Situations are viewed in terms of paradox and indeterminacy. Poststructural epistemologies suggest, in part, that all meaning is not definitive and shifts depending on perspective, is theoretically distant from practice, and as a result does not necessarily support individuals taking action. Although critical theory seeks consensus in decision-making, the poststructural focus relates to the nuances of dissensus (Cherryholmes, 1998). In this chapter, I examine the nature of power, change, decision-making, and the individual/subject from poststructural epistemologies.

Nature of power. Three key aspects of the nature of power within poststructural epistemologies include that power is not confined only within particular people or hierarchical positions, but that power is within all of us and everywhere – termed *disciplinary power.* Second, rather than oppressive, the exercise of power produces more power. That is, resistance and pushing back to power also constitutes a form of power; thus the exertion of power followed by resistance to power results in the production rather than the oppression of power. Third, surveillance serves as the primary strategy of disciplinary power.

Power is everywhere as disciplinary power. Critical theory and poststructural epistemologies both focus on power although with distinct differences. Critical theory considers power to be as all or nothing and as hierarchically centralized. Poststructural epistemologies consider power to be "decentralized, plural, complex, and web-like" (Capper, 1998, p. 364). Rather than specific and overt, Foucault (1988) described *disciplinary power* as power that exists everywhere (Capper, 1998). According to Foucault,

> Since the seventeenth century, individuals have been caught within a complex grid of disciplinary, normalizing, panoptic powers that survey, judge, measure, and correct their every move. There are no "spaces of primal liberty" in society; power is everywhere. What I am attentive to is the fact that every human relation is to some degree a power relation. We move in a world of perpetual strategic relations. (Foucault, 1988, p. 168, cited in Best & Kellner, 1991, p. 54)

Rather than being oppressive as is suggested from critical theory, power is productive. Burrell (1988) explains that rather than extreme forms of violence, power within the poststructural epistemology is "complex" and operates as "subtle forms of correction and training … as individuals, we are incarcerated within an organizational world. Thus, while we may not live in total institutions, the institutional organization of our lives is total" (p. 24).

Foucault (1980) developed the concept of *biopower,* which means that power is exercised on and through the physical body, spirit, and desire. Foucault believed that the strongest power comes not from oppressive rules and regulations per se, but from commonsense, natural activities and beliefs that sanction our bodies, souls, desires, and day-to-day living. Foucault believed that this sanctioning follows us everywhere, including into our homes and workplaces, and influences our interactions with our families and significant others (Cooper & Burrell, 1988).

The sanctioning function of power develops within "disciplinary blocks" or institutions, such as asylums, schools, the field of psychiatry, and discipline practices, and then radiates outward to society. Thus, government and similar macrostructures are not necessarily the center or base of power but are symptoms of power differences. Rather than only considering how those in power influence others, poststructural views of power consider how those in traditionally lower positions of power exert their influence over others and how power is constantly being circulated among and around us. ·

Power is productive rather than repressive. Foucault (1980) also believed that power was productive in that it did not necessarily repress people but that it multiplied the number of people under its rule, which served to reinforce this power. According to Foucault, power produces certain kinds of characteristics and behaviors in people. He further believed that power controls and produces the physical body. Modern forms of power also control the body, but the postmodern forms differ in their covertness. For example, Rouse (1987) explains that instead of being overtly punished or incarcerated, "the body was made visible and carefully scrutinized; instead of being tortured, it was programmed and exercised; instead of its simply being placed in servitude, its activities were reconstructed for efficiency and productivity" (p. 211).

Rouse (1987) explains the production of power, providing an example that reflects education's reliance on and promulgation of practices such as special education and the plethora of labels and programs (discussed in Chapter 10 on Disability Studies theories). Rouse argues that power is gradually refined in relation to the body and that the normalizing function of power is corrective.

> It reconstructs the person and her or his behavior by gradual steps and small impositions. The gaps between observed behavior and established norms are made thematic, and corrective procedures are invoked to bring the offender into line. Normalizing judgment does not aim to abolish deviance, for that would also obviate its own existence. Rather, it creates distributions around the norm, which can be classified, ranked, and dealt with differentially. It both continually corrects and reduces deviation and creates it in new forms so that the norms serve a distributive function. (pp. 217–218)

From poststructural epistemologies, power operates when educators seek to identify who is normal and who is not through remediation systems such as Response to Intervention and special education – and then seek to make these students more normal (Capper, 1998).

Strategies and tactics of disciplinary power. Rouse (1987) explains that surveillance is a primary strategy or tactic of disciplinary power. Surveillance connects with the organization or structure of space, which leads to "classification, description, and explanation, and documentation" (p. 217). In the past, people in power and those over whom power was exercised were both quite visible. With surveillance, however, the "exercise of power is hidden, while those upon whom it works are increasingly laid open to scrutiny" (Rouse, 1987, p. 214). Architecture is designed to increase this visibility and the ability for surveillance. Surveillance also contributes to the organization of people and space. The ways "people are enclosed, grouped, distributed, separated, and partitioned" determine physical space, which is related to power/knowledge (Rouse, p. 214). How we are spatially organized with people shapes our behaviors and interactions with one another. As one example, positioning chairs in a circle could be interpreted as a strategy for inclusion. However, a circle could also be considered as a form of surveillance; a circle configuration allows actions and behaviors to be more visible and thus more vulnerable to correction and control.

Nature of change. In addition to poststructural perspectives on the nature of power, poststructuralism can also inform the nature of change. Rather than working toward an end-point, in terms of change, educators who adopt poststructural epistemologies call into question the end-point itself – whether it is constituted by efficiency (structural functionalism), understanding (interpretivism), or social change (critical theory). Within poststructural epistemologies, change is not viewed in terms of progression, but, according to Lather (1991), change is considered "non-linear, cyclical, indeterminant, discontinuous, contingent" (p. 161). Educators who adopt poststructural epistemologies do not shy away from change, but they move away from causality regarding change. Derrida argues that change is personal and "must not be the same as that for anyone else in another place, another class, another country. From this standpoint, political action is ... constantly strategic" (Kaplan & Sprinkler, 1993, p. 215). The actions which educators take are amenable to change or may change each day; actions are not finite and are to be consistently re-evaluated.

Given their view that any suggestion for practice can be deconstructed, educators who adopt poststructuralist epistemologies would question leadership for social justice practice and point out the ambiguity of all social justice work. Accordingly, in the poststructural world, there is no final moment of knowing – no beginning point or end. Poststructural epistemologies shun elevating any idea, system, or symbol to the status of solution (Capper, 1992). Educators who adopt poststructuralist epistemologies seek instead to foster the natural tension and disagreement inherent in educational practices by deconstructing them. Poststructural epistemologies, by deconstructing social justice practice, can help educators to be conscious of developing new oppressive practices when trying to work toward equity and justice (Capper & Jamison, 1993).

Nature of decision-making. As discussed in the previous two sections, poststructural epistemologies can inform the nature of power and the nature of change.

In this section, I consider poststructural approaches to decision-making. Educators who adopt poststructural epistemologies question decision-making associated with dialogue and consensus (critical theory), which they believe oversimplify and mask power issues and which can create an illusion of community. Although consensus decision-making has merit, critical issues may be overlooked in reaching consensus – issues that could push the situation toward more meaningful change (Capper, 1992). Rather than consensus, "it is dissensus which continually compels our attention" (Cherryholmes, 1988, p. 98). Ellsworth (1989) asserts that sometimes it is better to support a coalition of "multiple, shifting, intersecting, and sometimes contradictory groups carrying unequal weights of legitimacy. Sometimes groups/persons need time to 'talk back' to the larger group, while the rest … listen without interruption" (p. 317).

Nature of the individual/subject. The nature of the individual/subject within the poststructural epistemology may be described by positioning it against feminist views of the same. As previously described, educators who adopt feminist perspectives tend to essentialize male and female, ascribing specific characteristics and behaviors to males and a different set to females, while ignoring the complexities of identity among and within individuals, regardless of gender.

Rather than an objective/essentialized male/female from feminist perspectives, educators engaged with poststructural epistemologies consider the individual as constructed of multiple, shifting identities Lather (1991) describes this nature of the individual as a "de-centered subject, culturally inscribed/constructed, contradictory, relational … continuously recreated and recreating … fractured" (p. 160). Accordingly, the agency of the subject, or the ability of a person to make a difference or to do something, also shifts and diminishes in poststructural thought. For some feminists, critiques of the subject are useful because it steers away from essentialism, which suggests that women and men "are just like that," to understanding how society and its institutions socially construct and shape the female/male subject. Some feminist theorists have raised additional concerns regarding poststructural epistemology. I explore these concerns in the section on feminist poststructuralism. When compared to critical theory, the postmodern epistemology could be considered as a way of viewing a situation rather than as a guide for action, although it does not preclude action.

In sum, rather than modernist views of change as being rational, evolutionary, and step-by-step, poststructural epistemologies consider change as "non-linear, cyclical, indeterminant, discontinuous, contingent" (Lather, 1991, p. 161). Modernist epistemologies view power as all or nothing, while poststructural epistemologies view power as complex, web-like, everywhere, related to the body, productive, and perpetuated by strategies such as surveillance and control of space. Diverging from a view of the nature of the subject/individual as essentialized, poststructural epistemologies consider the nature of the subject/individual to be multiple, shifting, "decentered … culturally inscribed/constructed, contradictory, relational … continuously recreated and recreating … fractured" (Lather, 1991, p. 160).

Poststructural Epistemologies and Leadership for Equity

In previous sections, I discussed how the postmodern epistemology informs decision-making and change theory, and embedded within that discussion lie implications for leadership as well. Poststructural epistemologies can inform leadership for equity related to the nature of power, the individual, and the role of individuals in equity work. Poststructural epistemologies provide for hope in social justice leadership. Rather than viewing oppression and marginalization as monolithic and immutable, poststructural epistemologies suggest that gaps and opportunities always exist for change and transformation within organizations. Likewise, rather than viewing individuals resistant to equity change as essentialist and unmovable, poststructural epistemologies ask us to view individuals as complex and that, like organizations, individuals shifting toward equity change is possible. Rather than believing that only one way exists to effect equity change (for example, from an activist standpoint), poststructural epistemologies suggest multiple ways to effect equity change and all ways are important in the equity change process at multiple levels. Instead of hoping for the lack of resistance to our equity work, poststructural epistemologies remind us to expect resistance and not to fear it.

Postmodern epistemologies have greatly influenced the critically oriented epistemologies that evolved during the time of postmodern epistemology formation, including Disability Studies theories (Chapter 10) and Queer Theory (Chapter 11). Critical scholars could not help but be influenced by postmodern epistemologies circulating at the time.

FEMINIST POSTSTRUCTURALISM

Feminist poststructural epistemology refers to the interactions and contradictions among subjectivity, power, and language that contribute to "common sense." Common sense relates to:

> Particular definitions of what is natural, normal, or commonsensical. … However, its power comes from its claims to be natural, obvious, and therefore true. … These supposed truths are often rhetorically reinforced by expressions such as "it is well known that," "we all know that", and "everybody knows that" which emphasize their obviousness and put social pressure on individuals to accept them. (Weedon, 1987, p. 77)

Feminist poststructuralists examine these unquestioned underlying assumptions to consider how power is exercised (Weedon, 1987) and the potential for change. The feminist poststructural epistemology claims some affinity with critical theory and poststructural epistemologies but is not fully at home with either of them. Here, I position feminist poststructuralist epistemologies against these epistemologies, unpacking the similarities and contradictions among them.

Tensions with critical theory. Educators engaged with feminist poststructural epistemologies of education avoid the limitations of critical theory and move beyond the gendered relations of feminist theories. These educators appreciate the messiness and complexity of poststructural epistemologies but maintain a focus on social change (Capper, 1994).

Educators working within critical theory do not explicitly take a stand and then recognize their own partiality and contradictions. In contrast, educators engaged with feminist poststructural epistemologies do not shy away from taking a stand, but they recognize the "undecidability, partiality, and uncertainty *within* a theoretical commitment" (Luke & Gore, 1992, p. 48). In short, a feminist poststructural epistemology suggests that an educator take a stand on an issue, overtly identify their own epistemological position, recognize the partiality and contradictions within the position, and then engage in self-interrogation of that position.

Tensions with the poststructural epistemology. Feminist theorists have not warmly embraced poststructural epistemologies. They have been suspicious of a theory, promulgated primarily by white males, that in part dismisses the importance of practice, does not adhere to any normative standard of right or wrong and, because of the structural constraints of a patriarchal society, removes the possibilities of persons in power to make a difference, especially when increased numbers of Anglo women and men and women of color are in positions of power (Nicholson, 1990; Scott, 1988). Consequently, the feminist contribution to the poststructural epistemology includes, in part, the retention of practice with the development of theory, the reinstatement of human potential to make a difference in practice, and the predisposition to take a stand amid continual self-reflection (Lather, 1991).

Irigaray accuses postmodern philosopher Derrida of appropriating feminine or feminist characteristics for his own use and support while simultaneously excluding women. Irigaray argues that "as soon as something valuable appears to be coming from the side of women, men want to become women" (cited in Whitford, 1991 p. 131). She also argues that:

> when male theoreticians employ women's discourse instead of male discourse, that act remains a phallocentric gesture. It means, We will become, and we will speak a feminine discourse in order to remain the master of discourse. What I would want from men is that, finally, they would speak a masculine discourse and affirm that they are doing so. (cited in Whitford, 1991, p. 131)

Fraser and Nicholson (1988) criticize Lyotard's view of postmodernism for privileging itself as the supreme view of theory and failing to consider its own history and that it is, itself, "simply one more discourse among others" (p. 87).

As such, theorists argue that modernist epistemologies have proved beneficial for equity work. For example, Best and Kellner (1991) explain that modernist approaches have:

> given women weapons to fight against their oppression. Modern[ist] categories such as human rights, equality, and democratic freedoms and power are used by feminists to criticize and fight against gender domination. ... Indeed, the very discourse of emancipation is a modern[ist] discourse. (pp. 208–209)

In addition to not wanting to disengage totally from the benefits of modernist epistemologies, educators engaged with feminist poststructuralist epistemologies find
continuities between the modernist and postmodernist project and prefer a dialectical stance between them (Flax, 1990; Lather, 1991; also see Irigaray, cited in
Whitford, 1991). For example, according to Best and Kellner (1991), the feminist
poststructural epistemology can contribute to poststructuralist perspectives and
could:

> help avoid the dead ends and traps of extreme postmodern theory by overcom-
> ing the nihilism and defeatism evident in some varieties of postmodern theory.
> We find pure postmodern theory without a strong dose of feminist or Marxism
> to be incapable of addressing concrete political problems. Postmodern theory
> in its more extreme forms tends to be exactly what it accuses modern theory of
> being: one-sided, reductionist, essentializing, excessively prohibitive ... polit-
> ically disabling ... reductive [and] dogmatically closed to competing perspec-
> tives. (p. 263)

Similarly, Lather (1991) believes that poststructural epistemologies offer feminism "less fixed, and determined ways of looking ... and avoid dogmatism and the
reductionism and single-cause analysis" (p. 39). Irigaray also advocates for a dialectic
between feminism and deconstruction. According to Whitford's (1991) interpretation of Irigaray, "It is not difficult to see that, if deconstruction can 'deconstruct'
feminism, feminism offers a standpoint from which to contextualize or interpret
deconstruction" (p. 132). Fuss (1989) agrees, and argues for a dialectic between essentialism and constructivism in relation to the subject/individual that I take up in
the next section.

Tension with the subject/individual. Subjectivity or subject positions within
feminist poststructural epistemology are defined as "ways of being an individual" or
personal identity (Weedon, 1987, p. 3). The term "identity" is used to refer to "the
conscious and unconscious thoughts and emotions of the individual, her knowledge
of herself and her ways of understanding her relation to the world" (Weedon, 1987,
p. 32). But a person does not possess just one identity (once and for all); instead,
identity is "precarious, contradictory, and in process" (p. 33), constantly being re-
shaped whenever we think, speak, or write. The feminist poststructural epistemology, rather than centering on class analyses reflective of traditional critical theory or
the holy trinity – gender, race, and class – of more contemporary critical theorists,
allows the exploration of the shifting, contradictory, incomplete, and competing
interpretations of personal identity. Weedon (1987) asserts that "the ways in which
people make sense of their lives is a necessary starting point for understanding how
power relations structure society" (p. 8).

Feminist poststructuralist scholars are uncomfortable shifting the emphasis away from a singular subject or individual and the ability to make a difference
as described within poststructural epistemology. At the time that scholars were
promulgating poststructuralism, feminist poststructuralists argued that typically

marginalized individuals were just beginning to be recognized as individuals in the first place – as individuals with power and as individuals capable of working toward equity systems change. In the past, typically marginalized individuals have been excluded from the conversation and discourse. Thus, feminist poststructuralists believe that, at the time, just when women were being recognized and accorded power, some (typically white, male, elite scholars) suggest that theory and practice must move beyond the singular subject/individual and that the conceptualization of the subject/individual must be a dispersed one. However, this dispersion may result in marginalized persons never being recognized as individuals effecting equity change. For example, Whitford (1991) argues that:

> "multiplicity" in one form or another has become one of the themes of contemporary French philosophy, and one of the characterizing features of what has come to be called postmodernism. … The problem is that "multiple" can exclude women just as certainly as the "one" or the "same". … One is still left with the fact that the move from the masculine subject to the disseminated or multiple subject bypasses the possibility of the position of woman-as-subject. … Women … are not in the same situation since (according to modem theory itself) they have never had a subject to lose. The problem for women, then, is that of acceding to subjectivity in the first place. (pp. 82–83)

Snitnow and Thompson (1984) concur, and suggest that "to close a discussion that began for some only very recently is to leave those speakers once again beyond consideration. … It is too soon, then, for silence" (cited in Whitford, 1992, p. 215).

Language and discourse. The language and discourse construct of feminist poststructuralism theory addresses the limitations of rationality, dialogue, and consensus. Feminist poststructuralists believe that "the way we speak and write reflects the structures of power in our society" (Lather, 1991, pp. 11–12). Feminist poststructuralists suggest that language should be examined and "understood in terms of competing discourses, competing ways of giving meaning to the world, which imply differences in the organization of social power" (Lather, 1991, p. 24). According to Cherryholmes (1988), the meanings of words or situations are "shifting, receding, fractured, incomplete, dispersed, and deferred" (p. 61). The meanings of language are always shifting and incomplete. According to Cherryholmes (1988), the language in schools, whether written, gestured, or spoken, "determines what counts as true, important, or relevant, what gets spoken, what remains unsaid" (p. 35).

The term "discursive fields" in feminist poststructuralist epistemology refers to language that is specific to the culture of a discipline. Weedon (1987) explains that "discursive fields consist of competing ways of giving meaning to the world and of organizing social institutions and processes" (p. 35). According to Cherryholmes, (1988), "discursive fields are generated and governed by rules and power" (p. 35). Cherryholmes (1988) interprets Foucault and frames questions such as: how do schools develop a language culture? How does the language used shape and influence educational practices? And how do schools regulate the language used?

Feminist poststructuralists question who and what structure and what cultures have power over what may be spoken or written in school. The authority of discourse relies on what is viewed as "natural" or "normal" (Weedon, 1987) in language.

Using feminist poststructuralism as a tool to act has often been questioned, since one of the main tenets of poststructuralism has been that discourses or societal systems largely shape our thoughts, feelings, and existence. Alcoff (1988), for example, suggested:

> The idea here (in poststructuralism) is that we individuals really have little choice in the matter of who we are, for as Derrida and Foucault like to remind us, individual motivations and intentions count for nil or almost nil in the scheme of social reality. We are constructs – that is, our experience of our very subjectivity is a construct mediated by and/or grounded on a social discourse beyond (way beyond) individual control. (p. 268)

However, many others have suggested that within given parameters, poststructuralism and feminism can ask critical questions and can inform practice and action (Lather, 1991; Sawicki, 1991; Scott, 1988; Weedon, 1987). As Ropers-Huilman (1998) described:

> Poststructuralist feminism does not claim that we have total control over our position in life; yet it advocates that we can recognize and choose to act within the social constructs that have acted to create the positions that we currently hold. (pp. 14–15)

Implications for educational leadership. I offer suggestions and questions for research and practice from the feminist poststructural epistemology. Although I rely on social structures such as race, class, gender, and sexuality, in the examples I recognize that these categories are not always consistent, stable, or even recognizable. I urge the reader to problematize the use of those categories and to consider the underlying assumptions and gaps inherent in the work.

Within feminist poststructural epistemologies, the educational system remains comprised of many discourses, all operating with various levels of power. Education, in turn, affects all who participate in the system. Education serves to both produce and reproduce societal norms and structures (Ropers-Huilman & Capper, 1995). Educators engaged with feminist poststructural epistemologies provide access to multiple knowledge sources and ways of knowing. These educators believe that teaching and learning take place everywhere by everyone in all interactions.

Within feminist poststructural epistemologies, effective "supervision" includes paying attention to the strategies and sources of normalization between the teacher and "supervisor." When educators view the curriculum from feminist poststructural epistemologies, the curriculum is never neutral and is simultaneously, never fully reflective of its contents; there is no "truth" to be conveyed; rather, the curriculum is constructed of knowledges that are not static. What is presented as valid knowledge is related to current power structures. Educational leaders within feminist poststructural epistemologies believe that a leadership vision reflects only particular voices, is a product of multiple discourses, and should be continually re-evaluated and problematized. Rather than striving for consensus or utopian views of "community," feminist poststructuralist epistemologies value dissensus, conflict, contradiction, and resistance, and would seek to understand and use this understanding to inform practice rather than to squelch conflict.

A few studies and theoretical essays in the field of educational leadership have been informed by feminist-poststructural epistemology. Capper (1992) first applied feminist poststructuralism as part of a mulit-paradigm framework for addressing educational leadership, diversity, and societal pluralism. Grogan (2000), in a special issue of *Educational Administration Quarterly* on women and the superintendency, framed her essay with feminist poststructuralism. She considered women and the superintendency for future research and practice with four dimensions of feminist-poststructuralism – discourse, knowledge and power, subjectivity, and resistance. She argued for reconceptualizing the superintendency from a feminist poststructural epistemology.

Guided by feminist poststructuralist theory, Wrushen and Sherman (2008) studied the leadership of eight female secondary principals: four Caucasian and two women who were African American, one Hispanic, and one Asian. The study addressed two research questions: (1) Who are women secondary school principals?, and (2) How are they experiencing their leadership roles at the secondary level? Through the conceptual framework of feminist poststructuralism and the tenets of language and discourse, power, and subjectivity, the analysis revealed the complexity of race and gender with their leadership. Wrushen and Sherman's study represents an example of research that considers the intersection of race/ethnicity and gender, and the methods included identifying the participants' age range, years of experience, and size of schools, but the authors are silent on their sexual/gender identity, disability status, their social class upbringing, and other identity markers and their intersections. While it is plausible to want to consider only two dimensions of identity and their intersections, the authors do not indicate their reasoning or the range of other possibilities.

Across poststructural and feminist poststructural epistemologies, educators analyze, take apart, or deconstruct policies and practices that emanate not only from structural functional (Chapter 3) and interpretive epistemologies (Chapter 4), but also from equity-oriented epistemologies such as critical theory (Chapter 5). As discussed in this chapter, while feminist theories emerged as one critique of critical theory, Critical Race Theory also emerged as a critique and advancement from Critical Legal Studies (undergirded by critical theory). We turn next in Chapter 7 to Critical Race Theory and its implications for organizational theory and educational leadership.

LEADERSHIP DEVELOPMENT ACTIVITIES

ACTIVITY 1: **Discussion and Critical Reflection on Your Own Leadership from Feminist, Poststructural, and Feminist Poststructural Epistemologies**

Language

1. How does the language used in my setting shape and influence educational practices? How do educational settings regulate the language used?
2. What labels and language are used in my educational setting and how does this language mask power inequities?
3. What are some examples in our setting of when something or someone is viewed as natural, normal, or commonsensical or as "the way we do things around here," "we all know that," "everybody knows," or "it is well known that" (Weedon, 1987)? Do I question this? Who is considered the authority, the expert, the knowledgeable one? How does this consideration maintain existing power relations?

Change

To what extent do I ...

4. Allow the nature of change to be messy, unpredictable?
5. Tend to try and control the process of change too much to reach my predetermined end-point?
6. Foster and am I comfortable with dissensus, resistance, contradiction, and conflict?
7. Recognize that there is not one solution to a so-called problem but multiple possibilities for a given situation? Do I recognize that these possibilities need to be personal, local, and close to the people in each situation and that these possibilities can change each day, that they are not finite?

Decision-making

8. To what extent am I conscious of the way in which consensus, dialogue, and democratic decision-making can serve to mask power inequities; that persons with differing opinions in the minority of the group are relegated to the side; and that consensus can lead to an illusion of community and stifle creative conflict?

Power

To what extent do I ...

9. Recognize that power is everywhere and that it can emanate from many different points?

10. Recognize that all people have the potential for power, that it can come from anyone, and that all people can exert normalizing power over others, but that some people have access to channels of power that others do not?

11. Recognize that power is operating on me in ways I may not expect or realize, governing my desire, needs, and my physical body?

ACTIVITY 2:   **Case Analysis Questions**

Feminist Epistemology

1. How is the situation "producing and reproducing gender differences and gender inequalities" (Kenway & Modra, 1992, p. 141)?

2. How does the situation (e.g., discourse, curriculum, policy, etc.) misrecognize, misrepresent, neglect, deny, or undervalue the "social contributions and culture experiences of [individuals who consider themselves girls and women]" (Kenway & Modra, 1992, p. 141)?

3. How and to what extent are outcomes, rationality, reason, competition, and the abstract conflated in the situation? How and to what extent are process, emotion, cooperation, nurturance, intuition, the relational, and experience suppressed in the situation?

Poststructural Epistemology

1. Does the case consider how space is set up in the organization in a way to manage and control people? Does the case consider how different groups of students/individuals are relegated to different spaces, and how this arrangement may maintain unequal power relations?

2. How is the language used in the situation influencing educational policy and practices? How is the situation regulating the language used?

3. How is the language used in the situation masking power inequities?

4. Identify the sources of power in the case.

NOTE

1   Adapted from Capper, C.A. Critical and postmodern perspectives: Sorting out the differences and implications for practice. *Educational Administration Quarterly, 34* (3), 354–379. © 2018, Sage Publications. Reprinted by permission of Sage Publications. doi: 10.1177/0013161X98034003005.

REFERENCES

Alcoff, L. (1988). Cultural feminism versus poststructuralism: The identity crisis in feminist theory. In E. Minnich, J. O'Barr, & R. Rosenfeld (Eds). *Reconstructing the academy: Women's education and women's studies* (pp. 257–288). Chicago: University of Chicago Press.

Althusser, L. (1969). *For Marx.* London: Allen Lane.

Anderson, G. (1990). Toward a critical constructivist approach to school administration: Invisibility, legitimation, and the study of non-events. *Educational Administrative Quarterly, 26*(1), 38–59.

André-Bechely, L. (2005). Public school choice at the intersection of voluntary integration and not-so-good neighborhood schools: Lessons from parents' experiences. *Educational Administration Quarterly, 41*(2), 267–305.

Best, S. & Kellner, D. (1991). *Postmodern theory.* New York: The Guilford Press.

Blackmore, J. (1999). *Troubling women: Feminist leadership & educational change.* Chestnut, PA: Open University Press.

Blackmore, J. (2007). *Performing and reforming leaders: Gender, educational restructuring, and organizational change.* Albany, NY: State University Press.

Blackmore, J. (2013). A feminist critical perspective on educational leadership. *International Journal of Leadership in Education, 16*(2), 139–154.

Blackmore, J. (2014). "Wasting talent"? Gender and the problematics of academic disenchantment and disengagement with leadership. *Higher Education Research and Development, 33*(1), 86–99.

Blount, J. (1998). *Destined to rule the schools: Women and the superintendency 1873–1995.* Ithaca, NY: State University of New York Press.

Brunner, C. (Ed.). (1999). *Sacred dreams: Women and superintendency.* Ithaca, NY: State University of New York Press.

Brunner, C. (2000). *Principles of power: Women superintendents and the riddle of the heart.* Ithaca, NY: State University of New York Press.

Brunner, C. & Grogan, M. (2007). *Women leading school systems: Uncommon road to fulfillment.* Lanham, MD: Rowman & Littlefield Education.

Burrell, G. (1988). Modernism, postmodernism, and organizational analysis 2: The contribution of Michal Foucault. *Organizational Studies, 9*(2), 221–235.

Capper, C.A. (1992). A feminist, poststructural critique and analysis of non-traditional theory and research in educational administration. *Educational Administration Quarterly, 28*(1), 103–124.

Capper, C.A. (1994). "We're not housed in an institution, we're housed in the community:" Possibilities and consequences of neighborhood-based interagency collaboration. *Educational Administration Quarterly, 30*(3), 237–277.

Capper, C.A. (1998). Critically oriented and postmodern perspectives: Sorting out the differences and applications for practice. *Educational Administration Quarterly, 34*(3), 354–379.

Capper, C. A. & Jamison, M.T. (1993). Let the buyer beware! Total quality management and educational research and practice. *Educational Researcher, 22*(8), 25–30.

Capper, C.A. & Green, T.L. (2013). Organizational theories and the development of leadership capacity for integrated, socially just schools. In L. Tillman & J.J. Scheurich and Associates, *Handbook of Educational leadership for equity and diversity* (pp. 62–82). New York: Routledge.

Cherryholmes, C.H. (1988). *Power and criticism: Poststructural investigations in education.* New York: Teachers College Press.

Cooper, R. & Burrell, G. (1988). Modernism, postmodernism, and organizational analysis: An introduction. *Organizational Studies, 9*(1), 91–112.

Derrida, J. (1981). *Positions.* Chicago, IL: University of Chicago Press.

Eckes, S.E. & McCall, S.D. (2014). The potential impact of social science research on legal issues surrounding single-sex classrooms and schools. *Educational Administration Quarterly, 50*(2), 195–232.

Eckman, E.W. (2004), Similarities and differences in role conflict, role commitment, and job satisfaction for female and male high school principals. *Educational Administration Quarterly, 40*(3), 366–387.

Ellsworth, E. (1989). Why doesn't this feel empowering? Working through the repressive myths of critical pedagogy. *Harvard Educational Review, 59*(3), 297–324.

English, F.W. (1998). The postmodern turn in educational administration: Apostrophic or catastrophic development? *Journal of School Leadership*, 8(5), 426–447.

Ferguson, K.E. (1984). *The feminist case against bureaucracy.* Philadelphia, PA: Temple University Press.

Flax, J. (1990). Postmodernism and gender relations in feminist theory. In L.J. Nicholson (Ed.), *Feminism/postmodernism* (pp. 39–62). New York: Routledge.

Foucault, M. (1980). *The history of sexuality (Vol 1).* New York: Pantheon.

Foucault, M. (1988). *The care of the self.* New York: Vintage.

Fraser, N. & Nicholson, L. (1988). Social criticism without philosophy: An encounter between feminism and postmodernism. In A. Ross (Ed.), *Universal abandon. The politics of postmodernism* (pp. 83–104). Minneapolis, MN: University of Minnesota Press.

Fuss, D. (1989). *Essentially speaking: Feminism, nature and difference.* New York: Routledge.

Grogan, M. (1996). *Voices of women aspiring to the superintendency.* New York: State University Press of New York.

Grogan, M. (2000). Laying the groundwork for a reconception of the superintendency from feminist postmodern perspectives. *Educational Administration Quarterly, 36*(1), 117–142.

Grogan, M. & Shakeshaft, C. (2011). *Women and educational leadership.* San Francisco, CA: Jossey-Bass

Grogan, M. & Smith, F. (1998). A feminist perspective of women superintendents' approaches to moral dilemmas. *Journal for a Just and Caring Education, 4*(2), 176–192.

Hallinger, P., Dongyu, L., & Wang, W.C. (2016). Gender differences in instructional leadership: A meta-analytic review of studies using the Principal Instructional Management Rating Scale. *Educational Administration Quarterly, 52*(4) 1–35.

Harding, S. (1991). *Whose science? Whose knowledge? Thinking from women's lives.* Ithaca, NY: Cornell University Press.

Holvino, E. (2010). Intersections: The simultaneity of race, gender and class in organization studies. *Gender, Work and Organization, 17*(3), 248–277.

Jackson, K., Chiu, C., Lopez, R., Simmons, J.M.C., Skrla, L., & Warner, L.S. (2013). An exercise in tempered radicalism: Seeking the intersectionality of gender, race, and sexual identity in educational leadership research. In L. Tillman & J.J. Scheurich (Eds), *Handbook on research on educational leadership for equity and diversity* (pp. 327–354). New York: Sage.

Kaplan, E.A. & Sprinkler, M. (Eds). (1993). *The Althusserian legacy.* London: Verso.

Kenway, J. & Modra, H. (1992). Feminist pedagogy and emancipatory possibilities. In C. Luke & J. Gore (Eds), *Feminism and critical pedagogy* (pp. 138–166). New York: Routledge.

Lacan, J. (1977). *Ecrits.* London: Tavistock.

Lather, P. (1991). *Getting smart: Feminist research and pedagogy with/in the postmodern.* New York: Routledge.

Luke, C. & Gore, J. (1992). *Feminisms and critical pedagogy.* New York: Routledge.

Lyotard, J. (1984). *The postmodern condition: A report on knowledge.* Minneapolis, MN: University of Minnesota Press.

Mahitivanichcha, K. & Rorrer, A. (2006). Women's choices within market constraints: Re-visioning access to and participation in the superintendency. *Educational Administration Quarterly, 42*(4), 483–517.

Mansfield, K.C. (2014). More than a school: Providing a safe space for girls to rewrite, direct, and act their life stories. In W.S. Newcomb & K.C. Mansfield (Eds), *Women interrupting, disrupting, and revolutionizing educational policy and practice* [Kindle version]. Retrieved from Amazon.com (pp. 1476–1897). Charlotte, NC: Information Age Publishing.

Mansfield, K.C., Welton, A., & Grogan, M. (2014). Truth or consequences: A feminist critical policy analysis of the STEM crisis. *International Journal of Qualitative Studies in Education, 27*(9), 1155–1182.

Marshall, C. (1997). *Feminist critical policy analysis I: Perspectives from K–12.* London: Falmer Press.

Marshall, C. & Young, M. (2013). Policy inroads undermining women in education. *International Journal of Leadership in Education, 16*(2), 205–219.

Mills, A.J. & Tancred, P. (1992). *Gendering organizational analysis.* Newbury Park, CA: Sage.

Newcomb, W.S. & Mansfield, K.C. (Eds). (2014) *Women interrupting, disrupting, and revolutionizing educational policy and practice.* Charlotte, NC: Information Age Publishing.

Newcomb, W.S. & Niemeyer, A. (2015) African American women principals: Heeding the call to serve as conduits for transforming urban school communities. *International Journal of Qualitative Studies in Education, 28*(7), 786–799.

Newton, R.M. (2006). Does recruitment message content normalize the superintendency as male? *Educational Administration Quarterly, 42*(4), 551–577.

Nicholson, C. (1989). Postmodernism, feminism, and education: The need for solidarity. *Educational Theory, 39*(3), 197–205.

Nicholson, L. J. (Ed.). (1990). *Feminism/postmodernism.* New York: Routledge.

Ropers-Huilman, B. (1998). *Feminist teaching in theory and practice: Situating power and knowledge in poststructural classrooms.* New York: Teachers College Press.

Ropers-Huilman, B., & Capper, C. A. (1995). *Ethical opportunities in school leadership: Guiding questions for revisioning and reform.* Unpublished manuscript.

Rouse, J. (1987). *Knowledge and power: Toward a political philosophy of science.* Ithaca, NY: Cornell University Press.

Santamaría, L.M. (2014). Critical change for the greater good. *Educational Administration Quarterly, 50*(3), 347–391.

Sawicki, J. (1991). *Disciplining Foucault: Feminism, power, and the body.* New York: Routledge.

Scott, J. (1988). Deconstructing equality-versus-difference: Or, the uses of poststructuralist theory for feminism. *Feminist Studies, 14*(1), 33–51.

Shakeshaft, C. (1987). *Women in educational administration.* Newbury Park, CA: Sage.

Shakeshaft, C. (2011). Wild Patience: The glass ceiling for women in school administration. In *Sage handbook of educational leadership.* Thousands Oak, CA: Sage.

Sherman, W. & Beatty, D. (2010). Using feminist phase theory to portray women in the principalship across generations in the USA. *Journal of Educational Administration and History, 42*(2), 159–180.

Sherman, W. & Wrushen, B. (2009). Intersecting leadership knowledge from the field: Diverse women secondary principals. *Journal of School Leadership, 19*(2), 172–199.

Sherman, W.H. (2005). Preserving the status quo or renegotiating leadership: Women's experiences with a district-based aspiring leaders program. *Educational Administration Quarterly, 41*(5), 707–740.

Sherman Newcomb, W. (2014). *Continuing to disrupt the status quo? New and young women professors of educational leadership.* Charlotte, NC: Information Age Publishing.

Sherman Newcomb, W. & Cummings Mansfield, K. (2014). *Women interrupting, disrupting, and revolutionizing educational policy and practice.* Charlotte, NC: Information Age Publishing.

Sherman Newcomb, W. & Niemeyer, A. (2015). African American women principals: Heeding the call to serve as conduits for transforming urban school communities. *International Journal of Qualitative Studies in Education, 28*(7), 786–799.

Snitnow, C. & Thompson, S. (1984). *Desire: The politics of sexuality.* London: Virago.

Tillman, L.C. (2009). The never-ending science debate: I'm ready to move on. *Educational Researcher, 38*(6), 458–462.

Weedon, C. (1987). *Feminist practice and poststructuralist theory.* Oxford: Blackwell.

Whitford, M. (1991). *Luce Irigaray: Philosophy in the feminine.* New York: Routledge.

Wrushen, B.R. & Sherman W.H. (2008). Women secondary school principals: Multicultural voices from the field. *International Journal of Qualitative Studies in Education, 21*(5), 457–469.

CHAPTER 7

Critical Race Theory, Black Crit[1]

Although the first published application of Critical Race Theory (CRT) to education occurred 20 years ago (Ladson-Billings & Tate, 1995), implications of CRT for educational leadership did not occur until López (2003) conducted a CRT analysis of the politics of education literature. Since then, including Lopez's work, few publications apply CRT directly to educational leadership as it relates to formal positions of authority (e.g., school principals or superintendents), and no publications identify implications for leadership practice guided explicitly by the CRT tenets. As such, the purpose of this chapter is to promulgate CRT as a framework to inform organizational theory and to guide the practices of educational leaders to eliminate racial inequities in their leading of equitable, socially just schools.

On the epistemology framework, Critical Race Theory is positioned across the subjective/objective nature of knowledge continuum and on the radical change end of the change continuum (see Figure 7.1). The next section describes the history of CRT and its lineage after critical theory and feminist theories discussed in the previous chapters.

BRIEF HISTORY OF CRT

Here, I offer a brief history of CRT. In each section of the chapter where I define and describe the central tenets of CRT, I refer back to some of the key scholars in the historic formation of CRT. In defining and explaining CRT, like Solórzano (1998),

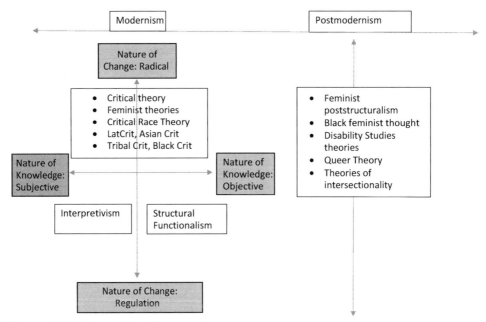

Figure 7.1 An Epistemology Framework

I do not view CRT as "uniform and static" (p. 123). Crenshaw (2011) agrees in her historical account of the formation of CRT:

> CRT is not so much an intellectual unit filled with natural stuff – theories, themes, practices, and the like – but one that is dynamically constituted by a series of contestations and convergences pertaining to the ways that racial power is understood and articulated in the post-civil rights era. … I want to suggest that shifting the frame of CRT toward a dynamic rather than static reference would be a productive means by which we can link CRT's past to the contemporary moment. (p. 1261)

Tate (1997), who published one of the first papers to apply CRT to education, concurs with this multiple view of the history and formation of CRT:

> I use the heading "One Historical Overview" to indicate that my historical interpretation of the origins of critical race theory is subject to critique and debate. Moreover, the heading reflects my belief that it is possible to construct more than one history of this scholarly movement. (p. 237)

Given these caveats, I draw upon Crenshaw's (2011) history of CRT, substantiated by other histories of CRT referred to in the initial applications of CRT to education (Ladson-Billings, 1998; Ladson-Billings & Tate, 1995; Parker, 1998; Parker, Deyhle, Villenas, & Nebeker, 1998; Solórzano, 1997, 1998; Solórzano & Yosso, 2000, 2001; Tate, 1994; 1997) and earlier (López, 2003) and later applications of CRT (Horsford, 2010a) to educational leadership.

Tate (1997) argues that "Although no identifiable date can be assigned to the conception of CRT, its foundation is linked to the development of African American thought in the post-civil rights era: the 1970s to the present (Bell, 1980a, b; Matsuda, Lawrence, Delgado, & Crenshaw, 1993)" (p. 206). Yet, as Solórzano and Yosso (2001) point out, it may be argued that "CRT's roots go back as far as the turn of the last century with DuBois' s (1903) work *The Souls of Black Folk*" (p. 474). Tate's (1997) CRT history presents key scholars in the CRT movement such as Bell (1980b), Delgado (1990), and Crenshaw (1988) who in the early 1980s identified the inadequacies of Critical Legal Studies (CLS) in addressing racism. According to Tate (1997), Crenshaw's contribution to the movement began when she was a Harvard Law student who helped organize student protests over the lack of faculty of color and the lack of courses in their program related to race and other dimensions of difference. Crenshaw helped create the Alternative Course developed by students and scholars external to Harvard based primarily on the work of Bell (1992). These scholars and others gathered for the first CRT Workshop in Madison, Wisconsin in 1989. Crenshaw (1988) and other scholars critiqued not only neoliberal aspects of the law but also CLS for its perpetuation of racism. Although Tate (1997) presented this CRT history in part, centered on these three scholars, Solórzano and Yosso's (2001) CRT history points out how "these criticisms had their roots and are still being influenced by similar criticisms that were developing in ethnic studies, women's studies, cultural nationalist paradigms, Marxist and neo-Marxist frameworks, and internal colonial models" (p. 474).

As such, some histories of CRT in CLS chronicle the central role of critical theory in its development (Solórzano, 1997; Solórzano & Yosso, 2001), in response to laws, associated policies, and legal practices that perpetuated oppression. Solórzano (1997, 1998) relies on Matsuda (1991) to define Critical Race Theory as:

> the work of progressive legal scholars of color who are attempting to develop a jurisprudence that accounts for the role of racism in American law and that works toward the elimination of racism as part of a larger goal of eliminating all forms of subordination. (Solórzano,1998, p. 1331)

López (2003) further explains: "CRT's premise is to critically interrogate how the law reproduces, reifies, and normalizes racism in society in particular for individuals of lower social classes and persons of color" (p. 83).

From this CRT history in law, the applications of CRT to education and educational leadership may be aligned with six primary, interrelated CRT tenets as identified in the education and educational leadership literature (Horsford, 2010a; Ladson-Billings, 2013; López, 2003). I briefly define these six tenets in Table 7.1.

CRT scholars in education moved the research on race in education (Tate, 1997) and educational leadership (López, 2003) from a racial deficit perspective to unearthing the prevalence and persistence of racism within society and reproduced in education and schools (*race is endemic to society*). CRT from law described how *whiteness is property* (Harris, 1993), and CRT education scholars identified

Table 7.1 Critical Race Theory Tenets

CRT Tenet	Definition	Source
Permanence of racism	Racism, both conscious and unconscious is a permanent component of American life	Bell (1992); Ladson-Billings & Tate (1995); Tate (1997); Ladson-Billings (1998)
Whiteness as property	Because of the history of race and racism in the U.S.A. and the role U.S. jurisprudence has played in reifying conceptions of race, the notion of whiteness can be considered a property interest	Harris (1995): Ladson-Billings (1998); Ladson-Billings & Tate (1995)
Counter-storytelling and majoritarian narratives	A method of telling a story that aims to cast doubt on the validity of accepted premises or myths, especially ones held by the majority; majoritarian narratives are also recognized as stories, and not assumed to be facts or the truth	Matsuda (1995); Ladson-Billings & Tate (1995); Tate (1997); Delgado (1995); Ladson-Billings (1998); Solórzano & Yosso (2001)
Interest convergence	Significant progress for blacks is achieved only when the goals of blacks are consistent with the needs of whites	Bell (1980a, 2004); Ladson-Billings (1998)
Critique of liberalism	Critique of basic notions embraced by liberal ideology to include color-blindness, meritocracy, and neutrality of the law	Crenshaw (1988), Ladson-Billings & Tate (1995); Tate (1997); Ladson-Billings (1998)
Intersectionality	Considers race across races and the intersection of race with other identities and differences	Crenshaw (1991)

how the white curriculum is defended as white property (Ladson-Billings, 1998) and, as a result, leaders can expect white resistance when seeking to address race in the curriculum (Pollack & Zirkel, 2013). CRT in legal studies identified the critical importance of experience and minoritized voices which paved the way for mining *counter-stories* in education (Solórzano & Yosso, 2001) and in educational leadership (Horsford, 2009, 2010a, 2010b), and how these counter-narratives push back against *majoritarian stories*. CRT in legal studies argued how seemingly legal advances only occurred when such advances also supported white interests at the same time and, in so doing, negated racial progress (Bell, 1980a) (*interest convergence*). CRT scholars in education (Ladson-Billings, 1998) echoed the legal studies critique of Brown vs. Board of education as a prime example of interest convergence, while educational leadership scholars revealed interest convergence in policies such as school finance (Aléman, 2007). In the same way that CRT scholars critiqued the critical discourse in Critical Legal Studies (Tate, 1997), CRT also provided a way to critique the liberal multicultural and diversity discourse in education (Ladson-Billings & Tate, 1995) and the leadership for social justice

Figure 7.2 Critical Race Theory Tenets

discourse in educational leadership (López et al., 2003) in that these progressive discourses submerge, marginalize, and perpetuate racism (*critique of liberalism*). Among the CRT in education scholars, Solórzano (1997, 1998) presented the most explicit extrapolation of *intersectionality* to education from legal studies (Crenshaw, 1988), followed by Parker (1998) and López (2003) in educational leadership with the importance of surfacing hidden oppression when examining the intersection of race with other identities.

Across the CRT in educational leadership publications, most scholars articulated similar CRT tenets, though they all chose to emphasize different tenets in their data analyses. Nearly all the publications viewed the data through the CRT lens of the endemic nature of racism (16) and counter-stories (16), while critique of liberalism (11), interest convergence (9), and whiteness as property (9) were nearly equally addressed. Only four articles identified intersectionality as a CRT tenet to be considered. None of the publications comprehensively traced the CRT pedigree in educational leadership in their reviews of literature. Although intersectionality emerged as a tenet of the CRT studies I reviewed, rather than discuss intersectionality in this chapter, I address intersectionality in Chapter 12

CRT TENETS AND IMPLICATIONS FOR LEADERSHIP PRACTICE

Next, I define and describe each of the six interrelated CRT tenets I apply to educational leadership. Within each tenet, I draw from the CRT in educational leadership literature, supported by related literature and my own analysis linked explicitly to the tenet to explicate implications for leadership practice to eliminate racism.

Permanence of Racism

López (2003) contends that many people perceive racism "as an individual and irrational act in a world that is otherwise neutral, rational, and just" (p. 69). Further, according to López (2003), "most people view racism … as the enactment of overt racial acts – for example, name calling, burning crosses, hate crimes, and so forth – while ignoring the deeper, often invisible, and more insidious forms of racism that occur on a daily basis" (López, 2003, pp. 81–82).

Thus, rather than viewing racism as random, infrequent, isolated, out-of-the ordinary events, CRT posits that racism has always been and always will be endemic and pervasive in society (Tate, 1997). Mentioned in 16 of the CRT in educational leadership publications, from this perspective, racism is understood to be normal (López, 2003), happening all the time, everywhere, at the individual, institutional, societal, and epistemological levels (Tate, 1997). CRT points to the importance of understanding the enormity and pervasiveness of the structural, political, economic embeddedness of racism throughout the history of and currently within the U.S. (Horsford, 2010a). As such, a challenge to ahistoricism is threaded throughout all CRT six tenets – a separate tenet identified by Tate (1997) and amplified throughout applications to education (Ladson-Billings & Tate, 1995; Ladson-Billings, 1998) and educational leadership (Horsford, 2010a).

The pervasiveness of societal racism remains true even with seeming societal racial gains and persons of color occupying positions of power and prestige in U.S. society. These facts do not mean that we now live in a "post-racial" society with racism in the past and not relevant today, as these gains most often prop up white privilege, perpetuate racism on other levels, and remain in stark contrast to the massive racial inequities that continue in society (Ladson-Billings, 2011). That is, that "race [still] matters" (Ladson-Billings, 1998, p. 8), and will always matter.

This tenet of the permanence of racism can help white educational leaders acknowledge that they themselves are racist, that all leaders regardless of race are complicit in racism (Khalifa et al., 2014), and that all schools and districts embody and perpetuate racism throughout the culture, organization, policies, and practices, and will always do so. This pervasiveness of racism exists even though educational leaders may have addressed their own racist assumptions and beliefs, participated in diversity training (Evans, 2007), engaged in meaningful work or relationships with persons of color, or made progress with students of color in their schools. These leaders understand that working against racism is a lifelong process personally, and is an ever-evolving and continuing process of working against organizational racism in their schools (Theoharis & Haddix, 2011).

The endemic and pervasiveness of racism at all levels of schools and society and within ourselves, however, is not without hope that progress can be made or that persons of color are without agency. Bell (1992), considered one of the godfathers of CRT, discusses racial realism as part of CRT which is "a philosophy [that] requires us to acknowledge the permanence of our subordinate status" which "enables us to avoid despair and frees us to imagine and implement racial strategies that can bring fulfillment and even triumph" (pp. 373–374). Bell believed that by acknowledging racial realism, individuals would be motivated to move beyond incremental, status quo change that, while addressing racial inequities in one form, spawns further racial inequities elsewhere. Ladson-Billings (1998) agrees: "Adopting and adapting CRT as a framework for educational equity means that we will have to expose racism in education and propose radical solutions for addressing it" (p. 22). As such, CRT in educational leadership literature suggests four interrelated practices educational leaders can take to recognize and eliminate the pervasiveness of racism.

First, educational leaders should work toward developing an anti-racist identity (Gooden, 2012; Theoharis & Haddix, 2011), which evolves through a series of stages and is ongoing through one's life. To date, the educational leadership scholarship on anti-racist leadership has focused on leadership preparation (Lightfoot, 2009; Young & Laible, 2000) and more work needs to be conducted that examines how leaders can further develop an anti-racist identity for themselves and how to develop such an identity with their staff and students. Gooden (2012) offers suggestions for anti-racist identity development based on his analysis of African American principals, including future and practicing principals, who need to understand individual, societal, and institutional racism. In doing so, leaders can investigate their own racial histories by writing racial autobiographies, then analyzing these autobiographies using racial identity development models. Horsford (2014) describes another model for developing an anti-racist identity, drawn in part upon the CRT tenet of the pervasiveness of racism where leaders move through a series of stages: racial literacy, racial realism, racial reconstruction, and racial reconciliation.

Importantly, developing an anti-racist identity cannot happen as the result of attending one workshop or reading a few articles or books on white racism. Evans (2007) studied school leader perspectives on the demographic changes in their schools. She found that even with white leaders who had participated in diversity training and who held authentic relationships with persons of color, they continued to hold deficit beliefs about students of color in their schools. In sum, an anti-racist identity occurs as a result of leaders being committed to lifelong work on their own racist assumptions and beliefs via professional development, readings, media, authentic relationships with individuals of color, and other experiences.

Successful principals of students of color in a study by Theoharis and Haddix (2011) did not avoid racial issues, but talked about race with their staff "plainly and often" (p. 1340). Thus, as a second strategy to address the pervasiveness of racism, educational leaders need to engage in informal individual conversations and whole-faculty conversations about race with their staff when issues arise at the school that are informed by race.

Educational leaders should be models of this process to facilitate the development of an anti-racist identity with their staff and students – a third way leaders can recognize the historical and current pervasiveness of racism and work toward eliminating racism (Theoharis & Haddix, 2011). These leaders themselves may facilitate race work with their staff and students or hire trained facilitators to do so. When facilitating race work with staff, CRT scholars argue that leaders must ensure that the work moves beyond diversity/multicultural training (Sherman, 2008; Stovall, 2004). According to Stovall (2004):

> Unfortunately, many diversity and cultural sensitivity workshops sanitize race and attempt to promote false senses of unity. ... Instead of confronting the difficult issues that race can present, some trainings amount to "we're a multicultural society and we should get along better." This is not enough. (p. 11)

Instead, leaders can evaluate the quality and effectiveness of professional development on race based on the extent to which the CRT tenets represented in this chapter are addressed.

Conducting equity audits of their schools constitutes a fourth way whereby leaders can recognize and eliminate the pervasiveness of racism in their schools. Leaders can collect and analyze race data (Gooden 2012; Theoharis & Haddix, 2011), develop concrete goals and implementation plans to eradicate these inequities, design effective measures of progress, and make all of these data and strategies transparent and easily accessible to the community.

In sum, CRT in educational leadership literature calls upon leaders to acknowledge the pervasiveness of racism within ourselves and our schools accompanied by hope that change is possible. To that end, this literature suggests four leadership practices that grapple directly with and work against the endemic nature of racism.

Whiteness as Property

The CRT tenant of whiteness as property refers to U.S. history where property rights were and are more important than human rights (Ladson-Billings, 1998; Ladson-Billings & Tate, 1995). From the founding of the U.S., a person who owned property was able to participate in the governance of the Union, whereas a person who did not own property could not participate. Starting with the take-over of Native American land, not only were whites the only people who could legally own property; African Americans could not own property and they themselves became property who could be traded and sold. To be able to own property accorded the property owner incredible power, privilege, status, and rights, based simply on skin color. Put simply, to be white meant something then, means something now, and will always mean something – an automatic affordance of rights and privileges – that whiteness *is* property.

According to Harris (1993), who penned the germinal scholarship on the concept of whiteness as property in legal studies, the legal right to exclude forms the conceptual anchor for understanding whiteness as property. She explains: "In particular, whiteness and property share a common premise – a conceptual nucleus – of a right to exclude. This conceptual nucleus has proven to be a powerful center around which whiteness as property has taken shape" (p. 1707). Harris further explains:

> The right to exclude was the central principle, too, of whiteness as identity, for mainly whiteness has been characterized, not by an inherent unifying

characteristic, but by the exclusion of others deemed to be "not white." The possessors of whiteness were granted the legal right to exclude others from the privileges inherent in whiteness; whiteness became an exclusive club whose membership was closely and grudgingly guarded.

In addition to the absolute right to exclude, legally, anyone who holds property holds "rights of disposition, rights to use and enjoyment, reputation and status property" (Harris, 1993, pp. 1731–1737).

In one of the earliest publications that applied CRT to education, Ladson-Billings and Tate (1995) linked the whiteness as property tenet in a literal way to property values; that is, because public school finance is based on local property taxes, wealthier communities are able to allocate more funding to education than economically poor communities. They explain, "The quality and quantity of the curriculum varies with the property values of the school" (p. 54). Alemán (2007) illuminated this link between property and curriculum in his analysis of Texas school finance policy on Mexican majority American school districts. He analyzed how Texas finance policy, which was hailed as transformative and more equity oriented than previous finance policy, continued to marginalize Mexican majority school districts and to perpetuate racism.

Thus, in public schools, aspects that uphold white privilege may be viewed as property that whites will fiercely protect for themselves. For example, the curriculum remains the most valued property in schools, and whites will fiercely defend the property of the school curriculum in at least two interrelated ways. First, whites defend the entire system of advanced placement (AP), gifted, and honors programs (collectively considered as the AP system) (Pollack & Zirkel, 2013) and the associated remedial, tracked, and special education system that upholds and reinforces the AP system. A second way in which whites uphold and defend the curriculum includes "the distortions, omissions, and stereotypes of school curriculum content" (Ladson-Billings, 1998, p. 18) which ignores and erases the perspectives of people of color.

While whiteness as property is defined or mentioned in nine of the CRT in educational leadership publications, only two of the publications provide an extensive analysis of race in educational leadership relying on this tenet. One of these two publications, by Pollack and Zirkel (2013), provides the most extensive examination of whiteness as property within the curriculum in the field of educational leadership in their study of equity failure at one high school. The specific equity practice that failed focused on changing the time of science labs that took place before and after school to during school time when more low-income students and students of color could participate. Pollack and Zirkel explain that the property interests of AP students and their families "include the entire AP system of material advantage – including a superior and more engaging curriculum, exclusivity, status, and a substantial competitive advantage in college admissions" (p. 301). They further explain, "we see that the AP students (and, by extension, their parents) clearly had a long-established, taken-for-granted hold on the rights of disposition, use and enjoyment, and status ... [and] their absolute right to exclude" (p. 302).

In this case, Pollack and Zirkel (2013) identified the competing interests as parents of students who were not benefitting from the times that labs were currently offered (these were primarily parents on low income and students of color) and parents of students who were in advanced placement (AP) science who were currently benefitting (these were primarily middle- and upper class white families). Within the school, the competing interests were teachers who believed that students of color had been systemically and historically disadvantaged at the school and thus change was needed, and teachers who believed that such a change was "eroding standards" (p. 301). The science teachers identified with the latter group and these teachers would also lose extra pay they had been receiving for teaching the labs outside of standard school time.

Pollack and Zirkel (2013) believed that the leaders in this study understood these competing interests. However, as Pollack and Zirkel point out:

> Unfortunately, merely identifying the competing interest groups and anticipating how they would be likely to respond to the change proposal was insufficient to prepare for the fierce resistance that ensued. What sets the groups apart are not simply different perspectives on educational processes and goals, but rather different underlying property interests and varying levels of power and privilege that can be exerted to protect those interests. We suggest, therefore, that it would have been far more helpful to first identify and address the specific property interests at issue. (p. 301)

Pollack and Zirkel seamlessly linked power, privilege, and property rights in their analysis of the situation. Although different power positions are clearly understood and visible such as power differences between teachers and leaders, privilege is less visible, and persons with the most privilege hold the strongest property concerns. Obviously, in this case, those who benefitted the most from the existing practices were the predominantly white and affluent students and families. Low-income students of color not only benefitted least from the before- and after-school labs, but the existing structure harmed these students.

When white families fiercely protect their property interests of the AP system, these actions also further prop up and maintain the remedial, tracked, special education system that serves to protect the AP system. The white AP system is protected when students of color are over-represented in special education and in Response to Intervention (RtI) programs (Orosco & Klinger, 2010), when students who are bilingual are segregated in particular classrooms or schools, and students of color are pulled out of the classroom and segregated for these separate programs, all under the well-intentioned but mythical guise of helping students succeed. When educators pull students of color out of classrooms and segregate them away from their white peers and from the core curriculum in these ways, whites exercise their "absolute right to exclude" (Harris, 1993, p. 1731) and further protect the general education classroom as property for white interests.

In addition to the AP system as property fiercely protected by whites, the typical white public school curriculum itself may be viewed as property for whites when perspectives of people of color are silenced. Ladson-Billings (1998) explains:

> Critical race theory sees the official school curriculum as a culturally specific artifact designed to maintain a White supremacist master script. ... This master scripting means stories of African Americans are muted and erased when they challenge dominant culture authority and power. (p. 17)

As one solution to a white curriculum and school culture, some schools engage in work on cultural diversity, multicultural, and culturally responsible teaching initiatives. Unless these initiatives directly address power, privilege, and the embeddedness of racism as explicated across all six CRT tenets, these initiatives serve as a distraction to white racism and further preserve and protect the curriculum for whites. Ladson-Billings (1998, 1999a) agrees that initiatives such as celebrating diversity and multiculturalism not only mute and sanitize the history of African Americans in this country, but further protect the white curriculum from change.

White families may rally against multicultural and social justice initiatives in their schools, since they perceive these initiatives as threats to their white curriculum property. One high school in Evans's (2007) CRT in educational leadership study held an annual black history assembly in which students were not required to attend, and over time an increasing number of white parents excused their children from attending the event. When the school board then canceled the program, Evans explained, "this occurrence illustrates the ways in which school curriculum and events, as intellectual property, serve as established property interests to be preserved and protected by those in power" (pp. 174–175).

Marx and Larson's (2012) CRT in educational leadership study discussed in detail how whiteness as property worked in principal Larson's middle school where Larson implemented curriculum improvements for Latino students:

> [C]ulturally relevant teaching, bilingual education, and Spanish for native speakers classes can be perceived as threatening to the White-dominant school culture and curriculum. ... Strategies for improving schooling for Latina/o students that required embrace of their culture(s) and language(s) were resisted as unnecessary by [the middle school]. These are examples of Whiteness as a property right that was protected and maintained ... even as it sought to better address the needs of its Latina/o students. ... That is, the White students in the school (who composed the majority of the student body population) were not perceived as needing or benefiting from these changes in curriculum and teaching. (p. 294)

Given this definition and description of whiteness as property across legal studies, education, and educational leadership, the CRT whiteness as property tenet suggests at least one implication for leadership practice. That is, many educational leaders may approach the elimination of inequities in their school from a place of naïve goodness. Leaders may assume that if they provide clear data and evidence that expose racial inequities, then all staff and community members also out of a sense of goodness and justice will fully support work to eliminate those inequities. Leaders may especially hold these community assumptions when the school is located in a liberal community, as were the schools in the studies by Pollack and Zirkel (2013) and Knaus (2014). However, this assumption does not consider the property interests at stake. Understanding the CRT whiteness as property tenet can help leaders anticipate, understand, and respond to the fierce backlash they will experience from white middle-/upper class families – including liberal families (Brantlinger, Majd Jabbari, & Gusin, 1996) protecting their property interests when leading equity work.

Toward this end, Pollack and Zirkel (2013) pose two questions for school leaders to consider prior to implementing equity change: "What forms of 'property' are at stake in this area in which we believe change is needed? Whose material interests are likely to be adversely affected?" (p. 300). Pollack and Zirkel argue that leaders should identify the property interests of upper class white students and families from the beginning of equity change. That is, for example, that these students and their families will strongly defend their property of the AP system that affords them enormous rights and privileges that will extend far beyond high school. The leaders should then anticipate that these students and families will also:

> use their considerable resources, access to media and social networks, and 'cultural capital' … to frame the debate in ways that serve their interests. … By anticipating this reaction, educational leaders [can play] a more central role in framing the narratives that defined the debate right from the start. (p. 302)

To help leaders learn how to frame narratives while working toward equity ends, leaders can learn from the CRT tenet of counter-narratives, which I discuss in the next section.

In sum, the CRT tenet whiteness as property views the entire AP system along with the typical public school curriculum with the perspectives of people of color silenced as white property fiercely protected by whites, while the school remedial system upholds and sustains that property. To lead toward the elimination of racism, leaders should identify the property interests at stake and anticipate the resistance from white families to this work.

Counter-narratives and Acknowledgment of Majoritarian Narratives

A third key tenet of CRT addresses the importance of personal experience shared via narratives of people of color (Ladson-Billings & Tate, 1995; Solórzano & Bernal, 2001; Solórzano & Yosso, 2001). These narratives are positioned as counter-stories to the white norm at the individual, institutional, societal, and epistemological levels (Solórzano & Yosso, 2001; Tate, 1997), and make visible the daily micro-aggressions and societal and institutional racism that people of color experience.

Solórzano and Yosso (2001) were among the first CRT in education scholars to develop counter-storytelling as a research method and further legitimize counter-stories as justifiable data and valid (Ladson-Billings, 1998) that "can be used as theoretical, methodological, and pedagogical tools to challenge racism, sexism, and classism and work toward social justice" (Solórzano & Yosso, 2001, p. 23). Delgado (1993) explains further: "Majoritarians tell stories too. But the ones they tell – about merit, causation, blame, responsibility, and social justice – do not seem to them like stories at all, but the truth" (p. 666). Smith, Yosso, and Solórzano (2007) agree and argue: "Counterstories challenge this facade of truth by revealing the perspectives of racialized power and privilege behind it" (p. 565).

While most CRT scholars in educational leadership emphasize the importance of legitimizing counter-stories of people of color, other scholars take up the converse idea of majoritarian stories which Delgado (1993) identifies as it applies to equity work. For example, Pollack and Zirkel (2013) explain how majoritarian narratives "help preserve the property rights of privilege and whiteness" (p. 297). In their study, privileged, white upper class families relied on majoritarian narratives to uphold and maintain their property rights. Understanding this linkage can help leaders understand why equity-oriented reforms are often subverted as they attempt to lead successful equity-focused changes in their schools.

Counter-narratives along with the permanence of racism were mentioned, defined, or relied on as a research method in the CRT in educational leadership articles more frequently than the other CRT tenets. This literature features counter-narratives of African American superintendents about school segregation (Horsford & McKenzie, 2008; Horsford, 2009, 2010a, 2010b), African American teacher experiences in "equity" schools (Knaus, 2014), an African American principal turning around a school (Brown, Beckett, & Beckett, 2006), African American and Latino mothers across social classes and school choice (André-Bechely, 2005), and Latino superintendents as they grappled with state finance policy (Alemán, 2006, 2007), though none of this literature offered implications for leadership practice.

In this literature, Pollack and Zirkel (2013) offer the most nuanced and detailed explanation of how counter- and majoritarian stories operate when educational leaders are engaged in equity work, and, given the purpose of this chapter that focuses on implications of CRT for organizational theory, and leadership practice, I review their study in detail. Pollack and Zirkel explain that whites use majoritarian narratives to "justify, legitimate, and help to maintain the status quo of racial inequities" (p. 298). Whites use these narratives to explain racial inequities – narratives that are "embedded with racialized omissions, distortions, and stereotypes" (Ladson-Billings, 1998, p. 18), deficit thinking, and blame the victim. For example, some whites may explain that racial inequities exist because "African American and Latina/o students 'do not value education,' or based on 'cultural differences' or 'deficiencies'" (Pollack & Zirkel, p. 298). These deficit-based explanations "fail to account for patterns of accumulation and disaccumulation of economic, social, and symbolic capital" (Pollack & Zirkel, p. 298) that produce and perpetuate the pervasiveness of racism. Pollack and Zirkel add,

> white people tend to view these narratives not as reflecting a particular perspective (theirs), but rather as uncontestable reality – simply the "way things are" … Narratives about who is deserving predominate – deserving of access to the best curriculum or access to the best colleges. Deserving in all these instances is defined in circumscribed ways that lead back to the most privileged people having the greatest right to additional privileges. (p. 298–299)

Pollack and Zirkel suggest two questions from the CRT tenet of counter-/majoritarian narratives to guide leaders attempting to make equity-oriented changes: "What are the narratives we might use to frame public debate? What are other narratives that might surface in response and how can we anticipate them?" (p. 300).

Pollack and Zirkel (2013) identified four majoritarian narratives of privilege in their case example: (a) to be fair means to not notice race, to be color-blind, nor to do anything different for/with students of color, to treat all students the same; (b) a belief that difference in intelligence or ability are genetically determined, and thus "normal, expected, and to be accepted" (p. 303), and further, that the racial inequities prevalent across the country in every school confirm this fact; (c) student achievement differences are due to talent and effort, and thus some students are more worthy than others, and it is best to invest resources into students who are worthy, rather than low performing students of color; and (d) if equity efforts aim to increase the achievement of students of color, then these efforts are unfair to students who are already successful and thus we are rewarding students who are unworthy and punishing students who work hard. These majoritarian narratives then make racial achievement inequities and racial segregation and stratification in schools via special education, remedial education, tracking, and response to intervention programs normal, acceptable, and in no need of change. These four narratives – centered on which students are deserving and which students are not – serve as a distraction to the central issue of privileged white families and students protecting their property rights of the Advanced Placement system.

These four majoritarian narratives also explain why simply sharing racial equity audit data with staff, families, and community members may not motivate these individuals to want to correct these inequities. In fact, the racial equity data can serve to reinforce stereotypes and deficit views of students of color and the four majoritarian narratives that Pollack and Zirkel (2013) describe. When school staff have not historically taken responsibility for low achievement for students of color, and instead hold deficit perspectives about students and their families, then equity audit data that show racial inequities may result in school staff feeling blamed about the inequities and react defensively, and blame the inequities on students of color for reasons that reinforce negative stereotypes and deficit thinking about students of color.

Counter-narratives and Decision-making

To counter the eruption and strengthening of these majoritarian narratives, the CRT tenet of counter-narratives suggests that leaders working to eliminate racism need to ensure that individuals and communities of color are authentically included in democratic decision-making about strategies and plans to eliminate racial inequities. At the beginning of equity work, leaders must seek the perspectives of students, families, and communities of color and make public their stories, views, and examples of how the current system is not working for them (Knaus, 2014). Seeking these perspectives must occur at the school and district level in multi-layered ways. For example, Horsford (2010a) suggests that "practicing and aspiring educational leaders … study the historical, political, economic, and social contexts of the school communities they serve to include informal interviews that capture the experiential knowledge of people who have been marginalized, underserved, or silenced in a particular community" (p. 313). The African American superintendents in her study offered counter-narratives of integrated schooling, including the strengths of African American schools pre-Brown. Thus, Horsford argues for the critical importance of deeply engaging with the history of marginalized individuals in the school community. Horsford also suggests:

> Exposing aspiring educational leaders to multiple perspectives of knowing and understanding, as uniquely experienced by veteran educational leaders of color, has educative value not only through the sharing of lived professional experiences but also through exposure to diverse leadership philosophies, styles, and practices that have proved effective in school communities of color. (p. 313)

Additional examples of ways to include the counter-stories of students of color include conducting focus groups with students of color and involving students of color in demographically proportional ways in school decision-making teams that include students. At the district level, district administration can conduct focus groups of community members at each school site and ensure that these focus groups are demographically representative of the school student population. Depending on the community context, district and school leaders may wish to solicit community family and school input particular to specific races/ethnicities; for example, hosting sessions with African American or Latino families and community members.

In addition to seeking the perspectives of educators and individuals of color in the school community, CRT scholars in educational leadership call for deep engagement with the community (Khalifa, Dunbar, & Douglas, 2013; Khalifa et al., 2014; Knaus, 2014; Sherman, 2008: Stovall, 2004) and with families of color (Theoharis & Haddix, 2011) as critical to racial equity. Stovall explains how this community engagement can lead to the development and use of community resource guides and positioning the schools as community centers.

This CRT tenet of counter-narratives in the educational leadership literature reiterates the importance of hiring educators of color and creating working conditions for these educators to thrive and to be genuinely mentored into leadership positions (Knauss, 2014; McCray, Wright, & Beachum 2007). Leaders must also aggressively ensure that district and school decision-making teams are racially representative of the school community. Of course, these staff of color cannot speak for all of their race or community; however, they offer important counter-narratives that are critical to equity decisions. Marx and Larson (2012) discuss how equity changes for Latino students at principal Larson's middle school were limited because all the individuals involved to bring about change were white. To this end, McCray, Wright, and Beachum (2007) analyzed the hiring of African American secondary principals in one southeastern state post-Brown. They found that African American principals are most likely to be hired in majority African American schools (which are often under-resourced), while white principals are hired for majority African American, diverse, and majority white schools. While African American leadership role models are important in majority black schools, at the same time leaders of color should be given the opportunity to lead diverse and white majority schools. Santamaría's (2014) study of diverse leaders in higher education and K-12 also confirms the importance of the leadership of individuals with differences across identity (race, class, ethnicity, language, gender, sexual identity), and how their identity can have a positive impact upon their leadership practice toward equity.

At least two interrelated factors converge for equity leaders to consider when inviting and integrating counter-stories from individuals and communities of color in their equity work: a) the ways in which white privilege and majoritarian narratives act upon and socialize individuals and communities of color (Alémán, 2009; Gooden & Dantley, 2012; Khalifa et al., 2014), and b) racial essentialism. Related to the first CRT tenet of the endemic nature of racism, all individuals have been subjected to and socialized with white, privileged majoritarian narratives about schools and education (Alémán, 2009; Gooden & Dantley, 2012; Khalifa et al., 2014). For example, students, families, and communities of all races may accept that the over-representation of students of color in special education, tracked into lower level courses and classes, or the over-representation of students of color in remedial efforts such as Response to Intervention programs are not only acceptable and immutable but are in fact the most effective ways to support and educate students of color. In addition, educators, families, and communities of all races may accept that the most effective way to educate students who are bilingual is within segregated classrooms. As Khalifa and colleagues (2014) explain in their study of the closure of a majority black high school:

> postracial, technical-rational administrative behaviors were enacted in the move to close [the high school] despite the fact that the superintendent was Latino and the principal was African American. This is another reminder that even minoritized school leaders can knowingly or unknowingly enact, reproduce, and reinforce systems of racial marginalization. (p. 168)

Thus, leaders must analyze and anticipate how students, families, and community members of color may react against equity work, and leaders may need to educate students, families, and community members in ways to undo the dominant majoritarian narratives which these individuals have believed in and bought into (Alémán, 2009; Gooden & Dantley, 2012; Khalifa et al., 2014).

Leaders also should not essentialize the perspectives of particular racial groups or identities. That is, for example, not all Latino families will respond in the same way when leaders wish to integrate students who are bilingual throughout the school rather than segregated into particular classrooms. In these two ways, then, leaders for equity cannot assume that when aggressively soliciting counter-narratives in the process of equity change these counter-narratives from families and students of color will unilaterally support these efforts, and in fact, these families and community members may join with the majoritarian narratives and rally to work against the leaders and equity work.

In sum, the CRT tenet of counter-narratives/majoritarian narratives refers to the importance of soliciting and listening to the perspectives and stories of students, families, and communities of color as integral to anti-racist leadership via community relationships, and hiring and supporting staff of color. In so doing, these counter-stories work against majoritarian stories by whites that mask as the only truth in opposition to equity work.

Interest Convergence and Change

A fourth tenet of CRT addresses interest convergence, meaning that any gains toward racial equality have only happened and can only happen when whites also benefit (Horsford, 2010a; López, 2003). CRT scholars critique apparent gains for racial equality, such as the Brown vs. Board of Education decision because that legal decision benefitted whites by increasing the positive stature of the U.S. with the rest of the world during the Cold War (Ladson-Billings & Tate, 1995). From a CRT perspective, the decision was also made to quell another potential African American uprising in the U.S.A. and the potential harm to whites in the U.S.A. should this happen (López, 2003). Further, this decision eroded black education and resulted in the widespread dismissal of black teachers and administrators across the south (Horsford, 2010a; Tillman, 2004). Thus, the Brown vs. Board of Education decision is one example of how apparent progress for people of color is made only when it meets the needs and interests of whites, and further, that liberal racial reform such as Brown exacerbates racial inequities.

Across the CRT in educational leadership publications through the lens of interest convergence, Khalifa, Dunbar, and Douglas (2013) detail how neoliberal reforms and high-stakes testing, though touted as ways to increase achievement for students of color, benefit whites and businesses more. Gooden (2012) points out why whites admire tough black principals like Joe Clark, as it converges with their own interests to alleviate themselves of racial guilt.

Marx and Larson (2012) explain how principal Larson's school implemented literacy and math classes for low-achieving white students and students who were linguistically diverse, and how these classes served as an example of interest convergence. In these classes, white students benefitted as well; thus the interests of white and Latino parents converged. However, these same families and educators impeded substantial changes for Latino students such as culturally relevant teaching, Spanish for native speakers' classes and bilingual education because these changes threatened the core school curriculum and worked against the unconscious or conscious assimilationist agenda of the school to maintain white cultural norms. Educators and families may reject these deeper changes by claiming that they do not benefit all students in the school, especially when white families believe the school is working well for most students. In this example, these changes for Latino students do not converge with white interests. Thus, the interest/convergence tenet suggests that if leaders expect their equity efforts to be successful, their work must be framed in such a way that middle- and upper class whites in the community will also benefit; otherwise white families will believe that the racial equity work is not worth doing.

Unlike the other CRT in educational leadership literature, Knaus (2014) offers a nuanced analysis of interest convergence in his study of "equity" principals. These principals identified an African American teacher in each of their schools as "most promising" for leadership potential, yet failed to support and promote these teachers to leadership positions in the same way they did white promising teachers. Knaus explains, "This research suggests that considering African American teachers as 'most promising' was in the interests of the principals because they could then claim to support equity-focused culturally responsive approaches (without even knowing what that meant)" (p. 440).

When applying interest convergence to leadership practice, Pollack and Zirkel (2013) argue that leaders must appeal to the concerns of parents across race, culture, and class to garner change support. They also suggest that leaders be specific about how current practices are harming students of color. Pollack and Zirkel pose two questions for leadership practice guided by interest convergence: "What commonalities of interests might exist [across races]? Can we identify and articulate areas of potential agreement among affected parties?" (p. 300). As such, educational leaders can strategically employ interest convergence as a tool for equity change.

At the same time, scholars caution about the limits of interest convergence, in that the change which results will typically be:

> limited, weak, and/or short-lived … perhaps interest convergence is best seen as one strategy in the arsenal, and a beginning rather than an end. Interest convergence can get change moving – but we need to be ever vigilant if those changes are to remain. (Pollack & Zirkel, 2013, p. 300)

Alemán and Alemán (2010) also articulate the limits of interest convergence for equity change and argue, instead, that using interest convergence as a political strategy can perpetuate racism. They conclude that relying on interest convergence as an equity practice to foster racial inequity is limited, yet they offer three suggestions to curb these limitations. One, relying on interest convergence as a change strategy, may result in leaders being resistant to discussions about race and racism, and being resistant to "strategies that focus centrally on the elimination of racism" (p. 15).

To counter this limitation of interest convergence, Alemán and Alemán (2010) argue that "discussions of race and racism and their implications for public policy and social life are central, regardless of how unpleasant these conversations may be perceived to be ... [these] discussions are foundational to CRT praxis" (p. 15).

Second, an interest-convergence perspective can also foster an acceptance of slow, incremental equity gains and these gains in racial equity rely on "notions of meritocracy, colorblindness, and 'fair play' within a democratic system, all without critiquing the power differentials that remain intact" (Alemán & Alemán, 2010, p. 16). While Alemán and Alemán acknowledge that racial gains have been made, they point to the persistent and pervasive educational racial inequities as just one example of evidence of the limitations of federal law and policies designed to purportedly eliminate these inequities. They explain further: "our critique with [the incremental change] approach is when community leaders present it as the *sole* (emphasis in the original) strategy in the struggle for change ... [the] interest-convergence principle should not be utilized as a justification for an incrementalist strategy of change" (p. 16).

Third, taking an interest-convergence approach may also lead to educators blaming racial inequities on individuals rather than on the "institutional and systemic racism that exists" (p. 15). Thus, Alemán and Alemán (2010) insist that educators "attack society's embedded racist structures, shifting blame and responsibility away from individuals" (p. 16).

In sum, educational leaders must address equity changes by considering how all students could benefit and how students of color are harmed by current practices. However, at the same time, leaders must keep race and the elimination of racism central to the equity work and not back down from the difficult racial conversations as a result of this work, ensure that race discussions focus on eliminating structures and systems of racism rather than becoming mired in blaming individuals, and understand that interest convergence is just one strategy among a plethora of strategies for eradicating racism.

Critique of Liberalism: Color-blindness and Critique of Equity Policies and Practices

CRT also critiques liberalism – a fifth CRT tenet applied to education. In this section, I focus specifically on concepts related to liberal ideas of color-blindness and the ways liberal equity policies and practices can perpetuate racial oppression.

Scholars in educational leadership who rely on CRT often refer to the problem of color-blindness in race equity work (Horsford, 2010a; López, 2003; Khalifa, Dunbar, & Douglas, 2013; Khalifa, et al. 2014; Valles & Miller, 2010). The concept of color-blindness can be manifested in two ways: first, when educators claim to not see a student's color or claim that race does not matter; and second, when educators do not realize the ways their school is not race neutral and reflects white culture, and, in turn, when they expect students of color to assimilate to and blend into the existing white school culture.

Across the CRT in educational leadership literature, five publications analyzed how color-blindness perpetuates racism initiated by López (2003), who illuminated the color-blindness of traditional political theory. Other studies examined how school leaders took a color-blind approach to issues such as demographic change (Evans, 2007) and closing a majority African American high school (Khalifa et al., 2014). Leaders in both studies downplayed race and approached these challenges from a supposedly neutral perspective and denied that race mattered. In Khalifa and colleagues' study, the leaders relied on policies and data to avoid race. Yet leaders in both studies relied on race to perpetuate a deficit perspective of African American students and families. Khalifa, Dunbar, and Douglas (2013) also analyzed how high-stakes testing and neoliberal reforms reflect color-blindness in insisting that school reforms are in the best interest of all students.

Phrases which educators may say related to the first example of color-blindness include "I do not see a student's color," "I treat all students the same," "I hold the same high standard for all my students," "A student's race does not matter to me." Marx and Larson (2012) explain that the majority of educators believe their "color-blind glasses" "prevent them from seeing any differences among children of varying racial, ethnic, cultural, and linguistic backgrounds" (p. 298). Marx and Larson explained how Larson as a white principal initially denied that race mattered, and claimed he was color-blind. Indeed, principal Larson believed, as do many white educators, that claiming to be color-blind is the right thing to do, and to intentionally attend to and respond to racial differences reflects racist beliefs and practices.

However, to claim color-blindness, or that race does not matter, or that educators need to treat all students the same and not differently, denies the atrocity of racial inequities in the past and the pervasive racial micro-aggressions, societal racism, and systemic racism that individuals of color experience daily and the way racism permeates all aspects of schools (Evans, 2007).

Educators also manifest color-blindness when they remain unconscious of or deny the ways their school reflects white culture. Marx and Larson (2012) explain how the majority of U.S. educators are "not cognizant of their Whiteness, nor that of the curriculum and schools within which they work. Rather than recognizing that they work in a cultural/racial/linguistic milieu, many educators believe their own school settings are culture free" (p. 293). As a result, educators expect students of color to "blend into the dominant White, English-speaking culture reflected in the school" (p. 293). Thus, when educators in principal Larson's school were asked to implement culturally responsive practices that address the needs of Latino students, principal Larson and his staff experienced these expectation as "vague, hard to achieve," "radical, inappropriate … a threat to the core curriculum," "and contrary to the assimilationist climate of the school" (p. 293).

In sum, many educators claim color-blindness, that they do not see a student's color, and are unconscious of the ways schools are not racially neutral but reflect white culture. In Marx and Larson's (2012) study, principal Larson's perspective shifted and "Rather than ignoring or denying the presence of the Latino students ... and their cultural and racial group in a colorblind manner," principal Larson sought to get to know the students and their families better. The principal took off his color-blind glasses and "recognize[ed] children for who they are: diverse people with diverse backgrounds, experiences, strengths, and weaknesses, qualities that can be built on only when they are recognized" (p. 298).

Thus, to counter a color-blind perspective, leaders need to know that "not seeing race" or being "color-blind" rather than neutral or positive reflect racist assumptions and beliefs. Leaders need to recognize the races and cultures in their school communities and reach out to families and students, and recognize their assets and value to the school and their unique needs. Leaders also need to help staff recognize the ways the school, its culture, and practices are not race neutral and reflect white culture (Valles & Miller, 2010), and the ways they expect students of color to assimilate and blend into the school. Instead, leaders must ensure that all aspects of the school – the curriculum, culture, structure, and policies – not only reflect the racial diversity in the school but also challenge and eliminate racist assumptions.

In addition to addressing color-blindness, the CRT tenet critique of liberalism also suggests that educational leaders be critical and discerning about equity policies and practices to ensure that these policies and practices do not perpetuate racial inequities (Valles & Miller, 2010). Scholars of CRT in educational leadership literature have demonstrated how Texas "equitable" school finance policy perpetuated inequities (Aléman, 2007), and how desegregation policies and practices aimed toward equitable ends can perpetuate inequities (André-Bechely, 2005; Horsford, 2010a). André-Bechely suggests that leaders for equity must examine how "the rules and processes that districts institutionalize to bring about access, equity, and equality may serve to hide the very real ways that race and class still support exclusion in our schools" (p. 302). Horsford (2010a) also cautions that:

> inclusion programs and initiatives that fail to recognize how race and racism work to maintain hierarchies, allocate resources, and distribute power will not do much to address gaps in student achievement, low school performance, and distrusting school communities. (p. 311–312)

Further, even effective practices such as culturally relevant pedagogy (Ladson-Billings, 1995, 1999b), if not fully understood or implemented properly, can fall far short of addressing racism. Ladson-Billings (2014) disappointingly notes:

> What state departments, school districts and individual teachers are now calling 'culturally relevant pedagogy' is often a distortion and corruption of the central ideas I attempted to promulgate. The idea that adding some books about people of color, having a classroom Kwanza celebration, or posting 'diverse' images makes one 'culturally relevant' seem to be what the pedagogy has been reduced to. (p. 82)

In the final section of this chapter, I discuss curriculum practices that purport to promote equity such as Universal Design for Learning and the social justice discourse in educational leadership as additional equity examples that can perpetuate racism.

In sum, the CRT tenet of the critique of liberalism requires leaders to understand how the concept of color-blindness reflects a racist perspective and denies historical racism and the current and pervasiveness of racism. Further, the critique of liberalism points to how school culture and practices are never race neutral, and perpetuate and require students of color to assimilate into white culture. This CRT tenet also calls on leaders to question and critique liberal and progressive equity work that does not directly address systemic and persistent racism.

CONCLUSION AND FUTURE DIRECTIONS FOR CRT AND EDUCATIONAL LEADERSHIP PRACTICE

This analysis of CRT in educational leadership suggests a CRT Inventory for Leading the Eliminating of Racism (see below). This inventory can help leaders assess the legitimacy and effectiveness of racial policies, practices, initiatives, and equity change efforts to help ensure that these efforts do not perpetuate racial inequities and racism, and to eliminate racism in public schools. While designed initially for practicing school leaders, faculty in leadership preparation programs can also adopt the CRT Inventory as a means to interrogate their own practice and program. Further, many questions in the inventory are under-researched and can guide future research in the field. Leaders and faculty who prepare them can rely on the inventory at regular intervals throughout the year for critical self-reflection of their own leadership practice in conjunction with using the inventory with their leadership team and with their entire faculty as a means to critically interrogate their educational practices in schools and leadership preparation programs.

In the same way that Ladson-Billings and Tate (1995) critiqued the diversity and multicultural discourse for marginalizing race, future scholarship on CRT and educational leadership must directly address and critique the current social justice discourse in the field and the ways in which the social justice discourse perpetuates racism (Knauss, 2014). As Knauss explains, "it is in the interest of White educators to adopt social justice language instead of integrating anti-racism into the foundation of academic programs" (p. 422). As I previously explained, CRT emerged out of a critique of radical, critical legal studies. In turn, the application of CRT to education was in part a critique of the multicultural discourse at the time (Ladson-Billings & Tate, 1995). As Crenshaw (2011) wrote about the emergence of CRT out of CLS: " it was difficult to imagine how to proceed with a conversation about race 'out there' without addressing race 'in here'" (Crenshaw, 2011, p. 1295). Scholars in educational leadership need to critique the "racism in here" that remains pervasive and unquestioned in the social justice discourse in the field.

LEADERSHIP DEVELOPMENT ACTIVITIES

ACTIVITY 1:   **Complete and Discuss the CRT Inventory for Leading the Elimination of Racism**

CRT Inventory for Leading the Elimination of Racism

Pervasiveness of Racism

1. Are we actively engaged in ongoing work on our own racism and ongoing work on developing an anti-racist identity?
2. Is the historical and current pervasiveness of racism in all of society, including schools, and within ourselves acknowledged and addressed?
3. Do we frequently engage in informal and formal conversations about race with our staff?
4. Are policies and practices in place to facilitate the ongoing development of an anti-racist identity with staff, students, families, and community members?
5. Do we conduct equity audits that include disaggregation of race data and establish concrete measurable goals, action plans, effective measures of progress, and follow-up as a result of the audit?
6. Is academic achievement for students of color and developing critical consciousness with all students the primary focus and measure of effectiveness for all the race work?

Whiteness as Property

7. Do we acknowledge that the curriculum itself and the AP/honors/gifted systems are white property, with all the rights and privileges afforded property, including the right to enjoyment and the fundamental right to exclude, and that whites will fiercely defend this property?
8. Have we identified the property interests at stake and prepared for how we will respond to the defense of that property by whites?
9. Do we acknowledge that the entire remediation system, including special education, remedial education, response to intervention, and other remediation practices, and the labeling of students for these programs, all purported to address racial achievement gaps, perpetuate racial inequities? Do we acknowledge that this remediation system upholds, maintains, and reinforces the AP system of privilege, and thus the primary task toward equitable change includes policies and practices that result in a highly rigorous curriculum for all students via integration, heterogeneous classrooms, de-tracking, proportional representation, and inclusive schooling?

(Continued)

10. Do the equity efforts include a focus on the voices and perspectives of people of color in the curriculum, moving beyond diversity and multiculturalism to culturally transformative practices?

Counter-narratives/Majoritarian Narratives

11. What strategies, policies, and practices are in place to ensure the hiring of leaders of color, that school and district conditions support their leadership success, and that these leaders are not always assigned to majority of color schools?
12. How and in what ways are the perspectives and stories of students, families, and community members of color solicited, drawn upon, and presented at the beginning of the equity change to frame the work proactively, and not as a reactive response to majoritarian resistance?
13. Have we identified why and how students, staff, families, and community members of color may resist the equity change because of their own socialization by the majoritarian narratives, and have we determined how we will re-educate all about the harms of current practices and benefits of the equity work?
14. Have we ensured that school and district decision-making, planning, and other teams are racially representative of the community and that in these team meetings all perspectives are heard and considered?
15. Have we identified what the majoritarian arguments will be against the equity change from staff, families, and community members, and how we will respond?

Interest Convergence

16. Have we identified the interests of the white privileged students, families, and communities and determined how the equity changes will benefit these students and families?
17. In identifying the interests of whites in the equity change, are we ensuring that the work on the pervasiveness and structural embeddedness of racism historically and currently does not abate, and that racial equity remains the public goal of equity work?
18. While we acknowledge positive results from incremental racial equity work, do we ensure that incremental change is not the only way for successful, enduring change to occur?

Critique of Liberalism

19. Have we acknowledged that claims of being color-blind, treating all students the same, not seeing color, and not acknowledging race all reflect racist beliefs and assumptions?
20. Have we analyzed and critiqued the equity change or new policy or practice to determine if or how it could perpetuate racism in its implementation?

ACTIVITY 2: CRT Analysis of Case Situation

Identify the issues in your case and then possible solutions for your case from a CRT epistemology.

Pervasiveness of Racism

1. How is the historical and current pervasiveness of racism in all of society, including schools, and within ourselves acknowledged and addressed?
2. How is the racial identity development of the actors a factor in the case?

Whiteness as Property

3. What aspects in the case could be considered an example of whiteness as property?
4. What property interests are at stake in the case?
5. To what extent is the case about the defense of white property?
6. To what extent are remediation systems as perpetuators of racial inequities a factor in the case?

Counter-narratives/Majoritarian Narratives

7. To what extent do the case issues consider proactively employing educators of color and supporting their success?
8. How and in what ways are the perspectives and stories of students, family, and community members of color solicited, drawn upon, and presented in the case proactively?
9. Have we identified why and how students, staff, families, and community members of color may resist the equity change because of their own socialization by the majoritarian narratives?
10. Has the case considered that school and district decision-making, planning, and other teams are racially representative of the community and that in these team meetings all perspectives are heard and considered?
11. Does the case consider the majoritarian arguments to resist change?

Interest Convergence

12. Does the case consider the interests of the white privileged students, families, and communities?
13. Does the case consider that in recognizing the interests of whites we are ensuring that the work on the pervasiveness and structural embeddedness of racism historically and currently does not abate, and that racial equity remains the public goal of the equity work?
14. Does the case consider that incremental change is not the only way for successful, enduring change to occur?

(Continued)

Critique of Liberalism

15. Does the case consider that claims of being color-blind, treating all students the same, not seeing color, and not acknowledging race all reflect racist beliefs and assumptions?
16. Does the case consider how the situation could perpetuate racism?

NOTE

1 Adapted from Capper, C.A. The 20th anniversary of Critical Race Theory in education: Implications for leading to eliminate racism. *Educational Administration Quarterly. 51* (5), 791–833. © 2015 Educational Administration Quarterly. Reprinted in part by permission of Sage publications. doi/10.1177/0013161X15607616.

REFERENCES

Alemán, E., Jr. (2006). Is Robin Hood the "prince of thieves" or a pathway to equity? Applying critical race theory to finance political discourse. *Educational Policy, 20*(1), 113–142.

Alemán, E., Jr. (2007). Situating Texas school finance policy in a CRT framework: How "substantially equal" yields racial inequity. *Educational Administration Quarterly, 43*(5), 525–558.

Alemán, E., Jr. (2009). LatCrit educational leadership and advocacy: Struggling over Whiteness as property in Texas school finance. *Equity & Excellence in Education, 42*(2), 183–201.

Alemán Jr, E. & Alemán, S.M. (2010). Do Latino interests always have to "converge" with White interests?: (Re)claiming racial realism and interest-convergence in critical race theory praxis. *Race, Ethnicity & Education, 13*(1), 1–21.

André-Bechely, L. (2005). Public school choice at the intersection of voluntary integration and not-so good neighborhood schools: Lessons from parents' experiences. *Educational Administration Quarterly, 41*(2), 267–305.

Bell, D.A. (1980a). Brown v. Board of Education and the interest-convergence dilemma. *Harvard Law Review, 93*(3), 518–533.

Bell, D.A. (1980b). *Race, racism and American law* (2nd edn). Boston: Little, Brown.

Bell, D.A. (1992). *Faces at the bottom of the well.* New York: Basic Books.

Bell, D.A. (2004). *Silent covenants: Brown v. Board of Education and the unfulfilled hopes for racial reform.* Oxford: Oxford University Press.

Brantlinger, E., Majd-Jabbari, M., & Gusin, S.L. (1996). Self-interest and liberal educational discourse: How ideology works for middle-class mothers. *American Educational Research Journal, 33*(3), 571–597.

Brown, L.H., Beckett, G.H., & Beckett, K.S. (2006). Segregation, desegregation, and resegregation in Cincinnati: The perspective of an African American principal. *Journal of School Leadership, 16*, 265–291.

Crenshaw, K W. (1988). Race, reform, retrenchment: Transformation and legitimation in anti-discrimination law. *Harvard Law Review, 101*(7), 1331–1387.

Crenshaw, K.W. (1991). Mapping the margins: Intersectionality, identity politics, and violence against women of color. *Stanford Law Review, 43*(6), 1241–1299.

Crenshaw, K.W. (2011). Twenty years of Critical Race Theory: Looking back to move forward. *Connecticut Law Review, 43*(5), 1253–1352.

Dantley, M., Beachum, F., & McCray, C. (2009). Exploring the intersectionality of multiple centers within notions of social justice. *Journal of School Leadership, 18*(2), 124–133.

Delgado, R. (1990). When a story is just a story: Does voice really matter? *Virginia Law Review, 76*, 95–111.

Delgado, R. (1993). Rodrigo's sixth chronicle: Intersections, essences, and the dilemma of social reform. *New York University Law Review, 68*, 639–674.

Delgado, R. (1995). Affirmative action as a majoritarian device: Or, do you really want to be a role model? In R. Delgado (Ed.), *Critical race theory: The cutting edge* (pp. 355–361). Philadelphia, PA: Temple University Press.

Evans, A.E. (2007). School leaders and their sensemaking about race and demographic change. *Educational Administration Quarterly, 43*(2), 159–188.

Gooden, M.A. (2012). What does racism have to do with leadership? Countering the idea of color-blind leadership: A reflection on race and the growing pressures of the urban principalship. *Educational Foundations, 26*(1), 67–85.

Gooden, M.A. & Dantley, M. (2012). Centering race in a framework for leadership preparation. *Journal of Research on Leadership Education, 7*(2), 237–253.

Harris, C.I. (1993). Whiteness as property. *Harvard Law Review, 106*(8), 1707–1791.

Harris, C.I. (1995). Whiteness as property. In K.W. Crenshaw, N. Gotunda, G. Peller, & K. Thomas (Eds), *Critical race theory: The key writings that formed the movement* (pp. 276–291). New York: New Press.

Horsford, S.D. (2009). From Negro student to Black superintendent: Counternarratives on segregation and desegregation. *Journal of Negro Education, 78*(2), 172–187.

Horsford, S.D. (2010a). Mixed feelings about mixed schools: Superintendents on the complex legacy of school desegregation. *Educational Administration Quarterly, 46*(3), 287–321.

Horsford, S.D. (2010b). Black superintendents on educating Black students in separate and unequal contexts. *Urban Review, 42*(1), 58–79.

Horsford, S.D. (2014). When race enters the room: Improving leadership and learning through racial literacy. *Theory into Practice, 53*(2), 123–130.

Horsford, S.D. & McKenzie, K.B. (2008). "Sometimes I feel like the problems started with desegregation": Exploring Black superintendent perspectives on desegregation policy. *International Journal of Qualitative Studies in Education, 21*(5), 443–455.

Khalifa, M., Dunbar, C., & Douglas T. (2013). Derrick Bell, CRT, and educational leadership 1995–present. *Race Ethnicity and Education, 16*(4), 489–513.

Khalifa, M.A., Jennings, M.E., Briscoe, F., Oleszweski, M., & Abdi, N. (2014). Racism? Administrative and community perspectives in data-driven decision making: Systemic perspectives versus technical-rational perspectives. *Urban Education, 49*(2), 147–181.

Knaus, C.B. (2014). Seeing what they want to see: Racism and leadership development in urban schools. *Urban Review, 46*, 420–444.

Ladson-Billings, G. (1998). Just what is critical race theory and what's it doing in a nice field like education? *International Journal of Qualitative Studies in Education, 11*(1), 7–24.

Ladson-Billings, G. (1999a). Preparing teachers for diverse student populations: A critical race theory perspective. *Review of Research in Education, 24*, 211–247.

Ladson-Billings, G. (1999b). Toward a theory of culturally relevant pedagogy. *American Educational Research Journal, 32*(3), 465–491.

Ladson-Billings, G. (2011). Race … to the Top, Again: Comments on the genealogy of Critical Race Theory. *Connecticut Law Review, 43*(5), 1439–1457.

Ladson-Billings, G. (2013). Critical race theory: What it is not! In M. Lynn and A.D. Dixson (Eds), *Handbook of critical race theory in education* (pp. 34–47). New York: Routledge.

Ladson-Billings, G. (2014). Culturally relevant pedagogy 2.0: a.k.a. the remix. *Harvard Educational Review, 84*(1), 74–84.

Ladson-Billings, G. & Tate, W.F. (1995). Toward a critical race theory of education. *Teachers College Record, 97*(1), 47–68.

Lightfoot, J. (2009). Toward a praxis of anti-racist school leadership preparation. In L. Foster and L.C. Tillman (Eds), *African American perspectives on leadership in schools: Building a culture of empowerment* (pp. 211–236). Lanham, MD: Rowan and Littlefield.

López, G.R. (2003). The (racially neutral) politics of education: A critical race theory perspective. *Educational Administration Quarterly, 39*(1), 68–94.

López, G., Tillman, L., Alston, J., Armendariz, A., Lopez-Marcano, R., Reyes, T., Cockrell, K., Gonzalez, M., Christman, D., & Gooden, M. (2003). *Justice or Just-us? A critical conversation with scholars of color surrounding leadership for social justice.* Panel presentation at the University Council for Educational Administration Annual Convention, Portland, OR.

Marx, S. & Larson, L.L. (2012). Taking off the color-blind glasses: Recognizing and supporting Latina/o students in a predominantly white school. *Educational Administration Quarterly, 48*(2), 259–303.

Matsuda, M. (1991). Voices of America: Accent, antidiscrimination law, and a jurisprudence for the last reconstruction. *Yale Law Journal, 100*, 1329–1407.

Matsuda, M. (1995). Looking to the bottom: Critical legal studies and reparations. In K. Crenshaw, N. Gotanda, G. Peller, & K. Thomas (Eds), *Critical race theory: The key writings that formed the movement* (pp. 63–79). New York: New Press.

Matsuda, M.J., Lawrence, C.R., Delgado, R., & Crenshaw, K.W. (Eds). (1993). *Words that wound: Critical race theory, assaultive speech, and the First Amendment.* Boulder, CO: Westview Press.

McCray, C.R., Wright, J.V., & Beachum, F.D. (2007). Beyond *Brown:* Examining the perplexing plight of African American principals. *Journal of Instructional Psychology, 34*(4), 247–255.

Orosco, M. J. & Klinger, J. (2010). One school's implementation of RTI with English language learners: "Referring into RTI." *Journal of Learning Disabilities, 43*(3), 269–288.

Parker, L. (1998). "Race is. Race isn't": An exploration of the utility of critical race theory in qualitative research in education. *Qualitative Studies in Education, 11*(1), 43–55.

Parker, L., Deyhle, D., Villenas, S., & Nebeker, K. (Eds). (1998). Guest editors' introduction: Critical race theory and qualitative studies in education. *International Journal of Qualitative Studies in Education, 11*(1), 5–6.

Parker, L. & Villalpando, O. (2007). A race(cialized) perspective on education leadership: Critical race theory in educational administration. *Educational Administration Quarterly, 43*(5), 519–514.

Pollack, T.M. & Zirkel, S. (2013). Negotiating the contested terrain of equity-focused change efforts in schools: Critical Race Theory as a leadership framework for creating more equitable schools. *Urban Review, 45*(3), 290–310.

Santamaría, L.J. (2014). Critical change for the greater good: Multicultural perceptions in educational leadership toward social justice and equity. *Educational Administration Quarterly, 50*(3), 347–391.

Sherman, W.H. (2008). No Child Left Behind: A legislative catalyst for superintendent action to eliminate test-score gaps? *Educational Policy, 22*(5), 675–704.

Smith, W.A., Yosso, T.A., & Solórzano, D.G. (2007). Racial primes and Black misandry on historically White campuses: Toward critical race accountability in educational administration. *Educational Administration Quarterly, 43*(5), 559–585.

Solórzano, D.G. (1997). Images and words that wound: Critical race theory, racial stereotyping, and teacher education. *Teacher Education Quarterly, 24*(3), 5–19.

Solórzano, D. (1998). Critical race theory, racial and gender microaggressions, and the experiences of Chicana and Chicano scholars. *International Journal of Qualitative Studies in Education, 11*(1), 121–136.

Solórzano, D.G. & Bernal, D.D. (2001). Examining transformational resistance through a Critical Race and LatCrit Theory framework. *Urban Education, 36*(3), 308–342.

Solórzano, D.G. & Yosso, T. (2000). Critical race theory, microaggressions, and campus racial climate: The experiences of African American college students. *Journal of Negro Education, 69*(1/2), 60–73.

Solórzano, D.G. & Yosso, T. (2001). Critical race and LatCrit theory and method: Counter-storytelling Chicana and Chicano graduate school experiences. *Qualitative Studies in Education, 14*(4), 471–495.

Stovall, D. (2004). School leader as negotiator: Critical theory praxis and the creation of productive space. *Multicultural Education, 12*(2), 8–12.

Tate, W.F. (1994). From inner city to ivory tower: Does my voice matter in the academy? *Urban Education, 29*(3), 245–269.

Tate, W.F. (1997). Critical race theory and education: History, theory and implications. *Review of Research in Education, 22,* 195–247.

Theoharis, G. & Haddix, M. (2011). Undermining racism and a Whiteness ideology: White principals living a commitment to equitable and excellent schools. *Urban Education, 46*(6), 1332–1351.

Tillman, L.C. (2004). African American principals and the legacy of *Brown. Review of Research in Education, 28,* 101–146.

Valles, B. & Miller, D.M. (2010). How leadership and discipline policies color school community relationships: A critical race theory analysis. *Journal of School Public Relations, 31*(4), 319–341.

Young, M.D. & Laible, J. (2000). White racism, antiracism, and school leadership preparation. *Journal of School Leadership, 10*(1), 374–415.

APPENDIX

Table 7.2 CRT Tenets Addressed in Educational Leadership

Publication	Permanence of racism	Whiteness as property	Counter- and majoritarian narratives	Interest convergence	Critique of liberalism (color-blindness, meritocracy, democracy)	Intersectionality[1]
Alémán (2006)	X		X			Latino superintendents

(*Continued*)

Publication	Permanence of racism	Whiteness as property	Counter- and majoritarian narratives	Interest convergence	Critique of liberalism (color-blindness, meritocracy, democracy)	Intersectionality[1]
Aléman (2007)	X	X	X	X	X	Latino communities in Texas state finance policy
Aléman (2009b)	X	X				Mexican American educational leaders
André-Bechely (2005)			X		X	Race, class, and gender – African American, Latino mothers of low and upper income
Brown, Beckett, & Beckett (2006)		X	X	X		Race, African American principal
Evans (2007)	X	X			X	Race, class, and gender – white male/female leaders' response to race/class
Gooden (2012)	X		X	X	X	African American principals
Horsford & McKenzie (2008)			X			African American superintendents
Horsford (2009)	X		X			African American superintendents
Horsford (2010a)	X	X	X	X	X	African American superintendents
Horsford (2010b)	X		X			African American superintendents
Khalifa, Jennings, Briscoe, Oleszweski, Abdi (2014)	X		X		X	Race – African American principal and Latino superintendent and an African American high school in a Latino community

Publication	Permanence of racism	Whiteness as property	Counter- and majoritarian narratives	Interest convergence	Critique of liberalism (color-blindness, meritocracy, democracy)	Intersectionality
Khalifa, Dunbar, and Douglas (2013)			X	X	X	African American and Latino youth
Knaus (2014)	X		X	X		Race
López (2003)	X		X	X	X	Race, class, gender, ability, sexual identity, and their intersections
Marx & Larson (2012)		X		X		Latino students
McCray, Wright, and Beachum (2007)	X	X				African American principals
Parker & Villalpando (2007)	X					Race, class, gender, ability, sexual identity, and their intersections
Pollack & Zirkel (2013)		X	X	X		Race and social class
Santamaría (2014)	X		X		X	Race, class, gender, ability, sexual identity, and their intersections
Sherman (2008)	X					Race and social class
Stovall (2004)	X					Race and social class
Theoharis & Haddix (2011)		X	X		X	Race, class, ability, gender, sexual identity, and their intersections

(Continued)

Publication	Permanence of racism	Whiteness as property	Counter- and majoritarian narratives	Interest convergence	Critique of liberalism (color-blindness, meritocracy, democracy)	Intersectionality
Valles & Miller (2010)					X	Race, gender

[1]An "X" in the box indicates that the article identified intersectionality as a CRT tenet. The text in the box indicates the identities addressed in the article and thus to what extent the article referred to race as it intersects with other identities, or the degree of intersectionality in the article.

CHAPTER 8

LatCrit, Tribal Crit, and Asian Crit Theories

In the previous chapter, I reviewed the literature on Critical Race Theory (CRT) in educational leadership, defined the key tenets of CRT, and described how CRT could inform leadership to eliminate racism. This chapter extends that work to examine LatCrit, Tribal Crit, and Asian Crit theories in educational leadership (see Figure 8.1). More specifically, the research question that anchors this chapter asks: How can LatCrit, Tribal Crit, and Asian Crit theories inform organizational theory and, in turn, how can these theories contribute to the leadership of socially just schools?

LATCRIT THEORY

Developed by the early founders of CRT, LatCrit theory originated in the late 1990s and early 2000s (Alemán, 2007). LatCrit theory complements rather than supplants CRT (Alemán, 2007, 2009), and expands the black/white binary that dominated racial discourse to address a broader spectrum of race and its intersections with other identities. Huber (2010) explains how LatCrit theory extends beyond CRT to address the unique histories and experiences of Latinos in the U.S.A.:

> LatCrit can be used to reveal the ways Latinas/os experience race, class, gender, and sexuality, while also acknowledging the Latina/o experience with issues of immigration status, language, ethnicity and culture. Thus, LatCrit theory enables researchers to better articulate the experiences of Latinas/os specifically, through a more focused examination of the unique forms of oppression this group encounters. (p. 79)

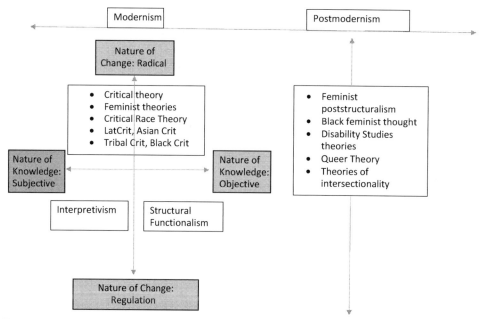

Figure 8.1 An Epistemology Framework

In addition to the tenets of immigration status, language, ethnicity, and culture, Alemán (2009) also identified Latinx essentialism and assimilation as key tenets of LatCrit theory. As such, LatCrit directly addresses moving beyond racial essentialism and addressing race across races, and also overtly addresses the intersection of Latinx identity with race, gender, social class, ability, and sexual/gender identity.

LatCrit theory is often combined with CRT within empirical studies where it has served as the theoretical lens, including research on pre-K-12 education in general (Gonzalez & Portillos, 2007; Huber, 2011; Irizarry & Raible, 2014; Malagon, 2010; Peralta, 2013; Portillos, Gonzalez, & Peguero, 2012; Solórzano & Bernal, 2001; Valdez & Lugg, 2010); the education of Latinx students in Chicago Public Schools (Davila & de Bradley, 2010); the experience of Latinx students in high school (Fernández, 2002); higher education in general (Flores & Garcia, 2009; Villalpando, 2003); Chicano college students' experiences (Bernal, 2002; Huber, 2010); pre-service teacher education (Franquiz, Salazar, & DeNicolo, 2011; Irizarry, 2011; Rodriguez, 2011); environmental education (Arreguin-Anderson & Kennedy, 2013); K-16 education (Urrieta & Villenas, 2013); mathematics education (Gutiérrez, 2013); community change (Quiñones, Ares, Padela, Hopper, & Webster, 2011); and education research (Huber, 2009; Solórzano & Yosso, 2001, 2002). One paper practically applied CRT, LatCrit, and Tribal Crit to social studies classrooms (Daniels, 2011). Only two studies viewed educational policy and finance through a LatCrit lens (Alemán, 2007, 2009).

Relative to educational leadership, Alemán (2009) studied the perspectives of eight Mexican American superintendents in Texas regarding their perspectives of changes in Texas school finance policy. Relying on a combination of CRT and

LatCrit theory for data collection and analysis, Alemán focused on the CRT tenets of interest convergence and whiteness as property in his analysis.

Alemán (2009) learned that though the superintendents recounted stories of racism in their families and lives growing up, they believed that underachievement of Latino students was due to lack of motivation or work ethic and not to systemic racism. In so doing, they framed racism at the individual level rather than pervasive, historical, and societal and, in turn, did not consider the inequitable Texas finance policy from a racial perspective.

As a result, when testifying before the legislature, even though the superintendents admitted that the current finance policy was unfair to their districts, they used a "majoritarian" rhetoric. Rather than testifying that the policy was inequitable, they instead thanked the politicians for the financial support their districts had been given. Alemán (2009) believed that "employing a majoritarian perspective as their sole political strategy, refuting the permanence of racism, and internalizing whiteness as property … cannot lead to a socially just school finance system" (pp. 194–195). Alemán defined this practice as "politically passing" (p. 197) which could be viewed as a form of interest convergence; that is, advocating for a particular equity policy or practice from a whiteness perspective in ways to ensure whites continue to benefit. Alemán argued that this "avoidance of racial analysis represents a traditional mode of leadership – one that allows the dominant, majority, political and racial hierarchy to continue its 'historical and continuing pattern of white racial domination'" (p. 186, cited in Harris, 1995, p. 1710).

Alemán (2007) also analyzed school finance policy in Texas, relying on Critical Race Theory and LatCrit theory to inform critical policy analysis. In so doing, he traces the history of Texas school finance policy to date and identifies the structural and institutional racism in the policy. Alemán makes the case that even though policy-makers sought to create finance policy which they believed was more equitable, a closer examination revealed how it continued to perpetuate inequalities based on property taxes.

As an extension of LatCrit theory, Huber (2010, 2011; Huber, Lopez, Malagon, Velez, & Solorzano, 2008) further developed a theory of racist nativism (Chang, 1993). Huber defines racist nativism as "the institutionalized ways people perceive, understand and make sense of contemporary US immigration, that justifies *native* (white) dominance, and reinforces hegemonic power" (p. 380). Huber developed this theory as a means to understand the experiences of undocumented Chicano college students, but the theory also applies to indigenous people or to anyone perceived as a "foreigner" in the U.S.A. Huber (2011) further explains: "A critical element of this definition is that racist nativism is based solely on perceptions. Thus, Latinas/os are racialized as nonnatives regardless of actual immigration status. This process of exclusion then, becomes a function of white dominance" (p. 382).

In sum, LatCrit theory extends beyond the black/white binary originally promulgated with CRT and explicitly considers race across races and the intersection of race with other identities such as class, gender, ability, and sexual/gender identity. Tenets of LatCrit theory can include CRT tenets but extends beyond those to also consider immigration status, language, ethnicity, culture, assimilation, and Latinx essentialism – all unique to the Latinx experience. With LatCrit theory as a base, Huber (2010, 2011) developed a theory of racist nativism. This theory helps explain how whites marginalize anyone who they believe is not "native" to the United States – labeling anyone with this status as a "foreigner" regardless of immigration status, and perceive individuals with this label as a threat and as justification for white dominance.

TRIBAL CRIT THEORIES

According to Brayboy (2005), who was the first to articulate the tenets of Tribal Crit theory, while the primary tenet of CRT is that racism is endemic in society, the primary tenet of Tribal Crit theory focuses on the fact that "colonization is endemic to society" (p. 429). In addition to this tenet, Brayboy identifies eight other tenets of Tribal Crit theory:

> 1) U.S. policies toward Indigenous peoples are rooted in imperialism, White supremacy, and a desire for material gain. 2) Indigenous peoples occupy a liminal space that accounts for both the political and racialized natures of our identities. 3) Indigenous peoples have a desire to obtain and forge tribal sovereignty, tribal autonomy, self-determination, and self-identification. 4) The concepts of culture, knowledge, and power take on new meaning when examined through an Indigenous lens. 5) Governmental policies and educational policies toward Indigenous peoples are intimately linked around the problematic goal of assimilation. 6) Tribal philosophies, beliefs, customs, traditions, and visions for the future are central to understanding the lived realities of Indigenous peoples, but they also illustrate the differences and adaptability among individuals and groups. 7) Stories are not separate from theory; they make up theory and are, therefore, real and legitimate sources of data and ways of being. 8) Theory and practice are connected in deep and explicit ways such that scholars must work towards social change. (pp. 429–430)

A few studies have applied these eight tenets of Tribal Crit theory to studies with Indigenous educators.[1]

For example, Castagno (2012) studied a teacher education program designed for the preparation of Indigenous teachers for Native American schools. The program was housed in a predominantly white university that had explicit goals about "serving Indigenous communities and that ... was founded and developed with the commitment to increase the number of culturally responsive Navajo teachers" (p. 16). Through the lens of Tribal Crit theory, she identified the ways the program perpetuated white colonialism and assimilation. The reasons for the programmatic assimilation included (a) the lack of buy-in and support from the College of Education; (b) divisions between program participants and those not in the program and among program participants, some whom spoke Navajo and some of whom did not, and (c) the ways that liberal multiculturalism anchor most teacher preparation programs. Castagno summarized the situation: "Indeed, throughout the College of Education, there exists a culture that values colorblindness, equality and sameness for all, and an extraordinarily slow pace of social change" (p. 16). The outcome of this programmatic assimilation included the fact that the Indigenous teachers were not fully prepared to teach in culturally responsive ways in Navajo schools.

Concluding that "good intentions and isolated strategic efforts are simply not enough to overcome entrenched patterns of assimilation and colonization" (p. 16), Castagno (2012) then identified specific ways in which teacher education could resist colonization and assimilation:

> (1) prepare Indigenous teachers with culturally responsive curricula driven by the goal of self-determination and centered around Indigenous knowledge systems; (2) are led and directed by Indigenous faculty and community members; and (3) are supported with hard-money funding sources... (p. 17)

Castagno further explained:

> Successful examples of this sort of culturally responsive teacher preparation share the following characteristics:
> (1) contextualizing and localizing curriculum and pedagogy so that it resembles the knowledge and learning of local communities; (2) the knowledge, values, resources, and epistemologies of communities are viewed as legitimate and are intimately integrated into schools; (3) students are engaged and learning 'school knowledge' at the same time and through experiences that also facilitate the learning of local community knowledge and ... (4) includes a central and explicit focus on sovereignty and self-determination, racism, and Indigenous Knowledge Systems. (Brayboy & Maughan, 2009; Castagno & Brayboy, 2008, cited in Castagno, 2012 p. 17)

Castagno's study offers several important implications for theory and practice that I discuss in the final section of this chapter. At the same time, Castagno's study reveals several limitations. First, the study does not address the importance of not essentializing Indigenous identity, even though one of the tensions in her study were differences among the Navajo students, some of whom spoke the Navajo language and some of whom did not. Further, the study does not address the intersections of Native American identity with gender, social class, ability, or sexual/gender identity. For example, she critiques the lack of culturally relevant pedagogy in the teacher preparation program and in the teaching practices of the Indigenous teachers; however, she does not address to what extent the students were prepared to teach across student differences by ability or how students labeled with disabilities were addressed in their schools. In this way, the study is one example of how addressing one area of difference (Indigenous identities) could further serve to mask and perpetuate oppression of other identities. The study also does not address the practicality of how to implement her ideas in diverse schools where students of many races are enrolled, including Native American students. Finally, the study does not consider how the implications could apply across other identities beyond Indigenous students and teachers.

In another study, Castagno and Lee (2007) relied on Tribal Crit theory to examine Native American mascots and ethnic fraud (where a person self-identifies as a Native American on university forms to gain advantage but who is not Native American) at a midwestern university. Along with the CRT tenant of interest convergence, Castagno and Lee relied on the Tribal Crit tenets of "colonization is endemic, Indigenous people are not just racialized but also occupy a unique political status within the United States, and that policies and practices aimed at tribal nations are generally rooted in assimilationist and white supremacist goals" (pp. 4–5) to analyze interviews with Native American female students and staff. They learned that though the university took steps to celebrate and confirm diversity, the university only did so to the extent that the policies continued to serve their own interests and stopped short of fully working toward equity and social justice with these particular policies.

In their study, Castagno and Lee (2007) indirectly addressed non-essentializing Native American identity when they identified differences in perspectives between Native American women with stronger affiliations with their tribe and with the Native American community compared to Native American women who were more strongly rooted in the white community. While Castagno and Lee focused their study on Native American perspectives and policies particular to this identity, they considered how their findings could inform university approaches to diversity, multiculturalism, and white racism more broadly. At the same time, their applications and examples centered on race rather than on other identities and their intersections.

Indigenous Knowledge Systems. As an extension of Tribal Crit theory, Brayboy and Maughan (2009) developed a theory of Indigenous Knowledge systems (IK). Importantly, Brayboy and Maughan (2009) argue that Western and Indigenous Knowledge systems can complement each other rather than be positioned as binaries against each other. According to Brayboy and Maughan (2009), Indigenous Knowledge systems:

> are processes and encapsulate a set of relationships ... entire lives represent and embody versions of IK ... are rooted in the lived experiences of peoples ... these experiences highlight the philosophies, beliefs, values, and educational processes of entire communities. (p. 3)

Characteristics of IK include that knowledge is a verb, not a noun, and is acted upon. Further, a premise of IK includes:

> A circular worldview that connects everything and everyone in the world to everything and everyone else, where there is no distinction between the physical and metaphysical and where ancestral knowledge guides contemporary practices and future possibilities. ... This fundamental holistic perspective shapes all other understandings of the world. (Brayboy & Maughan, 2009, p. 13)

From an IK framework:

> survival of a community is at the core of the matter. We simply cannot under-
> stand ways of knowing and being without a deep and abiding understanding of
> what community means and how, for many Indigenous peoples, community is
> at the core of our existence. (Brayboy & Maughan, 2009, p. 15)

Thus, in these ways, IK extended the tenets of Tribal Crit theory.

Critical Indigenous Pedagogy. As a further extension of critical pedagogy,
Garcia and Shirley (2012) relied on Critical Indigenous Pedagogy (CIP) as a theoretical lens to engage Indigenous educators and youth in a decolonization process as
a means toward activism. They define CIP as:

> theoretically grounded in critical methods that resist the injustices caused by
> colonization and oppression experienced by Indigenous peoples. CIP utilizes
> pedagogical methods that are critical, self-reflexive, dialogical, decolonizing and
> transformative while valuing and relying on Indigenous knowledge systems to
> promote, protect and preserve Indigenous languages, cultures, land and people.
> (Denzin & Lincoln, 2008, p. 80)

Garcia and Shirley focused on the importance of decolonization, defined as:

> developing a critical consciousness about the cause(s) of our oppression, the dis-
> tortion of history, our own collaboration, and the degrees to which we have
> internalized colonialist ideas and practices. Decolonization requires auto-
> criticism, self-reflection, and a rejection of victimage. Decolonization is about
> empowerment – a belief that situations can be transformed, a belief and trust
> in our own peoples' values and abilities, and a willingness to make change. It is
> about transforming negative reactionary energy into the more positive rebuild-
> ing energy needed in our communities. (Wheeler cited in Wilson, 2004, p. 71,
> cited in Garcia & Shirley, p. 81)

The purpose of decolonization is to develop a critical Indigenous consciousness, "which is 'the freeing up of the Indigenous mind from the grip of dominant
hegemony' in order to achieve transformation in Native communities" (Garcia &
Shirley, p. 82). Garcia and Shirley identified four steps of the decolonization process: "1) examining history and power; 2) engaging in a self-reflexive process and
critical dialogues; 3) becoming empowered to transform oppressive situations; and
4) taking action to reclaim and center Indigenous knowledge systems and values"
(p. 88). Importantly, Garcia and Shirley believe that Indigenous persons must engage in the decolonization process before they can effectively work toward social
justice for their own Indigenous communities. Garcia and Shirley reported cross-
study findings on two decolonization studies.

In the first study, Garcia and Shirley (2012) engaged a focus group of Hopi/
Tewa teachers and leaders about how they made curricular and pedagogical decisions for Hopi students (Garcia, 2011). To inform the decolonization process, these

educators learned about Tribal Crit and Red Pedagogy, deconstructed the history of Hopi/Tewa education, "explor[ed] Indigenous knowledge within curriculum and pedagogy; analyz[ed] Western curriculum materials and pedagogy; and discuss[ed] what self-education, self-determination and tribal sovereignty mean for Hopi/Tewa education" (p. 82).

In the second decolonialization study, a group of Diné youth aged 11 to 14 (Shirley, 2011) engaged in a focus group where:

> the youth self-reflected on their own identities, critiqued colonialism to expose the ways in which the presence of colonialism continued to exist among their people, and envisioned how they could actively engage in self-determination for themselves and their people. The topics within the focus group sessions centered on examining the history of the Diné long walks and boarding schools; critiquing the influences of popular culture and the media on Diné identities; and responding to and reflecting on Diné stories and philosophy in relation to their identities. (p. 82)

Across the educators and youth in the two studies, central themes included the importance of Indigenous youth and educators learning Indigenous history and how the educators and youth became aware of how they colluded with, adopted, and internalized Western ways. For the educators in the study, they realized they were not conscious about including Indigenous knowledge in the curriculum. In so doing, the Indigenous educators learned that they:

> are contributing to the issue of the loss of cultural identity with their Indigenous students. When teachers and educational leaders in our Indigenous school systems are unaware of their unconscious hegemonic tendencies toward Western culture, they fail to question their curriculum policies and practices in their schools and classrooms; thus perpetuating and privileging Western knowledge systems that contribute to such issues as the youth losing their Indigenous identities. (Shirley, 2011, p. 85)

Another theme, "It Made Me Think About My Life," emerged with the participants critically reflecting on their lives from the learning in the process and how they wanted to live their lives differently (for the youth) more in line with Diné culture and epistemologies. The educators critically reflected on their teaching practices that promulgated Western thinking. The final theme drew upon hope, empowerment, transformation, and personal agency with the participants seeking to live their lives differently to reflect their history, identity, and culture. Thus, Tribal Crit theory has spawned Indigenous Knowledge systems and Critical Indigenous Pedagogy

Tribal Nation Building. Brayboy, Castagno, and Solyom (2014) drew upon principles of Tribal Crit theory and Indigenous Knowledge systems to develop the concept of tribal nation building as a foundation for graduate education. They describe tribal national building as being grounded in "reciprocity rooted in relationships and responsibilities that suggests individuals serve their nation and communities while being supported by that same nation and its communities" (p. 587). Brayboy and colleagues (2014) explain how tribal nation building can inform graduate education through its investments in tribal communities:

> [It] insists that graduate programs work with and through tribal nations and Indigenous leaders to identify critical issues, problems, and opportunities facing their community as well as how they might be addressed ... higher education can fold into a larger agenda of tribal nation building and vice versa – since nation building cannot be fully or adequately pursued without some agenda of higher education [it] encourages graduate education to invest in tribal nations and Indigenous communities ... [and] commit[ed] to tribal nation building goals.

In addition to the mutual investment of higher education and tribal nations with each other, Brayboy et al. (2014) suggest how tribal nation building can inform graduate education in program development, including culturally relevant pedagogy and the location of courses in Native American communities.

Brayboy and colleagues (2014) offer several recommendations on the ways in which tribal nation building can inform student recruitment and admissions. First, "institutions and Nations ought to work together to identify, recruit, and encourage individuals for graduate programs" (p. 591).

Second, for admissions, rather than focusing on single test scores for graduate admissions like GPA or GRE scores and admissions which consider only the past "success" of students, the primary criterion for graduate admissions should be the extent to which the student will be able to contribute back to his or her community. They argue that admissions and the evaluation of the effectiveness of the institution as a whole should center on the idea of democratic merit. They explain:

> At the individual level, democratic merit calls for an investment-based system whereby individuals are invested in (and, thus, "rewarded") based on their potential for contributing to the larger democratic project (Dodson, 2008). Therefore, individuals who have promise and capacity for becoming leaders and for giving back to their communities, for creating good and sustainable relationships, are the ones who graduate programs should be recruiting, admitting, and investing in. (Brayboy et al., 2014, p. 586)

Brayboy and colleagues (2014) further explain how the concept of democratic merit should be applied not only at the individual level in the admissions process but also at the institutional level as part of evaluating the effectiveness of graduate education:

> Institutions are rated highly (or not) based on the prior accomplishments of the individuals they admit. Instead, Guinier argues, universities should focus on and be held accountable according to treatment effects, which would be the value added that they invest in individuals and the larger society toward the

democratic project. Under this system, an institution would be rated highly (or not) based on the degree to which their graduates are better off than when they entered the institution – with better off assessed by their capacity to contribute to a healthy democratic society. (Dodson, 2008, p. 587)

Thus, in these ways, tribal nation building can inform action at the individual and institutional level.

Importantly, when applying tribal nation building to higher education, Brayboy et al. (2014) moved beyond essentializing Native American identity:

[A] great deal of diversity exists among Indigenous peoples. For example, there are over 560 federally recognized tribes in the United States and at least half that many state-recognized tribes (US Government Accountability Office, 2012). Indigenous peoples live within the borders of these nations, in rural communities, in urban centers, and everywhere in between. Therefore, the vision, goals, and needs of a community are likely to vary depending on their unique population and context. (p. 580)

Regarding intersectionality, however, Brayboy et al. (2014) applied nation building only to Native American students in a teacher education program and graduate education in general and did not consider how these graduate school changes could or should apply across other racial identities. In addition, they focused on transforming graduate school for Native American students but did not consider the intersections of Native American identity with other identities. For example, they explained how the teacher education program of which they were a part included two additional courses: one on the history of Native American education and the other on Indigenous Knowledge systems. They did not address how the intersections of identities with Native American identity were considered in these courses, such as sexuality (e.g., "two spirited" people in Native American culture), gender, gender identity, social class, or ability.

In sum, Tribal Crit theory emerged in 2005, first articulated by Brayboy (2005). Building upon CRT, Brayboy identified eight tenets of Tribal Crit theory, yet all eight tenets are unique to the Native American experience. Several studies have applied Tribal Crit theory alone to Indigenous teacher preparation (Castagno, 2012), or in combination with CRT; for example, to the study of Native American policies in higher education (Castagno & Lee, 2007). As an extension of Tribal Crit theory, Garcia and Shirley (2012) identified Critical Indigenous Pedagogy (CIP) as a means for a decolonization process for Indigenous educators and youth. Similar to the Alemán (2007, 2009) and Huber (2010) LatCrit studies, their studies demonstrate how Indigenous educators and youth often collude in their own oppression. As such, Garcia and Shirley (2012) argue that the decolonization process remains an essential prerequisite for social justice work. Brayboy and Maughan (2009) expanded on Tribal Crit theory to identify what they term Indigenous Knowledge systems to characterize Indigenous ways of knowing. Brayboy and colleagues (2014) further extended Brayboy's earlier Tribal Crit work to create the concept of tribal nation building as the anchor for graduate education. Across all these associated Tribal Crit theories, no studies have applied these theories to educational leadership, organizational theory, and socially just schools.

ASIAN CRIT THEORY

Among the race-based critical theories (e.g., CRT, Black Crit, LatCrit, Tribal Crit), Asian Crit theory is the least developed and the least applied to education. Developed initially within critical legal studies, Chang (1993) argued for Asian American legal scholarship which began the formation of Asian Critical theory. Chang emphasized the importance of Asian American history and the Asian American perspective or counter-stories. Yet, subsequent education scholarship on Asian Americans and Pacific Islanders (AAPI) has not taken up this theory. For example, a special 2006 issue of *Race, Ethnicity, and Education* devoted to and authored by the leading scholars of AAPIs in education did not mention Asian Crit theory. In that special issue, Coloma (2006) suggests four conceptual frameworks for examining the AAPI experience in education: pan-ethnic, intersectional, cultural, and transnational. In that same issue, Kumashiro (2006) calls for the expansion of theory in the study of AAPIs in education, including Critical Race Theory, cultural studies, feminist post-colonial theories, Queer Theory, and psychoanalysis. Similar to Tribal Crit theory, no studies have applied Asian Crit theory to organizational theory or to educational leadership for equity.

LATCRIT, TRIBAL CRIT, ASIAN CRIT, AND ORGANIZATIONAL THEORY

As may be seen by a review of this literature, only two studies have applied LatCrit, Tribal Crit, and Asian Crit theories to the field of educational leadership (Alemán, 2007, 2009). Across the theories, none have been applied to the study of educational leadership within schools; nor have these theories been applied to organizational studies. In this next section, I identify lessons from these theories and the studies that have been guided by these theories that can inform our understanding of traditional dimensions of organizational theory: leadership, change, and decision-making. Although I discuss leadership as a separate dimension from change and decision-making, as does traditional organizational theory, in fact the practice of leadership for equity remains entwined with change and decision-making. I then consider how these epistemological perspectives can inform organizational theory beyond these traditional dimensions of organizational theory and, in turn, can inform leading for equity.

Leadership

Alemán's (2009) study offers important implications for leadership. First, for leadership practice, Alemán proposes a LatCrit educational leadership framework which he defines as an alternative social justice framework from which to practice educational leadership and activism:

> LatCrit educational leadership is foundationally political and just as LatCrit scholars complicate notions of race and racism and problematize the black/white binary. … The framework centers the permanence of racism, values multiple voices, understands and utilizes the histories of Latina/o peoples, and endorses activism to achieve social transformation. A LatCrit educational leadership framework requires that coalition building occur, interest convergence analysis be utilized, and internalized racism and notions of whiteness be refuted. (p. 195)

Thus, Alemán suggests that a LatCrit educational leadership framework move beyond a generalized liberal social justice leadership approach. Instead, a LatCrit leadership framework centers on race/ethnicity and in so doing moves beyond the black/white binary. A LatCrit educational leadership framework pivots on the CRT tenets of the permanence of racism, counter-stories and histories of Latina/o people, and interest convergence with social justice at its core. Enacting LatCrit theory-inspired leadership for social justice requires disrupting internalized racism and coalition building.

A second implication for leadership from LatCrit, Tribal Crit, and Asian Crit theory centers on the hiring of leaders and educators of color. As Alemán's (2007, 2009), Garcia and Shirley's (2012), and Huber's (2010) studies suggest, hiring leaders and educators of color does not guarantee that these leaders will advance equity and social justice, since it depends on where these educators are in their own racial identity development. Instead, these studies illuminate how educators of color can internalize and collude in their own oppression and support policies and practices that perpetuate white racism. For example, Alemán (2009) argues that given that many districts in the southwest of the United States are led by leaders of color proportional to the student racial demographics and that inequities persist in these districts, then "What appears evident is that solely increasing numbers of leaders of color is not sufficient to garner social change" (p. 183). Alemán believes that the reason the leaders in his study did not push for more significant change in finance policy centered on evidence of internalized oppression as described by Padilla (1999, 2001). Alemán explains:

> Padilla (1999, 2001) discusses how assimilation issues and internalized oppression or racism (i.e., the problem of the colonized mind) affect Latina/o identity and leadership. Explaining that 'internalized oppression and racism are insidious forces that cause marginalized groups to turn on themselves, often without even realizing it' (2001, p. 61), Padilla asserts that 'destructive behavior' is the

result of 'self-fulfilling negative stereotypes' (p. 61) and can stymie empower-ment of their communities. She also writes that it is often 'survival instincts' that trigger an 'unquestioned acceptance of liberal ideology' that encourages Latina/os to 'claim a White identity' (p. 186).

Garcia and Shirley (2012) revealed similar findings with indigenous educators, leaders, and youth who colluded in their own oppression.

Thus, when hiring leaders regardless of race, we need to ensure that their beliefs, experiences, and expertise align with disrupting oppression and marginalization in schools. Further, regardless of our race, we are responsible to continue to deepen our own racial identity development and facilitate the racial identity development of others. The Tribal Crit empirical studies provide evidence of the power and impor-tance of simultaneous decolonization and racial identity development as a prereq-uisite to social justice leadership across youth and adults (Garcia & Shirley, 2012).

Change

Like change from Critical Race Theory perspectives, change from LatCrit, Tribal Crit, and Asian Crit theories ask the question "change to what end?" with the only answer being racial justice. Thus, unlike how typical change is carried out in schools such as in the math curriculum, change from LatCrit, Tribal Crit, and Asian Crit theories means that individuals are being asked to address their own racism and how they are complicit in all levels of racism as they work to initiate change that works against white racism toward racial justice.

Castagno's (2012) Tribal Crit study in a school of education demonstrates, similar to Pollack and Zirkel's (2013) Critical Race Theory study in a high school, how good intentions are not enough, and that leaders must be cognizant that their social change efforts may morph into colonization and assimilation. In the Castagno (2012) study, many aspects were in place in the predominantly white school of education to support the preparation of Indigenous teachers for Indigenous students, including holding explicit goals about: "serving Indigenous communities and that … was founded and developed with the commitment to increase the number of culturally responsive Navajo teachers" (p. 16). Yet, the Indigenous teacher education program failed to be effective. Castagno quoted Ladson-Billings and Tate (2006), who describe how liberal, multicultural approaches do not support social change and, as a result, anti-racist work ends up being "sucked back into the system":

> We argue that the current multicultural paradigm functions in a manner similar to civil rights law. Instead of creating radically new paradigms which ensure justice, multicultural reforms are routinely "sucked back into the system"; and just as traditional civil rights law is based on a foundation of human rights, the current multicultural paradigm is mired in liberal ideology that offers no radical change in the current order. (Castagno, 2012, p. 25)

Thus, as Castagno's (2012) study illustrates, leaders are constantly working against social justice change becoming sucked back into the structural functionalist, interpretive, or liberal, progressive system. Yet, as Castagno suggests, social justice efforts are not without hope and we can take steps to effect significant social change against the odds.

Similarly, Castagno and Lee's (2007) study of how a university responded to policies about Native American mascots from other universities revealed the limits of racial change from a Tribal Crit perspective. Their study suggested how the university engaged in interest convergence related to changes in equity policies and practices in that the university was willing to attend to issues of diversity and equity only to the extent that these changes continued to align with university interests.

Alemán's (2007) study of Mexican superintendents in Texas also revealed how the actions of these Texas superintendents to bring about change in school finance policy collapsed into interest convergence. These superintendents relied on the majoritarian narrative as a way to maintain their current school funding and so as not to appear "too racially radical" to white policy-makers. In so doing, the superintendents aligned their interests with the white policy-makers and urged finance policy change only to the extent that it continued to support the interests of the legislators.

In sum, in all of these examples, LatCrit and Tribal Crit theories reveal the limits of structural functional changes toward efficiency, interpretive changes that revolve around collaboration, and critical changes toward social justice ends in general. LatCrit and Tribal Crit theories reveal the limits of yet possibilities for change toward racial justice in a context of liberal multiculturalism and interest convergence.

Decision-making

Similar to Critical Race Theory, decision-making from a LatCrit, Tribal Crit, and Asian Crit lens means that equity leaders are aware that all decisions are racial justice decisions. Thus, the outcome of any decision has an impact upon racial justice – for good or for worse. Further, LatCrit, Tribal Crit, and Asian Crit perspectives on decision-making require demographically representative/proportional representation in all decisions. Thus, leaders must ensure that communities are demographically represented on all decision-making teams and, at the same time, not essentializing these perspectives.

In sum, from the perspectives of LatCrit, Tribal Crit, and Asian Crit, traditional organizational theories such as those related to leadership, change, and decision-making are fundamentally and epistemologically shifted from the goals of structural functionalism of efficiency, the goals of interpretivism of understanding, and the goals of critically oriented theories of equity and social justice, to the goal of racial equity and eliminating racial oppression. More specifically, LatCrit, Tribal Crit, and Asian Crit theories call for considerations of identity unique to the individual Latino/a, Indigenous, and Asian history and experience within a context of white hegemony as those experiences intersect and collide with gender, social class, sexual identity, gender identity, ability, and their intersections. Thus leadership, change, and decision-making from LatCrit, Tribal Crit, and Asian Crit epistemologies are not generic practices. Likewise, from the perspectives of LatCrit, Tribal Crit, and Asian Crit, equitable leadership, change, and decision-making aims not for a generic liberal, progressive, social justice leadership, but instead, leadership, change, and decision-making are anchored in the unique, lived, individual Latino/a, Indigenous, Asian experiences with the goal of racial justice.

LATCRIT, TRIBAL CRIT, ASIAN CRIT THEORY: IMPLICATIONS BEYOND TRADITIONAL ORGANIZATIONAL THEORIES

LatCrit, Tribal Crit, and Asian Crit Theory offer theoretical implications beyond traditional organizational theories of leadership, change, and decision-making. These theoretical implications apply across leadership, change, and decision-making, and include considering how theories associated with individual identity at the micro-level can reflect back to organizations at the macro-level and the importance of pedagogy. I discuss this further in Chapter 12 when I propose a theory that links individual identity development with organizational identity development toward social justice ends. In the final section of this chapter, I consider applications of LatCrit, Tribal Crit, and Asian Crit theories beyond their individual identities.

Individual Identity and Organizations

Brayboy and colleagues' (2014) essay which proposed tribal nation building for graduate education moved beyond single identity theories that focus on the individual as the unit of analysis and applied principles of nation building to higher education as an institution. Likewise, Castagno and Lee's (2007) study applied Tribal Crit theory to higher education policies and practices. Castagno's (2012) study also relied on Tribal Crit theory to analyze the policies and practices in teacher education that prevented the effective preparation of Indigenous teachers. Further, Huber's (2011) research promised to "better articulate the relationship between individual experiences with microaggressions and the institutionalized, systematic forms of racism from which they emerge to expose a process of domination over Latina/o students and communities" (pp. 380–381). In so doing, she connects the individual experience of Chicana/o K-12 students to the larger institution. Unlike traditional organizational theories that completely ignore individual identity, all these examples illustrate how considerations of individual identity can and should inform organizational and institutional policies and practices.

Beyond Instructional Leadership: Culturally Relevant Pedagogy

Castagno's Tribal Crit study (2012) reiterates the critical importance of culturally relevant pedagogy for preparing Indigenous educators and, in turn, for Indigenous educators to be proficient teachers of culturally relevant pedagogy for Indigenous students. Garcia and Shirley's (2012) studies also demonstrate the significance of culturally relevant pedagogy as one tool for disrupting the power of colonization. In one of their studies, Indigenous educators assimilated and colluded with Western thinking and ideals and in so doing perpetuated this assimilation with Indigenous students. Their study illuminated how Indigenous youth and educators experienced culturally relevant pedagogy as part of the decolonization process along with learning about Tribal Crit and Indigenous history. Their study also demonstrated how a purposeful process, such as the decolonization process which includes culturally relevant pedagogy, not only can move individuals along the identity development continuum toward social justice action, but is a prerequisite for such action. Further, Brayboy and colleagues (2014) centered the importance of culturally relevant pedagogy in graduate education linking pedagogy to tribal communities.

As such, rather than the benign calls for generalized instructional leadership (Neumerski, 2013), or leadership for learning (Hallinger, 2011), LatCrit, Tribal Crit, and Asian Crit asks instructional leadership toward what end, and what kind of leadership for learning exactly what? Further, instructional leadership and leadership for learning rarely address the means to learning. To this end, then, rather than instructional leadership, LatCrit, Tribal Crit, and Asian Crit epistemologies require culturally relevant instructional leadership. Further, these theories call for culturally relevant instructional leadership for learning that advances achievement and racial justice. As such, culturally relevant instructional leadership requires leaders to become proficient in culturally relevant pedagogy and to be able to teach and support classroom teachers to become experts in culturally relevant pedagogy as well. In this sense, then, culturally relevant pedagogy becomes a means to disrupt colonization of staff and students and a prerequisite for racial justice action. As such, culturally relevant instruction, rather than an "add-on" special program or short-term initiative, forms the core instructional work of the school. In so doing, educators must consider culturally relevant pedagogy across races and their intersections with other identities such as gender, social class, sexual/gender identity, and ability.

Applications beyond Identity

LatCrit, Tribal Crit, and Asian Crit may be applied to studies and practice relative to these identities and their intersections, but not necessarily inclusively so. For example, if an educator is examining Latinx education policy or practice in education, LatCrit theory may be one lens for that examination. At the same time, many empirical studies exist that have examined populations who are linguistically diverse, including Latinx students, but these studies do not necessarily rely on LatCrit theory (Kanno & Kangas 2014). Theoretical perspectives in addition to LatCrit can offer important insights on Latinx education policy and practice. Further, educators need to consider whether and to what extent LatCrit theory may be applied to the experience of other U.S. immigrants such as Hmong immigrants to the U.S.A. who also experience issues of immigration, status, language, ethnicity, and culture (DePouw, 2012). In addition, though most aspects of Tribal Crit Theory and its derivatives have been applied to Indigenous individuals and communities, many aspects of these theories can and have yet to be applied across identities and their intersections.

CONCLUSION

To conclude, LatCrit theories have only been applied to two studies in educational leadership, while no studies in educational leadership have relied on Tribal Crit or Asian Crit as a theoretical lens. Yet, these epistemologies offer several important implications for organizational theory in education and for leading socially just schools. With the increasing population of Latinx students and immigrant students in U.S. schools, and the persistent, historical oppression of Indigenous students, more studies are needed from these epistemologies that examine schools as organizations and the leaders within them as they work toward racially just education.

LEADERSHIP DEVELOPMENT ACTIVITIES

After reading the chapter, leadership development activities that I describe below for the Lat Crit, Tribal Crit, and Asian Crit epistemologies include: (1) questions for whole class discussion; (2) critical analysis of the educator's own leadership, and (3) case study analysis. It is best to work through all the activities in the order they are presented here.

ACTIVITY 1:   Discussion Questions for LatCrit, Tribal Crit, and Asian Crit Epistemology

1. What are the organizational goals?
2. What does leadership look like?
3. How is the organization structured?
4. What does organizational culture look like?
5. What does decision-making look like?
6. What does change look like?
7. What aspects of education emanate from this epistemology?
8. What is the goal of education?
9. What does the curriculum look like?
10. What does instruction look like?
11. What does assessment look like?
12. What does evaluation/supervision look like?
13. How does this epistemology respond to differences and diversity?

ACTIVITY 2:   Critical Reflection on Your Own Leadership from LatCrit, Tribal Crit, and Asian Crit Epistemologies

Table 8.1 Critical Reflection on Your Own Leadership from LatCrit, Tribal Crit, and Asian Crit Epistemologies

Leadership	Critical Self Reflection
"[C]enters the permanence of racism, values multiple voices, understands and utilizes the histories of Latina/o peoples, and endorses activism to achieve social transformation" (Alemán, 2009, p. 195).	To what extent does your leadership reflect each of these three points? What are your leadership strengths and in what ways do you need to further develop your leadership relative to these three points?
"A LatCrit educational leadership framework requires that coalition building occur, interest convergence analysis be utilized, and internalized racism and notions of whiteness be refuted" (Alemán, 2009, p. 195).	To what extent does your leadership reflect each of these three points? What are your leadership strengths and in what ways do you need to further develop your leadership relative to these three points?
"Racial identity development serves as a prerequisite to social justice leadership" (Garcia & Shirley, 2012).	Assess your own racial identity development to date.
Change	
From LatCrit, Tribal Crit, and Asian Crit epistemologies, the goal of change is racial justice.	If someone evaluates your leadership as measured by the extent to which your change efforts are having a positive impact upon racial justice, how would your change efforts fare?
Leaders must be cognizant of how their social change efforts may morph into colonization and assimilation and being sucked back into the white racist system.	What evidence do you have that your equity change efforts have morphed into reinforcing white ideology? What evidence do you have that your equity change efforts have resisted being sucked back into the white racist system?
Decision-making	
From these epistemologies, all decisions are racial justice decisions.	To what extent do you consider all your leadership decisions as racial justice decisions?
Decision-making teams are demographically representative of the school/community.	To what extent are the teams that you participate in demographically representative of the school/community? If not, what can you do about this?
Beyond Instructional Leadership: Culturally Relevant Pedagogy	To what extent is culturally relevant pedagogy the central core of your instructional leadership?

ACTIVITY 3: LatCrit Epistemology Case Analysis

Note: I offer an example of case analysis from LatCrit epistemology given that Tribal Crit and Asian Crit have not yet been applied to educational leadership or organizational theory.

"LatCrit can be used to reveal the ways Latinas/os experience race, class, gender, and sexuality, while also acknowledging the Latina/o experience with issues of immigration status, language, ethnicity and culture" (Huber, 2010, p. 79).

Alemán (2009) also identified Latinx essentialism and assimilation as key tenets of LatCrit theory. LatCrit directly addresses moving beyond racial essentialism and addressing race across races, and also overtly addresses the intersection of Latinx identity with race, gender, social class, ability, and sexual/gender identity.

1. *LatCrit Tenets:* Are the issues or solutions to your case related to issues of immigration status, language, ethnicity, culture, assimilation, or essentialism? If not, could it be expanded to consider these aspects? That is, even though not directly addressed in the case, did you inadvertently not address these aspects, but these aspects could be or should be considered?

2. *Intersectionality:* Similar to LatCrit theory, how do your case issues or solutions address intersectionality of two or more identities (e.g., the intersection of race, class, gender, ability, gender identity, language)?

   a. How *could* your case address intersectionality in its issues or solutions?

3. *Politically Passing:* Alemán's (2009) study of Latino superintendents revealed that they argued for funding equity using majoritarian perspectives only. Alemán defined this practice as "politically passing" (p. 197), which may be viewed as a form of interest convergence; that is, advocating a particular equity policy or practice from a white perspective in ways to ensure that whites continue to benefit.

   a. To what extent are issues in your case related to any individuals in your case "politically passing?"; that is, working for equity but from a white perspective?

   b. To what extent could politically passing or interest convergence be a short-term solution for your case?

4. *Equity Practices Perpetuating Inequities:* Alemán (2007) analyzed Texas finance policy and learned that though policy-makers sought to create finance policy they believed was more equitable, a closer examination revealed how it continued to perpetuate inequalities based on property taxes.

   a. To what extent is the issue or solution in your case a situation of how what was perceived to be a more equitable policy or practice is actually perpetuating inequities?

(Continued)

5. *Racist Nativism:* Huber defines racist nativism as "the institutionalized ways people perceive, understand and make sense of contemporary US immigration, that justifies *native* (white) dominance, and reinforces hegemonic power" (p. 380); the theory also applies to Indigenous people or anyone perceived as a "foreigner" in the U.S.A. Huber (2011) further explains, "racist nativism is based solely on perceptions. Thus, Latinas/os are racialized as nonnatives regardless of actual immigration status. This process of exclusion then, becomes a function of white dominance" (p. 382). This theory helps explain how whites marginalize anyone who they believe is not "native" to the United States – labeling anyone with this status as "foreigner" regardless of immigration status and perceive individuals with this label as a threat and as justification for white dominance.

   a. Are the issues or solutions in your case related to an individual or individuals perceived as a "foreigner" (i.e., not of this community, an outsider, "different from us")?

NOTE

1   For language, I adopt the position of Castagno and Lee (2012), who explain: "[W]e use the terms 'Indigenous,' 'Native,' 'American Indian,' 'Indian' and 'Native American' interchangeably to refer to the peoples indigenous to what is now the United States. Scholars, educators, and other Indigenous people have not come to an agreement over the use of these terms. . ." (p. 10)

REFERENCES

Alemán, E., Jr. (2007). Situating Texas school finance policy in a CRT framework: How "substantially equal" yields racial inequity. *Educational Administration Quarterly, 43*(5), 525–558.

Alemán, E. (2009). LatCrit educational leadership and advocacy: Struggling over Whiteness as property in Texas school finance. *Equity & Excellence in Education, 42*(2), 183–201.

Arreguin-Anderson, M.G. & Kennedy, K.D. (2013). Deliberate language planning in environmental education: A CRT/LatCrit Perspective. *Journal of Environmental Education, 44*(1), 1–15.

Bernal, D. (2002). Critical race theory, Latino critical theory, and critical raced-gendered epistemologies: Recognizing students of color as holders and creators of knowledge. *Qualitative Inquiry, 8*(1), 105–126.

Brayboy, B.M.J. (2005). Toward a Tribal Critical Race Theory in education. *The Urban Review, 37*(5), 425–446.

Brayboy, B.M.J. & Maughan, E. (2009). Indigenous knowledges and the story of the bean. *Harvard Educational Review, 79*(1), 1–21.

Brayboy, B.M.J., Castagno, A.E., & Solyom, J.A. (2014). Looking into the hearts of Native Peoples: Nation building as an institutional orientation for graduate education. *American Journal of Education, 120*(4), 575–596.

Castagno, A. (2012). "They prepared me to be a teacher, but not a culturally responsive Navajo teacher for Navajo kids:" A Tribal Critical Race theory analysis of an Indigenous teacher preparation program. *Journal of American Indian education, 51*(1), 3–26.

Castagno, A. & Brayboy, B.M.J. (2008). Culturally responsive schooling for Indigenous youth: A review of the literature. *Review of Educational Research, 78*(4), 941–993.

Castagno, A. & Lee, S. (2007). Native mascots and ethnic fraud in higher education: Using Tribal Critical Race theory and the interest convergence principle as an analytic tool. *Equity & Excellence in Education, 40*, 3–13.

Chang, R.S. (1993). Toward an Asian American legal scholarship: Critical race theory, post-structuralism, and narrative space. *California Law Review, 19*, 1243.

Coloma, S. (2006). Disorienting race and education: Changing paradigms on the schooling of Asian Americans and Pacific Islanders. *Race, Ethnicity, and Education, 9*(1), 1–15.

Daniels, E.A. (2011). Racial silences: Exploring and incorporating critical frameworks in the Social Studies. *Social Studies, 102*(5), 211–220.

Davila, E.R. & de Bradley, A.A. (2010). Examining education for Latinas/os in Chicago: A CRT/LatCrit approach. *Educational Foundations, 24*(1–2), 39–58.

Denzin, N. & Lincoln, Y. (2008). *Handbook of critical and indigenous methodologies.* Thousand Oaks, CA: Sage.

DePouw, C. (2012). When culture implies deficit: Placing race at the center of Hmong American education. *Race Ethnicity and Education, 15*(2), 223–239.

Dodson, A.P. (2008). Q&A: Lani Guinier and the Pimple on Adonis' Nose. *Diverse Issues in Higher Education,* December 5. http://diverseeducation.com/article/12033/.

Fernández, L. (2002). Telling stories about school: Using Critical Race and Latino Critical Theories to document Latina/Latino education and resistance. *Qualitative Inquiry, 8*(1), 45–65.

Flores, J. & Garcia, S. (2009). Latina "Testimonios": A reflexive, critical analysis of a "Latina Space" at a predominantly White campus. *Race, Ethnicity and Education, 12*(2), 155–172.

Franquiz, M.E., Salazar, M.C., & DeNicolo, C.P. (2011). Challenging majoritarian tales: Portraits of bilingual teachers deconstructing deficit views of bilingual learners. *Bilingual Research Journal, 34*(3), 279–300.

Garcia, J. (2011). *A critical analysis of curriculum and pedagogy in Indigenous education: Engaging Hopi and Tewa educators in the process of praxis.* (Unpublished doctoral dissertation). Purdue University, West Lafayette, IN.

Garcia, J. & Shirley, V. (2012). Performing decolonization: Lessons learned from Indigenous youth, teachers and leaders' engagement with Critical Indigenous Pedagogy. *Journal of Curriculum Theorizing, 28*(2), 77–91.

Gonzalez, J.C. & Portillos, E.L. (2007). The undereducation and overcriminalization of U.S. Latinas/os: A post-Los Angeles riots LatCrit analysis. *Educational Studies: Journal of the American Educational Studies Association, 42*(3), 247–266.

Gutiérrez, R. (2013). The sociopolitical turn in mathematics education. *Journal for Research in Mathematics Education, 44*(1), 37–68.

Hallinger, P. (2011). Leadership for learning: Lessons from 40 years of empirical research. *Journal of Educational Administration, 9*(2), 125–142.

Harris, C.I. (1995). Whiteness as property. In N. Krenshaw, G. Gotanda, G. Peller, & K. Thomas (Eds), *Critical race theory: The key writings that formed the movement* (pp. 276–291). New York: The Press.

Huber, L.P. (2009). Disrupting apartheid of knowledge: Testimonio as methodology in Latina/o critical race research in education. *International Journal of Qualitative Studies in Education, 22*(6), 639–654.

Huber, L.P. (2010). Using Latina/o Critical Race Theory (LatCrit) and Racist Nativism to explore intersectionality in the educational experiences of undocumented Chicana college students. *Educational Foundations, 24*(1), 77–96.

Huber, L.P. (2011). Discourses of racist nativism in California public education: English dominance as Racist Nativist microaggressions. *Educational Studies, 47*(4), 379–401.

Huber, L.P., Lopez, C.B., Malagon, M.C., Velez, V., & Solórzano, D.G. (2008). Getting beyond the "symptom," acknowledging the "disease": Theorizing racist nativism. *Contemporary Justice Review, 11*(1), 39–51.

Irizarry, J.G. (2011). En La Lucha: The struggles and triumphs of Latino/a preservice teachers. *Teachers College Record, 113*(12), 2804–2835.

Irizarry, J.G. & Raible, J. (2014). "A Hidden Part of Me": Latino/a students, silencing, and the epidermalization of inferiority. *Equity & Excellence in Education, 47*(4), 430–444.

Kanno, Y. & Kangas, S.E.N. (2014) "I'm not going to be, like, for the AP": English Language Learners' limited access to advanced college-preparatory courses in high school. *American Educational Research Journal, 51*(5), 848–878.

Kumashiro, K. L. (2006). Toward an anti oppressive theory of Asian Americans and Pacific Islanders in education, *Race Ethnicity and Education, 9*(1), 129–135.

Ladson-Billings, G. & Tate, W. (2006). Toward a critical race theory of education. In A. Dixson & C. Rousseau (Eds), *Critical race theory in education: All God's children got a song* (pp. 11–30). New York: Routledge.

Malagon, M.C. (2010). All the losers go there: Challenging the deficit educational discourse of Chicano racialized masculinity in a continuation high school. *Educational Foundations, 24*(1–2), 59–76.

Neumerski, C.N. (2013). Rethinking instructional leadership, a review: What do we know about principal, teacher, and coach instructional leadership, and where should we go from here? *Educational Administration Quarterly, 49*, 310–347.

Padilla, L.M. (1999). Social and legal repercussions of Latinos' colonized mentality. *University of Miami Law Review, (53)*, 769.

Padilla, L.M. (2001). "But you're not a dirty Mexican": Internalized oppression, Latinos, and law. *Texas Hispanic Journal of Law and Policy, (7)*, 59.

Peralta, C. (2013). Fractured memories, mended lives: The schooling experiences of Latinas/os in rural areas. *Bilingual Research Journal, 36*(2), 228–243.

Pollack, T.M. & Zirkel, S. (2013). Negotiating the contested terrain of equity-focused change efforts in schools: Critical race theory as a leadership framework for creating more equitable schools. *The Urban Review, 45*(3), 290–310.

Portillos, E.L., Gonzalez, J.C., & Peguero, A.A. (2012). Crime control strategies in school: Chicanas'/os' perceptions and criminalization. *Urban Review, 44*(2), 171–188.

Quiñones, S., Ares, N., Padela, M.R., Hopper, M., & Webster, S. (2011). ¿Y Nosotros, Qué?: Moving beyond the margins in a community change initiative. *Anthropology & Education Quarterly, 42*(2), 103–120.

Rodriguez, T.L. (2011). Stories of self, stories of practice: Enacting a vision of socially just pedagogy for Latino youth. *Teaching Education, 22*(3), 239–254.

Shirley, V. (2011). *Indigenous subjectivities: Diné youth (de)construct identity.* (Unpublished doctoral dissertation). Purdue University, West Lafayette, IN.

Solórzano, D.G. & Bernal, D. (2001). Examining transformational resistance through a Critical Race and LatCrit Theory framework: Chicana and Chicano students in an urban context. *Urban Education, 36*(3), 308–342.

Solórzano, D.G. & Yosso, T.J. (2001). Critical race and LatCrit theory and method: Counter-storytelling. *International Journal of Qualitative Studies in Education (QSE), 14*(4), 471–495.

Solorzano, D.G. & Yosso, T.J. (2002). Critical Race methodology: Counter-storytelling as an analytical framework for education research. *Qualitative Inquiry, 8*(1), 23–44.

Urrieta, L.J. & Villenas, S.A. (2013). The legacy of Derrick Bell and Latino/a education: A Critical Race testimonio. *Race, Ethnicity and Education, 16*(4), 514–535.

US Government Accountability Office. (2012). *Indian Issues: Federal Funding for Nonfederally Recognized Tribes.* GAO-12–348: a report to the Honorable Dan Boren, House of Representatives, Washington, DC.

Valdez, T.M. & Lugg, C. (2010). Community cultural wealth and Chicano/Latino students. *Journal of School Public Relations, 31*(3), 224–237.

Villalpando, O. (2003). Self-segregation or self-preservation? A critical race theory and Latina/o critical theory analysis of a study of Chicana/o college students. *International Journal of Qualitative Studies in Education, 16*(5), 619–646.

Wilson, W. A. (2004). Reclaiming our humanity: Decolonization and the recovery of Indigenous knowledge. In D. A. Mihesuah & A. C. Wilson (Eds), *Indigenizing the academy* (pp. 69–87). Lincoln, NE: University of Nebraska Press.

CHAPTER 9

Black Feminism and Black Feminist Epistemology

The purpose of this chapter and its central research question asks: How can the literature on Black feminist epistemology in educational leadership inform organizational theory and equity leadership? As Tillman (2009) noted, "It is likely that research questions about African-Americans in school leadership are important to African-Americans as well as to the field of educational leadership as a whole" (p. 461).

Similar to feminist poststructuralism (Chapter 6), Black feminist epistemology includes elements from the radical change end of the change continuum within modernism and also draws from poststructuralism (see Figure 9.1).

In the literature, about a dozen studies focused on black female leaders but did not rely on Black feminist epistemology to conceptually frame the study. I confined my analysis only to those studies that explicitly relied on Black feminist epistemology because of their explicit attention to interlocking oppressions of gender, race, and class and other identities and to theoretically explore how Black feminism and organizational theory could inform each other toward social justice ends. Hill Collins (1991, 2000) articulated the dimensions of an African American feminist epistemology more than 25 years ago and I located a little over two dozen empirical studies in educational leadership that relied on Black feminist epistemologies (Atlas & Capper, 2003). For example, a special issue of the *International Journal of Qualitative Studies in Education* (February, 2012) features emerging African American female scholars writing about black female K-12 leadership. This special issue was conceptually framed by "Black Feminist Thought, leadership theory, and intersectionality" (Horsford & Tillman, 2012, p. 2). Although this special issue focuses on the intersections of race and gender, the editors point out: "it is important to assess whether or not other factors such as age, professional experience, sexuality, ability, and context have an impact" (p. 2). I conducted a content analysis of all the publications

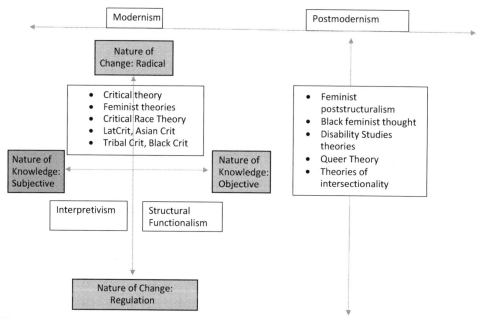

Figure 9.1 An Epistemology Framework

I located, identifying themes of Black feminism that not only inform black female leadership but also inform educational leaders of all races and genders in leading to eliminate inequities.

BLACK FEMINIST EPISTEMOLOGY

Sociologist Patricia Hill Collins (1991) articulated Black feminist epistemology in the early 1990s. Hill Collins explicitly positions African American feminist epistemology against white Eurocentric masculinist epistemologies (i.e., structural functionalism and interpretivism discussed earlier in this book), and offers not only an alternative epistemology to positivism but also provides a different set of knowledge validation "rules" based on African American feminism. In so doing, Hill Collins explains that though positivists can easily dismiss and marginalize alternative epistemologies based on their rules of validation, identifying a different set of knowledge validation rules calls into question the entire positivist epistemology.

Hill Collins's (1991, 2000) framework for Afrocentric feminist epistemology includes the following four tenets of African feminist epistemology that comprise the epistemology and at the same time serve as a set of knowledge validation rules to determine the validity of knowledge claims: concrete experience as a criterion of meaning, the use of dialogue in assessing knowledge claims, the ethic of caring, and the ethic of personal accountability. That is, for knowledge to be valid, it must be grounded in concrete experience; developed and assessed through dialogue; emanate from an ethic of caring derived from individual uniqueness, emotion, and empathy; and make visible the relationship between personal identity and the knowledge claims.

Concrete Experience as a Criterion of Meaning

For Hill Collins (1991, 2000), the concrete experience of African American women forms a fundamental underlying criterion for developing and assessing knowledge claims. According to Hill Collins, (1991):

> For most African-American women those individuals who have lived through the experiences about which they claim to be experts are more believable and credible than those who have merely read or thought about such experiences. Thus concrete experience as a criterion for credibility frequently is invoked by Black Women when making knowledge claims. (p. 209)

With concrete experience as a criterion of meaning,[1] Hill Collins distinguishes between wisdom and knowledge or "book learning," and argues that for African American women, their central criterion of life meaning is the wisdom they garner from concrete life experiences. They rely on this wisdom to survive in a repressive world. From this view, black women are more valued, believed, and accepted based on the extent of their life experiences. According to Hill Collins (1991):

> This distinction between knowledge and wisdom, and the use of experience as the cutting edge dividing them, has been key to Black women's survival. In the context of race, gender, and class oppression, the distinction is essential. Knowledge without wisdom is adequate for the powerful, but wisdom is essential to the survival of the subordinate. (p. 208)

Hill Collins then points out how most black women are supported in this importance of concrete experience by their communities, their churches, their families, and by their sisterhood with each other in ways that are different than for white women.

The Use of Dialogue in Assessing Knowledge Claims

In addition to relying on concrete experience as one measure of assessing claims and developing knowledge, an African American feminist epistemology calls on the use of dialogue to assess knowledge claims. Unlike qualitative or quantitative research methods and unlike structural functional and interpretive epistemologies, Hill Collins (1991) argues that knowledge claims can only be worked out in dialogue with others:

> For black women, new knowledge claims are rarely worked out in isolation from other individuals and are usually developed through dialogues with other members of a community. A primary epistemological assumption underlying the use of dialogue in assessing knowledge claims is that connectedness rather than separation is an essential component of the knowledge validation process. (p. 212)

For Hill Collins, for dialogue to work out this knowledge validation process two criteria must be met: (1) all must participate equally in the dialogue, no one can be left out; and (2) all must truly say what they believe in the dialogue: "To refuse to join in, especially if one really disagrees with what has been said is seen as 'cheating'" (p. 213).

The Ethic of Caring

For Hill Collins (1991, 2000), the knowledge validation process and the creation of knowledge must include the ethic of caring, "and that personal expressiveness [or individual uniqueness], emotions, and empathy are central to the knowledge validation process" (1991, p. 215). According to Hill Collins, individual uniqueness is "Rooted in a tradition of African humanism, each individual is thought to be a unique expression of a common spirit, power, or energy inherent in all life" (p. 215).

Hill Collins (1991) then links the black church to the ethic of caring with the appropriateness of emotions in dialogue, moving beyond the intellect/emotion binary. Supported by the black church, she explains, "Emotion indicates that a speaker believes in the validity of an argument" (p. 215). The third aspect of caring – empathy – emanated from black women's lives of struggle and history of overcoming oppression. Black women held empathy for individuals who struggle because of their own lives of struggle. These three aspects of caring pervade and are supported by African American culture, including black families and the black church.

The Ethic of Personal Accountability

An African American feminist epistemology insists on the importance of the relationship between the personal identities of the knower and that which is claimed to be known: "every idea has an owner and … the owner's identity matters" (Hill Collins, 1991, p. 218). From this epistemology, an individual's knowledge claims are not separate from the individual's character, values, and ethics. Hill Collins (1991) argues that for African Americans, they must take personal positions on issues and should "assume full responsibility for arguing their validity" (p. 218). Individuals need to have confidence in their ideas when they speak and be willing to take a stand on their personal beliefs.

BLACK FEMINIST THOUGHT AND EDUCATIONAL LEADERSHIP THEORY AND PRACTICE

Nine themes emerged from the Black feminist epistemology and educational leadership research that can inform educational leadership to eliminate inequities. Some of these themes have implications for traditional concepts of organizational theory, including leadership theory, change theory, and decision-making theory. One theme emerged from this literature that contributes beyond traditional categories of organizational theory. Taken together, these themes constitute fresh ways to theorize about organizations and leadership.

Black Feminist Epistemology and Leadership Theory

Three themes emerged from the literature on Black feminist epistemology that demonstrate the limitations of traditional leadership theories in the organization literature and the utility of Black feminism for equity leadership: (a) Moral Obligation from Within, (b) Community Other Mothers, and (c) Education as Political Liberation.

Moral Obligation from Within

Black feminist epistemology suggests that leaders for equity use their social capital, not to advance their own careers but for "collective racial and community uplift" (Wilson & Johnson, 2015, p. 106). These leaders realize that their position of authority brings with it a communal and societal responsibility to make the world a better place, starting with their schools.

According to Dillard (1995), equity leadership actions "arise from personal biographies, which are always located in a more collective (and sometimes connected) history" (p. 558). As such, the motivation for addressing inequities comes from the leaders' own experiences with oppression, marginalization, discrimination, growing up in families that developed this worldview, or encounter experiences (Bass, 2012). These leaders feel "they are morally obligated to do everything in their power to remedy oppressive situations" (Bass, 2012, p. 74).

This moral obligation stemming from personal experience then helps sustain these leaders when facing opposition to their work and when faced with the enormity of pushing back against centuries of oppression. Bass (2012) learned in her study of African American female principals that they demonstrated resilience by continuing to work in a system they knew to be unjust to make it better: "These women demonstrated resilience in that they were able to effectively navigate and function within a system they perceived as unjust to accomplish their purpose of helping those for whom they cared" (Bass, 2012, p. 193).

Because of their personal marginalized identities (e.g., gender, race, ability, sexual/gender identity, language, and their intersections) or because of leading toward social justice in white, masculinist environments regardless of personal identities, these leaders lead as outsiders/within (Hill Collins, 2000; Bass, 2012). That is, these leaders view and experience themselves or their ideas often as marginal as they are seeking social justice ends within white, masculinist environments.

Community Other Mothers

As well, leaders leading from a Black feminist epistemology feel morally responsible to be advocates for all students in their school, especially for students of color, and they also feel a moral responsibility and advocacy for their communities outside the school (Newcomb & Niemeyer, 2015). Leaders informed by Black feminist epistemology view their leadership as an expression of love and care

(Newcomb & Niemeyer, 2015). Deliberately engaging with families and their communities, and viewed as "mothers of others' children" or "other mothers," these leaders affirm students' home cultures and center students' learning experiences in the students' history, culture, and communities (Dillard, 1995). They advocate for and support families in advocating for their own children and how to navigate the dominant system. Yet, at the same time, Reed (2012) and Reed and Evans (2008) report that district leaders should not assume that black female principals assigned to predominantly black schools will be able to experience a positive connection with black male students and may need professional development toward this end.

From a Black feminist epistemology, this support and love for community forms a reciprocal circle back of love and support from the community. Black female educational leaders recognize how others have supported them to be where they are as leaders, mothers, grandmothers, and, because of that, they want to give back to their families and communities (Angel, Killacky, & Johnson, 2013). These leaders experienced high standards of achievement and behavior from family and community and an expectation that they would go to college and do well and do better than earlier generations (Angel, Killacky, & Johnson, 2013). These leaders cited critical support from family, community, and the church that formed a network of support for their equity leadership, ensuring that these leaders were not isolated in the work (Bloom & Erlandson, 2003).

Education as Political Liberation

From Black feminist epistemologies, leadership is not just about rhetoric or holding the position; leadership credibility and authority stem from the leaders' relationships and actual critical work on behalf of students of color (Dillard, 1995). As such, unlike traditional leadership theory where the "what" or "target" or outcomes of leadership are generically defined, if at all, Black feminist educational leadership focuses on the critical importance of academic achievement, "creating ways and means for students to achieve at all costs" (Dillard, 1995, p. 552). The African American female principals across the studies emphasized how their black families and communities valued the importance of education (Dillard, 1995) because black communities "regard educational attainment as a tool for political liberation and socioeconomic advancement" (Wilson & Johnson, 2015, p. 13). The black female principal in Dillard's (1995) study provided clear rules and expectations for students and was direct in her admonishments and equally direct in her praise as a means to hold her highest expectations of students for their achievement and growth.

In sum, Black feminist epistemology contributes to traditional conceptions of leadership theory in three ways. Black feminist epistemology suggests that leadership derives from a moral obligation within leaders stemming from leaders' personal biographies that position equity leaders as outsiders/within their schools and districts (Hill Collins, 2000). In addition, leading from Black feminist epistemology, leaders feel a moral obligation to be advocates for students of color and all students who struggle and their communities as "other mothers" as a way to give back to families and communities who have supported the leader in their lives. Third,

Black feminist epistemology contributes to leadership theory by being explicit about the target, goal, or outcome of leadership; thus, equity leaders are adamant about the critical importance of education as political liberation from oppression.

Black Feminist Epistemologies and Leadership and Change Theory

One theme from Black feminist epistemology holds implications for change theory (Multiple Approaches to Equity). I also identified three themes that can inform both leadership and change theory: (a) Leadership as Activism, (b) Everyday Acts of Resistance, and (c) Bridge Leaders. I discuss both of these sets of implications in this section.

Multiple Approaches to Equity

For change theory alone, Black feminist epistemology suggests that equity leaders must lead at multiple levels of change – grassroots, community, professional, and institutional levels. These leaders "pursue varied paths of resistance toward similar goals" (Wilson & Johnson, 2015, p. 105). Historically, some black feminists engaged in public protests; others "pursued quieter, yet still courageous, change oriented measures implemented within institutions" (Wilson & Johnson, 2015, p. 105); as such when pursuing change, all change is directed toward equity ends, and leaders work toward this equity change at multiple levels.

Leadership is Activism

Informing leadership and change theory, Black feminist epistemology suggests that leadership is not neutral but rather leadership is activism, and that "effective leadership is transformative political work" (Dillard, 1995, p. 560). Loder-Jackson (2011) learned in her study from black female educators that "Although the professional practices of teachers and school administrators are veiled behind the schoolhouse wall, these practices constitute daily individual struggles for group or professional survival … that teaching and leading [are] legitimate expressions of activism" (p. 166). For example, leadership as activism requires not just enacting a policy as it is but also leading as a change agent toward equitable ends (Newcomb & Niemeyer, 2015). Rather than being merely receivers of federal and state policy, leaders as activists know how to take any federal or state policy or law and translate and leverage it toward equitable ends in their schools.

Everyday Acts of Resistance

A second implication for leadership and change theory refers to the daily small acts of leadership that are critical for equity work (Dillard, 1995), which provide congruence in all the leader says and does toward equitable ends, and that all add up to more equitable outcomes. Dillard's (1995) study of a black female high school principal revealed how this principal's "simple, ordinary acts" (p. 548), such as speaking or teaching, "may also be interpreted as powerful acts of resistance – of talking back or acting up – particularly for African American women working within power-ful White male dominated sites such as high school principalship" (Dillard, 1995, p. 548). While activist leadership conjures up radical, expansive, public acts, "Collins (1990, p. 746) … validated the notion that 'everyday acts of resistance' can contrib-ute to communal, institutional, and/or societal transformation" (cited in Wilson & Johnson, 2015, p. 104). According to Dillard (1995), "What looks like something or-dinary, is in fact disrupting the status quo" (Dillard, p. 548). Reed's (2012) study of three African American female principals also reflects how these principals quietly went about making significant steps in addressing inequities in their schools. These "Black women school leaders [made] quiet, but steady advancements on behalf of the children they serve" (p. 55).

As an additional example of everyday acts of resistance, Frattura and Capper (2015) discuss the importance of language in leading to eliminate inequities and how language drives equity practice. They refer to the importance of using person first language, for example, putting the person first and then the descriptor after, such as instead of saying "autistic student," saying "student with autism"; instead of "poor students," saying "students from low-income homes"; instead of ELL or English Language Learners, saying, "students who are bilingual" or "students who are linguistically diverse." They also suggest not using other deficit language such as "minority students" and instead using "students of color"; not using "subgroups" which connotes deficit thinking and labeling. Instead of referring to education prac-tices that meet the needs of learners in their classrooms as "push-in" services which denotes a practice that is unusual or harsh and the opposite of a loving school com-munity, they suggest not using the phrase "push-in" at all, and instead that services are provided in the classroom. District administrators have attributed these small, everyday acts of resistance as the underlying basis and the driver of the entire equity change efforts and resultant more equitable outcomes in their districts and schools (personal communication, Lisa Dawes, July 25, 2015).

Bridge Leaders

A third implication of Black feminist epistemology for leadership and change theory refers to bridge leadership and the importance of "serving as a bridge for others, to others, and between others in oppressive and discriminatory contexts over time" (Horsford, 2012, p. 17). Equity leaders serve as bridge leaders between work at the individual and at the institutional levels. Enacting bridge leadership "foster[s] ties between the social movement and the community; and between prefigurative strat-egies (aimed at individual change, identity, and consciousness) and political strat-egies (aimed at organizational tactics designed to challenge existing relationships with the state and other societal institutions)" (Horsford, 2012, pp. 15–16). Bridge leaders challenge top-down, hierarchical leadership "that fail[s] to meet the needs of people where they are and even worse are unable to connect with who they are" (Horsford, 2012, p. 18). Bridge leadership also refers to equity leaders who are able to navigate complex "community-based, institutional, and political terrains" (Wilson & Johnson, 2015, p. 105).

Horsford (2012) importantly emphasizes that work on individual change, identity, and consciousness and identity development (discussed in Chapter 12), while important, on its own will not change the historical, structural oppression in schools – that this identity development work must be paired with political strategies and the deliberate dismantling of oppressive school structures such as tracking, ability grouping, and pull-out programs. Hill Collins (1999) agrees, noting that a focus on the individual level of identity work perpetuates white American individualism and that "questions of individual identity resonate with distinctly American beliefs that all social problems can be solved by working on oneself" (p. 86).

In sum, Black feminist epistemology informs leadership theory in organizational theory: first, by emphasizing the importance of leading as a moral obligation that emanates from within the leader. Second, leaders practice their leadership as "community other mothers" by leading as advocates for students of marginalized identities who struggle in their schools and as advocates for and with their families and communities. Third, leaders drawing upon Black feminist epistemologies view education as a way out of oppression, as political liberation, and thus hold the highest of expectations for student achievement and growth.

Black Feminist Epistemology and Decision-making Theory

The literature on Black feminist epistemology in educational leadership did not directly mention decision-making, except for Beard's (2012) study of an African American district superintendent's decision-making related to closing opportunity and achievement gaps in her district. Beard learned that the district superintendent's identity centered all her decision-making about achievement: "She attributed her decision-making to being informed by her cultural membership, life experiences, values developed through socio-historical circumstances, and her world view" (Beard, 2012, p. 60).

The Black feminist epistemology literature suggests that – unlike traditional categories of organizational theory that address decision-making, leadership, and change as separate, distinct entities – all the previous themes discussed here associated with leadership theory and change theory are intertwined with decision-making. From a Black feminist epistemology perspective, leadership is about making decisions and change toward social justice ends; all decisions are about equity, even seemingly mundane decisions. This leadership ensures that community and students not only inform but are key players in all decisions.

Black Feminist Epistemologies Extending beyond Traditional Organizational Theory Categories

Absent from traditional categories of organizational theory are any considerations of historical context; traditional categories of organizational theory are ahistorical. In contrast, Black feminist epistemologies hold leaders responsible for deeply understanding racial history and that this understanding constitutes a prerequisite for equity leadership.

UNDERSTAND RACIAL HISTORY AND INTERLOCKING SYSTEMS OF OPPRESSION

Black female educational leaders hold a strong sense of their own racial history. Likewise, Black feminism requires that leaders for equity must hold a critical consciousness about the history of racism in the U.S.A. (Bloom & Erlandson, 2003), "and the impact of structural racism and micro-to-macro level oppression" (Wilson & Johnson, 2015, p. 105). These leaders understand how educational inequities are not because of students, families, or communities but are a result of the structural, historical inequalities in society and schools (Bloom & Erlandson, 2003). In addition, equity leaders must understand this history and interlocking systems of oppression related to gender, race, class, language, ability, sexual identity, gender identity, and their intersections (McClellan, 2012) as they are played out in schools.

BLACK FEMINIST EPISTEMOLOGY AND CHALLENGES TO EQUITY LEADERSHIP

The Black feminist epistemology literature suggests at least three challenges to equity leadership. First, black female educational leaders experience blatant racism, sexism, or other forms of discrimination (Bloom & Erlandson, 2003; Dillard, 1995; Gaetane, 2013; McClellan, 2012). More research is needed to explore in detail how leaders who are not white, male, and heterosexual experience macro- and micro-aggression when leading to eliminate inequities, and how heterosexual, white males who lead for equity experience marginalization in leading for social justice pushing against historical systems and structures of white racism.

Second, the studies of Black feminist epistemology in educational leadership literature suggest that at times the leadership and change previously described make for complicated relationships with teachers and staff in the school and with district leadership. Doing what is fair and advocating for students can at times put the leader at odds with teachers and with district leadership (Dillard, 1995). Across these studies, the principal intervened directly with teachers for two reasons – first, to mentor and support those who align with her beliefs; and second, to address the teachers' lack of effort or inequitable outcomes in their work (Bloom & Erlandson, 2003). In Dillard's study, the principal declared that, in the midst of politicized labor relations with teachers, "if it is not good for kids, it is not good for Rosefield" (p. 556). One black female principal in Bloom and Erlandson's (2003) study reported on consequences that resulted from her focus on students:

> What I did not know hurt me. I did not understand or believe that the welfare of children was subordinate to the needs of adults. The politics within the district was astounding. ... When I started stirring the pot, and parents became too involved, and the students wanted more opportunities, and the teachers were expected to teach, I got the boot. I became the problem. (p. 354)

Black female principals also report feeling isolated and not supported by the district when working against the status quo (Bloom & Erlandson, 2003; Gaetene, 2013; Peters, 2012).

They reported that to move up in position, they were expected to conform to the status quo and not disagree with their superiors or other people; otherwise district administrators would not support or hire them (Beard, 2012). For example, the black female district administrator in Beard's (2012) study reported:

> Several principal mentors told me if you really want to move up, you need to hold your tongue and straighten your hair – they don't hire people to lead school districts with your hairstyle. Here, I thought it was about the content of my character; the intellectual horsepower, now you're telling me it's about appearance? You've got to be kidding. They told me to change my hairstyle and don't let people know you disagreed with them. (p. 65)

This leader countered and knew that if she had the data to show improvement, the district would finally support her. According to Beard, "Dr. S. rejected being defined by outsiders and articulated her self-valuation. She created her own standard for evaluating herself based on her values, and her confidence in her vision, ability, intellect, and self-efficacy" (p. 65). Theoharis's (2007) research on social justice educational leaders confirms that a major source of resistance to their work flowed from the district office where district leaders did not necessarily support the work and district mandates and demands served as distractions to the equity work.

Third, black female leaders experience a lack of mentoring because there are so few black female leaders (Gaetene, 2013) or other equity leaders. The black female leaders in this literature reported the importance of being mentored by other black female leaders, yet these leaders were not available. In addition, locating equity mentors for principals leading for equity of all races and genders may be difficult when there may be so few principals actually leading for equity, and few university supervisors who understand equity work, the unique challenges of equity work, and how to support principal candidates in this work. Typical state and national administrator associations may also not provide relevant professional development to support this leadership.

In sum, Black feminist epistemology suggests a rethinking of traditional categories of organizational theories for leadership theory (Moral Obligation from Within; Community Other Mothers; Education as Political Liberation); change theory (Multiple Approaches to Equity); and leadership and change theory (Leadership as Activism; Every Day Acts of Resistance; and Bridge Leader). Black feminist epistemologies also inform organizational theory beyond these traditional categories with the critical importance of leaders understanding U.S. racial history and how it is currently manifested in schools. The literature also revealed challenges to leadership, including discrimination, complicated relationships with teachers and the district, and lack of mentors.

Across the critically oriented epistemologies discussed thus far, critical theory (Chapter 5); feminist, poststructural, and feminist poststructural (Chapter 6); Critical Race Theory and Black Crit (Chapter 7); LatCrit, Asian Crit, and Tribal Crit (Chapter 8); and Black feminism (Chapter 9), none mention ability. Even when all these critical epistemologies lay claim to some aspect of intersectionality in their formation and application, this literature fails to even include ability/disability in the list of intersectional identities and thus does not substantively engage disability at all. Chapter 10 redresses this blatant omission in critically oriented epistemologies by addressing Disability Studies in Education (DSE) for the first time in relation to organizational theory.

LEADERSHIP DEVELOPMENT ACTIVITIES

ACTIVITY 1: Discussion Questions and Critical Self-reflection on Our Leadership from Black Feminist Epistemologies

Table 9.1 Discussion Questions and Critical Self-reflection on Our Leadership from Black Feminist Epistemologies

Black Feminist Epistemology Theme	Traditional Organizational Theory Category	Discussion//Critical Reflection Questions
Moral Obligation from Within	Leadership Theory	- Do you have a desire to lead for "collective racial and community uplift" and, if so, where does that originate within you? - To what extent do you feel you lead as an outsider within? - To what extent do you believe you have a moral obligation to equity work? If you have a moral obligation, how does your moral obligation to the work sustain you when facing resistance?
Community Other Mothers	Leadership Theory	- To what extent do you feel morally responsible to be an advocate for students who typically struggle in your school and their communities? Name some ways you advocate for students. - Have others supported you in your equity leadership work in a way that you feel you want to give back? Explain.

Black Feminist Epistemology Theme	Traditional Organizational Theory Category	Discussion//Critical Reflection Questions
Education as Political Liberation	Leadership Theory	- How is academic achievement a tool of political liberation? - Leader credibility stems from actual work on behalf of students of color. What actual work have you done in this regard?
Multiple Approaches to Equity	Change Theory	- What have you done to advance racial and equity change at multiple levels?
Leadership as Activism	Leadership and Change Theory	- To what extent do you view yourself as a leader activist?
Everyday Acts of Resistance	Leadership and Change Theory	- Name seemingly "simple, ordinary acts" that you engage in that are disrupting the status quo.
Bridge Leaders	Leadership and Change Theory	- Identify examples where you serve as a bridge between doing critical consciousness work and concrete practices that dismantle racist structures in your school. - What are other ways that you "serve as a bridge for others, to others, and between others" (Horsford, 2012, p. 17)?
Identity Informs Decisions	Decision-making Theory	- Describe how your identity informs your decisions. - To what extent do you recognize that all decisions you make are equity decisions?
Understand Racial History and Interlocking Systems of Oppression	Beyond Traditional Categories of Organizational Theory	- Assess your understanding of the racial history of the U.S.A. and the impact of structural, institutional racism upon schools. What structures and practices continue to be in place in your educational setting that perpetuate this racial oppression?
Challenges		- How have you experienced discrimination/bias in your leadership? - Describe a time where your advocacy for students created push-back from teachers and how you responded. - Describe ways the district could better support you in this racial equity work. - Describe the quality of your mentoring as it relates to being equity focused and supportive of your identities.

ACTIVITY 2: Case Analysis Questions from Black Feminist Epistemologies

1. First, each educator reviews the epistemology case analysis handout below (5 minutes).
2. Individual case analysis: What are the issues in your case from the epistemology? What are the possible solutions in your case from the epistemology? (Write down notes to these questions, 7 to 10 minutes.)
3. With a partner, exchange and read each other's case (5 minutes).
4. With the same partner, share the issues and possible solutions to your case from the epistemology. The partner can add additional ideas they noticed that you may have missed; next, switch partners and repeat (7 minutes each, 14 minutes in total).
5. Due the following week, educators then write up a Black feminist epistemology case analysis – the issues and possible solutions – supported by the literature, and limited to about two to three pages.

Table 9.2 Case Analysis Questions from Black Feminist Epistemology

Black Feminist Epistemology Theme	Traditional Organizational Theory Category	Case Analysis Questions
Moral Obligation from Within	Leadership Theory	- To what extent are the participants in your case acting from a moral obligation within? - To what extent are the participants in your case leading as an outsider within?
Community Other Mothers	Leadership Theory	- To what extent are the participants in your case acting as advocates with individuals along the axis of oppression?
Education as Political Liberation	Leadership Theory	- In your case, to what extent do the participants in your case view education as a tool of political liberation? - In your case, to what extent do the participants hold credibility due in part to their work with typically marginalized communities?
Multiple Approaches to Equity	Change Theory	- To what extent is your case addressing racial and equity change at multiple levels?
Leadership as Activism	Leadership and Change Theory	- To what extent are the participants in your case engaged in activism?
Everyday Acts of Resistance	Leadership and Change Theory	- To what degree are the participants in your case engaged in "simple, ordinary acts" of resistance?

Black Feminist Epistemology Theme	Traditional Organizational Theory Category	Case Analysis Questions
Bridge Leaders	Leadership and Change Theory	- To what extent are the participants in your case engaged in both critical consciousness work and concrete practices that dismantle racist structures in the setting?
Identity Informs Decisions	Decision-making Theory	- How are the participant identities in the case informing decision-making? - To what extent do the actors in your case view all decisions as equity decisions?
Understand Racial History and Interlocking Systems of Oppression	Beyond Traditional Categories of Organizational Theory	- To what extent do the actors in your case understand the racial history of the U.S.A. and the impact of structural, institutional racism upon education? - To what extent does your case address structures and practices in the setting that perpetuate racial oppression?
Challenges		- To what extent does your case suggest push-back to equity work? - What kind of support for anti-racist work is being provided in the upper administration to support that work in the case?

NOTE

1   Adapted from Atlas, B.L.H. & Capper, C.A. (2003). *The spirituality of African-American women principals in urban schools: Toward a reconceptualization of Afrocentric Feminist epistemology.* Paper presented at the Annual Meeting of the American Educational Research Association, Chicago, IL.

REFERENCES

Angel, R., Killacky, J., & Johnson, P.R. (2013). African American women aspiring to the superintendency: Lived experiences and barriers. *Journal of School Leadership, 23,* 595–614.

Atlas, B.L.H. & Capper, C.A. (2003). *The spirituality of African-American women principals in urban schools: Toward a reconceptualization of Afrocentric Feminist epistemology.* Paper presented at the Annual Meeting of the American Educational Research Association, Chicago, IL.

Bass, L. (2012). When care trumps justice: The operationalization of Black feminist caring in educational leadership. *International Journal of Qualitative Studies in Education, 25*(1), 73–87.

Beard, K.S. (2012). Making the case for the outlier: Researcher reflections of an African-American female deputy superintendent who decided to close the achievement gap. *International Journal of Qualitative Studies in Education, 25*(1), 59–71.

Bloom, C.M. & Erlandson, D.A. (2003). African American women principals in urban schools: Realities, (re)constructions, and resolutions. *Educational Administration Quarterly, 39*(3), 339–369.

Collins, P.H. (1991). *Black feminist thought: Knowledge, consciousness, and the politics of empowerment*. New York: Routledge.

Collins, P.H. (1999). Reflections on the outsider within. *Journal of Career Development, 26*(1), 85–88.

Collins, P.H. (2000). *Black feminist thought: Knowledge, consciousness, and the politics of Empowerment* (2nd edn). New York: Routledge.

Dillard, C.B. (1995). Leading with her life: An African American feminist (re)interpretation of leadership for an urban high school principal. *Educational Administration Quarterly, 31*(4), 539–563.

Frattura, E.M. & Capper, C.A. (2015). *Integrated Comprehensive Systems for Equity* (www. icsequity.org).

Gaetane, J.M. (2013). The subtlety of age, gender, and race barriers: A case study of early career African American female principals. *Journal of School Leadership, 13*, 615–639.

Horsford, S.D. (2012). This bridge called my leadership: An essay on Black women as bridge leaders in education. *International Journal of Qualitative Studies in Education*, 25(1), 11–22.

Horsford, S.D. & Tillman, L.C. (2012). Inventing herself: Examining the intersectional identities and educational leadership of Black women in the USA. *International Journal of Qualitative Studies in Education, 25*(1), 1–9.

Loder-Jackson, T.L. (2011). Bridging the legacy of activism across generations: Life stories of African American educators in post-civil rights Birmingham. *Urban Review, 43*, 151–174.

McClellan, P. (2012). Race, gender, and leadership identity: An autoethnography of reconciliation. *International Journal of Qualitative Studies in Education, 25*(1), 89–100.

Newcomb, W.S. & Niemeyer, A. (2015). African American women principals: Heeding the call to serve as conduits for transforming urban school communities. *International Journal of Qualitative Studies in Education, 28*(7), 786–799.

Peters, A.L. (2012). Leading through the challenge of change: African-American women principals on small school reform, *International Journal of Qualitative Studies in Education, 25*(1), 23–38.

Reed, L.C. (2012). The intersection of race and gender in school leadership for three Black female principals. *International Journal of Qualitative Studies in Education, 25*(1), 39–58.

Reed, L. & Evans, A.E. (2008). "What you see is [not] always what you get!" Dispelling race and leadership assumptions. *International Journal of Qualitative Studies in Education, 21*(5), 487–499.

Tillman, L.C. (2009). The never-ending science debate: I'm ready to move on. *Educational Researcher, 38*(6), 458–462.

Theoharis, G. (2007). Social justice educational leaders and resistance: Toward a theory of social justice leadership. *Educational Administration Quarterly, 43*(2), 221–258.

Wilson, C. & Johnson, L. (2015). Black educational activism for community empowerment: International leadership perspectives. *International Journal of Multicultural Education, 17*(1), 102–120.

CHAPTER 10

Disability Studies in Education Epistemology

Disability Studies in Education (DSE) has evolved more recently than the other epistemologies discussed in this book. Similar to feminist poststructuralism (Chapter 6) and Black feminist epistemology (Chapter 9), DSE lies on the radical end of the change continuum within modernism (see Figure 10.1) and has also been heavily influenced by postmodernism (Chapter 6).

To date, not a single published study exists in the field of educational leadership that is conceptually grounded in DSE. Likewise, Disability Studies theory has been minimally addressed in the study of organizations. Williams and Mavin (2012) explain that in spite of "a wider range of theoretical perspectives and voices in organization studies ... disability theory and disabled people's voices have remained marginal" (p. 159). Connor and Gabel (2013) catalogued the research on DSE in education and not a single study addressed leadership, principals, or whole-school social justice approaches. Likewise, disability has been minimally addressed in the field of educational leadership. Capper, Theoharis, and Sebastian (2006) reviewed the literature on social justice leadership preparation in the field and noted that none of the publications addressed disability. To locate implications for leadership preparation related to disability required the authors to review the literature on special education. Across 16 years of equity research in educational leadership as reviewed in Chapter 2, not a single study has been grounded in DSE, and few of these studies examined special education or disability. At the same time, O'Malley and Capper (2015) found in their national study of educational leadership preparation programs that 79.7 percent of the social justice programs claimed they attended to disability in their programs to a moderate or high degree (compared to race/ethnicity 95.4 percent, social class 94.9 percent, and culture 93.8 percent). What we do not know

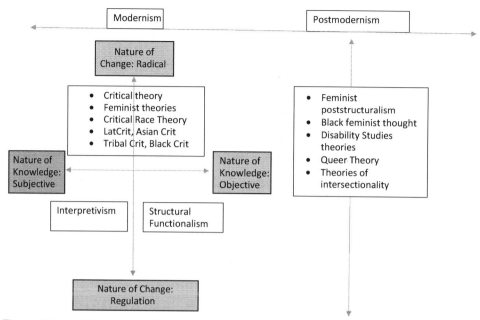

Figure 10.1 An Epistemology Framework

SF
or
critical?

from their study is how disability and special education are attended to, and as I discuss further in this chapter, whether in these programs disability is addressed in structural functional or critical ways.

In this chapter, I first discuss how disability has been addressed in the field of educational leadership. I next review the history of Disability Studies in Education, define it, and discuss its central tenets. I then consider the implications of DSE for the field of educational leadership and how some current research in educational leadership can inform DSE. To close the chapter, I discuss the implications of DSE for organizational theory, including leadership theory, change theory, and decision-making theory.

DISABILITY AND EDUCATIONAL LEADERSHIP

The relationship of disability to the field of educational leadership is depicted in Figure 10.2. The figure shows how disability or special education is typically not addressed in educational leadership at all, even in studies of social justice leadership (Pazey & Cole, 2013). Exceptions are research on principals grappling with the complexities of including students with disabilities in schools (DeMatthews & Mawhinney, 2014; DeMatthews, 2014; Frick, Faircloth, & Little, 2013), case studies of principals implementing inclusive schooling (Hoppey & McLeskey, 2011; Ryan, 2010; Waldron, McLeskey, & Redd, 2011), and entire school districts implementing inclusive practices (Ryndak, Reardon, Benner, & Ward, 2007). The literature also includes calls for principal preparation programs to address special education (Pazey & Cole, 2013). These calls for addressing special education in educational leadership

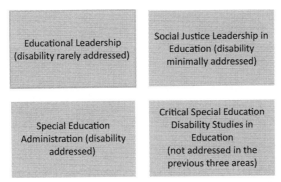

Figure 10.2 How Special Education/Disability is Addressed in Educational Leadership

over the past several decades have been largely ignored by the educational leadership field based on conference/convention sessions, publications, and the latest educational leadership preparation standards. Special education administration continues to stand as a field apart, with its own national and state organization through the umbrella organization Council for Exceptional Children and its associated journals.

The underlying epistemologies of most of the few studies in educational leadership that do address disability or special education are essentially structural functional and uncritical. A critical special education/DSE perspective would ask an entirely different set of questions of these studies which I will discuss further in this chapter. Danforth and Gabel (2006) concur with this assessment:

> [W]ith few exceptions, special education researchers have struggled little with the complexities and ambiguities of social categories, giving little attention to the processes and practices that actively construct disability types in the public schools, and perhaps paying even less attention to the interactions of power and identity across categories of race, class, gender, etc. (Danforth & Gabel, 2006, p. 12)

The way disability has been represented in educational leadership is similar to how Danforth and Gabel (2006) portray Disability Studies and educational research: "educational research has long perpetuated the myth of the need for distinctions between research about disabled students and research about all other students" (p. 3). Only a few scholars (Capper & Frattura, 2008; Frattura & Capper, 2007; Theoharis, 2007, 2010) address students labeled with disabilities and the importance of inclusive practices along with eliminating tracking and pull-out programs as part of an overarching principal leadership for social justice across student differences (e.g., race, social class, ability, gender, sexual/gender identity, language, and their intersections).

DISABILITY STUDIES IN EDUCATION

Connor, Valle, and Hale (2015) offer the most recent history of DSE, building on the histories of Disability Studies in Education by Danforth (2006), Taylor (2006), Connor, Gabel, Gallagher, and Mortond (2008), Baglieri, Valle, Connor, and

Gallagher (2011a), Ferguson and Nusbaum (2012), and Connor and Gabel (2013). A distinct field of Disability Studies formed in the late 1970s across disciplines. In the early 1990s, educators interested in a critical view of special education participated in an international conference on Disability Studies. In 1999, U.S. scholars who considered themselves critical special educators joined together at the first conference in New York City to explore these ideas. Some of these scholars then formed the Disability Studies in Education special interest group of the American Educational Research Association.

DSE as a field of study evolved in part in response to the limits of other critically-oriented epistemologies discussed in previous chapters. Danforth and Gabel (2006) explain how the social justice discourse and the critical epistemologies that inform that discourse often do not address disability:

> Another source of the growing interest in DSE builds from an awareness that the critical educational research traditions – areas that ask serious and deep questions about power, identity, and justice – have left something out. The standard critical trinity of class, race, and gender, even if fortified by constructs such as sexual orientation or immigrant status, fails to provide relevant, persuasive insight into the dynamics of power and identity within public schools by ignoring the most vulnerable students (those with significant cognitive impairment, for example) or by adding-on disability without fully exploring the ways in which disability transforms arguments about power, identity, and justice. (Danforth & Gabel, 2006, p. 3)

According to Danforth and Gabel (2006), DSE is defined as understanding *"what disability means*; how it is interpreted, enacted, and resisted in the social practices of individuals, groups, organizations, and cultures" (p. 5). They further explain:

> Done well, DSE leaves readers with a nagging sense of discomfort with the reified status quo, a lingering pang of guilt for accepting what went unnoticed before, and a flicker of anger over the customs, complacencies, and good intentions that mask social injustices on a daily basis. (Danforth & Gabel, 2006, pp. 6–7)

Taylor (2006) defines DSE as a field that "examines disability in social and cultural context. Constructions of disability are questioned and special education assumptions and practices are challenged" (p. 19).

Tenets of Disability Studies in Education

DSE scholars have been reticent to identify specific DSE tenets, as doing so works against their stance of not wanting to develop another limiting paradigm (Connor, Gabel, Gallagher, & Mortond, 2008). Yet, Connor and colleagues (2008) reported that the DSE special interest group of the American Educational Research

Association agreed on DSE tenets that "centre on engagement in research, policy, and action that:

- contextualize disability within political and social spheres;
- privilege the interests, agendas, and voices of people labelled with disability/ disabled people;
- promote social justice, equitable and inclusive educational opportunities, and full and meaningful access to all aspects of society for people labelled with dis- ability/disabled people; and
- assume competence and reject deficit models of disability" (Connor et al., 2008, p. 447–448).

Ferguson and Nusbaum (2012) identified five core concepts of Disability Studies and considered their implications for individuals with significant intellectual dis- abilities, and scholars and practitioners for whom this aspect of disability is their focus. These five core concepts include: (a)The study of disability must be social. (b) The study of disability must be foundational. (c) The study of disability must be interdisciplinary. (d) The study of disability must be participatory, and (e) The study of disability must be values based.

    With my analysis of the DSE literature, I identified DSE tenets that align with these previous tenets and core concepts, but I also identified additional tenets to inform organizational theory, leadership practice, and research. I derived the tenets from the DSE literature, though DSE scholars may or may not agree that these tenets characterize DSE. I also identify and describe each tenet separately; however, their assumptions are fully integrated, and each informs the other. These seven DSE tenets include (a) hegemony of normalcy, (b) denouncement of labeling, (c) disability is socially constructed, (d) critique of special education (e) importance and critique of inclusion, (f) disability voice, and (g) intersectionality.

Hegemony of Normalcy

According to Baglieri et al (2011c), "There is clearly a normative center around which schools gravitate. Like gravity itself, the force exists despite being invisible (p. 2136) … our aim is not only to focus on the margins, but also, perhaps more critically, to deconstruct the center" (p. 2146). Thus, DSE exposes how all of society is based on a standardized norm, and society deems anyone who does not fit this norm as deficient. Connor and Gabel (2013) refer to the "Hegemony of Normalcy" (p. 101) and explain: "The hegemony of the special–general education bifurcation, therefore, is very much alive and, in turn, continues to reinforce the Hegemony of Normalcy – a concept that has been used in oppressive ways to segregate, mar- ginalize, devalue, and abnormalize children" (Connor & Gabel, 2013, p. 101). DSE scholars believe that "DSE, in concert with other criticalist perspectives, can edu- cate citizens to question school organization, personnel, and practices that perpet- uate the damaging ideologies and discourses of difference that conjure the myth of normal/average/ordinary/typical/standard children" (Baglieri, Bejoian, Broderick, Connor, & Valle, 2011b, p. 2119).

This hegemony of normalcy is pervasive in society and contributes to the pathology of difference. That is, when a student displays learning differences, these differences are pathologized and then we marginalize these students in the name of helping them. As Erevelles (2011) explains, special education holds a "persistent commitment to pathologize difference in order to provide 'appropriate' services in contexts that ultimately exclude" (p. 2157).

This concept of normalcy cuts across race, class, language, ability, gender, gender identity, sexual identity, and their intersections, in that what is considered normal is most often white, male, middle to upper class, for whom English is his first language, heterosexual, able-bodied, and cisgender, and any student who deviates from those identities we often identify as different and deficient. Parallel to the whiteness as property tenet within CRT, the pervasiveness of normalcy renders normalcy as it intersects with identities as valuable property – in Leonardo and Broderick's (2011) terms "smartness as property" – with all the attendant privileges to the best curriculum and education in the school.

Denouncement of Labeling

Student labeling becomes the primary outcome of the hegemony of normalcy, the pathology of difference, and normalcy as property. As Connor and Gabel (2013) explain, "The increasing number of students labeled is evidence of an obsession within education to locate, and then often relocate, children who are viewed as insufficiently normal in behaving, learning, focusing, following instructions, speaking correctly, and so on" (Connor & Gabel, 2013, p. 103). As such, I use the phrase throughout this chapter "students labeled with disabilities" versus students with disabilities. The former phrase makes clear that students have been labeled with disabilities by educators in the school and such labeling is socially constructed, variable, and arbitrary compared to the latter phrase "students with disabilities" that positions the disability within the student: that the student "has" "within them" a disability which represents the medical model of special education that DSE disputes. At the same time, I recognize the prerogative of disability activists who reclaim disability as an identity marker of power and who place disability first for this reason.

Disability is Socially Constructed/An Ideological System

Given that schools and society are centered in normalcy, difference is pathologized, these pathologies are then labeled, and students with these labels are marginalized, DSE scholars believe that disability is socially constructed: "[DSE] … frames disability as a social, cultural, political, and historical phenomenon situated in a specific time and place rather than a medical, scientific, or psychological 'objective fact'" (Baglieri, Bejoian, Broderick, Connor, & Valle, 2011c, p. 2130). That is, disability is not a medical or psychological diagnosis, but a function of the environment and how people respond to difference. The social construction of disability applies not only to non-medical categories such as emotional disturbance and learning disabilities but to all categories that may typically be seen as medical, such as visual impairments. A person may have a visual impairment but how the school responds to and supports the student determines whether the visual impairment becomes a disabling condition in the school.

At the same time, Leonardo and Broderick (2011) discuss the limits of the social construction of disability concept and, instead, that disability should be viewed as an ideological system:

> By locating 'mental retardation,' 'competence,' or 'smartness' primarily as social constructions rather than systems of ideology that operate to constitute and sustain unequal relations of power, there is an as of yet incomplete exploration of the oppressive and mystifying ways in which power and privilege operate. (p. 2219)

Thus, DSE views disability not as a medical diagnosis but as an ideological system that perpetuates structures and systems of power and privilege in schools.

Critique of Special Education

Critical special education served as a precursor to DSE. Because the field of special education is based on a history of normalization and the medical model, DSE practitioners critique special education practice as it is typically conceived with its emphasis on identification, labels, interventions, and subsequent isolation and segregation. Special education operates as one of the primary managers and perpetuators of normalcy in the school. In the special education administration literature, the goal of special education leadership is to manage special education programs to be as efficient and effective as possible, and the focus of leadership is often legal compliance. Special education administration focuses unquestioningly on child deficits and not on how the school has created and perpetuated those deficits and the ideological systems of oppression that create and perpetuate deficits. In contrast, from a critical special education perspective, Connor and Gabel (2013) explain, "By focusing on the overall system rather than on the child as the site of responsibility, teachers and scholars in the field of DS engage in combating structural ableism that is embedded in the everyday arrangements of schooling" (p. 107)

Importance and Critique of Inclusion

Most DSE scholars advocate for inclusive practices as a matter of civil rights for individuals labeled with disabilities and an associated curriculum that is universally designed (Connor & Gabel, 2013). Yet, DSE scholars point out the ironic limits of inclusive practices, arguing that most inclusion stops at inclusive spaces and does not address curriculum and other school features that are not inclusive across student differences (Baglieri et al., 2011b, 2011c; Erevelles, 2011). Further, educators often view inclusion as including students within an ideological norm and as a form of "assimilation and normalization rather than changing and actually moving toward coexistence within a broader notion of diversity" (Valle, Connor, Broderick, Bejoian, & Baglieri, 2011, p. 2285). Erevelles (2011) agrees and argues: "inclusion as it is currently conceived, appears more as a synonym for assimilation and normalization, then we need to challenge the ways its rhetoric efficiently manages difference by allowing schools to essentially stay the same" (p. 2159). As such, DSE scholars argue for the following parameters around inclusive practices:

> that inclusive education (a) is fundamentally about all learners (rather than just about disabled learners), (b) is fundamentally about striving to make all learners' experiences with schooling inclusive and participatory rather than exclusionary and marginalizing (rather than just being concerned with where particular learners are physically placed), and (c) is concerned with aspirations for democratic and socially just education, and therefore fundamentally concerned with interrogating the cultural practices of schooling (rather than just seeking to prescribe procedural, techno-rational definitions of inclusive schooling to be implemented). (Baglieri et al., 2011c, p. 2128)

While most educators claim that their schools are "inclusive" or that they practice inclusion of students with disabilities, educators most often practice many different iterations of what I call the ironic limits of inclusion (Scanlan, 2006). The eight ironic limits of schools which claim to be practicing inclusion, not all of which are fully addressed in the DSE literature, include the following: (a) students labeled with disabilities are included only in particular courses or classes for parts of the day, (b) only students with particular disability labels are included (e.g., students labeled with learning disabilities) but students with significant intellectual disabilities are included only in limited ways or not at all, (c) some students labeled with disabilities are included but only within lower track courses in co-teaching models, (d) students labeled with disabilities are included in particular classrooms/processes, while students labeled English Language learners (ELL) are included only in certain other classrooms, (e) students labeled with disabilities are included for part of the day, but students with other labels (e.g., response to intervention, students who are ELL, students labeled gifted) are pulled out for parts of the day, (f) the over identification of students labeled with disabilities (more than 10–12%) is ignored, such that inclusion is happening in a context where the needless labeling of students is not addressed, (g) a concern for student labeling is highlighted, but students who are labeled speech and language are not considered in this labeling, even though students from low income families and students who are linguistically diverse are often over-labeled for speech and language and they and their families are signaled as deficient as a result, and segregated for parts of the day for this deficit, and (h) inclusive practices are targeted only for students labeled with disabilities and the needs of other students, such as students experiencing teasing and bullying because of their gender identity are not addressed (Baglieri et al., 2011b, 2011c). As to the latter point, Erevelles

(2011) concurs and argues: "the rhetoric of inclusion currently in vogue does little to critique how Other students, not just students with recognizable disabilities, are excluded by the normative discourses of schooling" (Erevelles, 2011, p. 2159).

Theoharis (2007, 2010; Theoharis & Haddix, 2011) remains one of the few scholars who has studied social justice principals and their inclusive practices related to students with disabilities and students labeled ELL (Theoharis & O'Toole, 2011). What we do not know from Theoharis's work is the extent to which any of the ironic limits of inclusion were taking place in the schools that were studied. Likewise, we have experienced schools devoted to community-building processes and classrooms engaging in community-building activities while students with disabilities are pulled out of the classroom and excluded from the community-building activity, or districts committed to racial consciousness work while students labeled with disabilities are bussed across the district and are unable to attend their neighborhood schools. In sum, I agree with Graham and Slee (2008), who argue that "inclusive education is now no longer a progressive educational practice because it is more often used to explain, defend, and protect the status quo" (cited in Erevelles, 2011, p. 2158).

Disability Voice

Similar to Critical Race Theory, DSE advocates what could be considered counter-narratives – seeking the perspectives of individuals with disabilities. I extend this tenet to include the perspectives of individuals with disabilities but also families and students across differences. In Theoharis's (2010) study, the principals ensured that staff were involved in decisions about the school and the principals explicitly reached out to typically marginalized families to engage them with the school. Ryan's (2010) study of principals at a new inclusive school also described how the principals extensively involved the participation of students, staff, and families in school decision-making.

Intersectionality

None of the DSE definitions or DSE tenets I reviewed explicitly addressed intersectionality. Some DSE scholars have described how the deficit perspectives of some educators:

> about *certain* children according to race, social class, and dis/ability results in referrals for pseudoscientific testing, the inscription of labels, and the likelihood of situating these students outside the general classroom – a literal placement outside of the norm. Echoing the concerns of Leonardo and Broderick (2011), the authors likewise identify school practices that reinforce intelligence as whiteness (and conversely, disability as color) and argue for a conscious shift toward cultural responsiveness in pedagogical practices and structural arrangements. (Valle et al., 2011, p. 2286)

Thus, even though some DSE scholars acknowledge how students of color, of low income, and labeled with disabilities are similarly marginalized in schools, these scholars do not identify the intersections of these identities.

Some DSE scholars address the "double jeopardy" of students of color, including their over-representation in special education, and how, once they are identified for special education they are placed in more segregated settings than white students labeled with disabilities (Fierros & Conroy, 2002; Zion & Blanchett, 2011). Zion and Blanchett examined the intersection of race, social class, and ability in their critique of inclusion in the United States that continues to segregate and marginalize students of color. Recent DSE scholarship examines the theoretical intersections of Disability Studies in Education and Critical Race Theory (DisCrit) and the intersections of race, gender, and social class (Annamma, Connor, & Ferri, 2013; Connor, Ferri, Annamma, 2015), Other DSE scholars have examined the intersections of disability, race, social class, and sexual identity (Erevelles, 2011).

In sum, seven tenets of DSE include (a) the hegemony of normalcy, (b) denouncement of labeling, (c) disability is socially constructed/an ideological system, (d) critique of special education, (e) the importance and critique of inclusion, (f) disability voice, and (g) intersectionality. In the next section, I consider the implications of these DSE tenets for educational leadership and organizational theory.

IMPLICATIONS OF DSE FOR EDUCATIONAL LEADERSHIP AND ORGANIZATIONAL THEORY

In this section, I consider the implications of DSE for educational leadership to build the foundation for further implications for organizational theory. DSE demands a different set of questions and lens for disability and special education in educational leadership than previously asked. The limited research studies in educational leadership related to disability and special education have all made important contributions to the field. I take a similar view of this research as do Leonardo and Broderick (2011) in their critiques of Disability Studies and whiteness studies in that "although we [can] take theoretical and political strategies from [this work], [this work] on its own is theoretically and politically incomplete" (Leonardo & Broderick, 2011, p. 2225).

Danforth and Gabel (2006) acknowledge that one major critique of DSE is its limited connection to practice and lack of consideration of how practice can inform DSE. To that end, a recent text in DSE includes practice in the title, *Practicing disability studies in education. Acting toward social change* (Connor, Valle, & Hale, 2014). This text includes a section on applying DSE to educational practices, yet all the papers in that section focus on higher education. This lack of implications for practice in DSE is due in part to the, at times, conceptual complexity of DSE, but also it can be difficult to imagine DSE in practice without re-inscribing oppressive ideologies of normalcy while doing so. In this sense, when considering DSE for educational leadership practice, we are always working against limits of normalcy, though, at the same time, we are always working to expand those limits.

Even with these limits, however, Theoharis's scholarship (2010) on social justice principals identifies explicit strategies they employed to address inequities in their schools – practices that align with DSE theory and the DSE tenets I discussed previously. While no studies in educational leadership have been conceptually framed by DSE, nonetheless, DSE scholars have much to learn from some of the limited research in educational leadership on the practical strategies of school principals leading for social justice. Theoharis's (2010) study of social justice leaders provides one exemplar of DSE for leadership practice to eliminate inequities from which DSE scholars could learn.

To review, Theoharis (2010) studied six social justice public school principals at the elementary, middle, and high school levels who were working toward eliminating inequities in their schools. Their schools each evidenced equity data toward that end related to achievement, attendance, and suspensions among other data. Theoharis did not rely on DSE as the conceptual framework for his study; however, the strategies these principals employed to eliminate inequities reflect some of the DSE tenets. I rely on examples from Theoharis's (2010) study to illustrate four implications of DSE for educational leadership and organizational theory toward equitable ends: (1) dissolve the hegemonic normative core, (2) denounce labeling, (3) engage in substantive inclusion, and (4) critique special education.

Dissolve the Hegemonic Normative Core

All the principals in Theoharis's (2010) study anchored their leadership in inclusive practices across student differences, not for assimilation or normalization, but in a way that sought to transform the core of teaching and learning to be responsive across student differences. Theoharis describes the situation:

> The principals described the conditions they found upon starting at their respective schools as built on norms that separated students into various fragmented programs. In these programs, students of color, students from low-income families, students learning English, and students with disabilities were continually removed from general education classes to receive a fragmented curriculum from a range of teachers, much of which did not have a connection to the core or general education curriculum of the school" (p. 341–342).

As such, the first injustice the principals addressed were "School structures that marginalize, segregate, and impede achievement" (p. 341). The strategies the principals engaged in to disrupt this injustice included: "(a) Eliminate pullout/segregated programs, (b) Increase rigor and access to opportunities, (c) Increase student learning time, and (d) Increase accountability systems on the achievement of all students" (p. 341). These principals truly practiced what DSE scholars call for, including substantive inclusion, beyond the rhetoric, and that moves beyond spacial inclusion (Erevelles, 2011). Their inclusive practices were not just about general education space but also included dissolving the normative core of the school

(Baglieri et al., 2011b) and establishing a rigorous and responsive curriculum, a welcoming and inclusive community, and developing staff capacity to effectively teach across student differences.

Importantly, among the strategies the principals in Theoharis's (2010) study employed to address injustices did not include a "hunt for" deficiencies in students (Baker, 2002) by evaluating students, diagnosing the students as deficient, and then labeling them under the guise that their teachers could better support them. The principals in Theoharis's (2010) study did not focus on more effective special education practices or ensure that responses to interventions were implemented with fidelity (Ferri, 2012). They did not spend time on restructuring the school day to ensure that particular students were identified and sorted into "intervention blocks." These principals were not engaged in inclusive practices to make their students more normal. They did not label, segregate, and marginalize students in the name of helping them. These principals did not pathologize student differences nor perseverate on screening, early identification, labeling, and progress monitoring in the name of helping. The principals did not seek to fix the students or their families.

Instead, all the principals' efforts to address the injustices in their schools focused on changes that the principal and staff could make, locating students' issues as a problem of the system, not of the students and their families. In addition to the four strategies the principals engaged in to address injustice which I discussed previously, Theoharis identified three additional injustices and eight strategies to respond to those injustices – none of which blames or focuses on fixing students or families (see Table 10.1).

Table 10.1 Injustices and Principal Strategies to Disrupt (Theoharis, 2010)

Injustice 2: Deprofessionalized teaching staff

Strategies to disrupt

- Address issues of race.
- Provide ongoing staff development focused on building equity.
- Hire and supervise for justice.
- Empower staff.

Injustice 3: A disconnect with the community, low-income families, and families of color

Strategies to disrupt

- Create a warm and welcoming climate.
- Reach out intentionally to the community and marginalized families.
- Incorporate social responsibility into the school curriculum.

Injustice 4: Disparate and low student achievement

Strategies to disrupt

- Confluence of all efforts and strategies.

Denounce Labeling

DSE suggests that educational leadership scholars and practicing leaders must become critically conscious about the extensive damaging problems of labeling, including disability labels, speech/language labels, RtI labels, gifted labels, tracking labels, and ability grouping labels. Hattie and Yates (2014) report that not labeling students has an effect size of .61 on student learning (with .40 effect size as the hinge point above which has a larger impact on student learning). DSE suggests that educational leadership research that considers special education or disability must not tacitly accept, but instead take a critical perspective on the growing numbers of students labeled with disabilities as a problem not within the students themselves (e.g., that there are just simply more students with disabilities), but as a problem of how educators respond to students who learn differently, intent on preserving the normative core of the school, as discussed in Chapter 3 (this volume). Thus, from a DSE epistemology, this aversion to labeling necessitates working to dismantle separate programs that require a need for labels in the first place such as Response to Intervention, lower tracked courses, or alternative schools.

In addition, research in educational leadership that addresses disability or special education should include the extent to which students in the setting are labeled as one of the contexts of inquiry. Two concerning aspects of Theoharis's (2010) study regarding labeling emerged. First, four of the six principals' schools labeled an extraordinarily high percentage of students with a disability, ranging from 20 to 25 percent. Yet, federal law suggests that about 8 to 10 percent or fewer of students should be considered as having a disability across all schools. (Given the constructs of DSE, I realize that this 8 to 10 percent could be contested as to why even this lower percentage of students needs to be labeled). In schools that are working to widen or dissolve the normative core of schools to encompass all student differences, the percentage of students labeled with disabilities drops, in many schools by half (Frattura & Capper, 2015). Moreover, schools engaged in intensive early literacy result in far fewer students labeled with learning disabilities. Yet, none of the principals in Theoharis's study identified the high percentage of students labeled with disabilities in their school as an issue, and none of their social justice strategies resulted in fewer students requiring special education services.

Further, Theoharis (2010) reports that the percentage of students labeled with disabilities in these schools did not include students labeled for speech and language. Educators tend to downplay the negative consequences of students being labeled for speech/language, yet the ascription of this label and response to the label is much the same as any other disability label – including pathologizing the child's speech and language and remediating via pull-out programs. Further, students from low-income families and students who are linguistically diverse, or both, are often over-identified for speech/language programs. Related to the previous points, principals may work to provide speech/language services within general education and develop the capacity of teachers to address speech and language needs across the school day to avoid the negative consequences of pull-out programs. Yet, in do-ing so, they are not addressing why so many students have been labeled for speech and language and the extensive negative ramifications of this labeling in the first place.

In addition, much research has drawn attention to the over-representation of students of color in special education and that students of color, once identified, receive more segregated placements than do white students labeled with disabilities (Zion & Blanchett, 2011). Yet, DSE scholars point out that even if students of color were proportionally represented, it leaves unexamined students being identified and labeled in the first place (Leonardo & Broderick, 2011). Thus, students could be racially proportionally represented in special education, but if a high percentage of students are labeled with a disability, disproportionality is not the underlying problem.

In sum, DSE suggests that principals must become critically conscious about the extensive damaging effects of student labels. Addressing this issue will require a dismantling of separate programs that require students being labeled in the first place. Further, research in educational leadership related to student differences, in-cluding research on social justice leadership, leadership related to racial inequities, and related equity research, should include the percentage of students labeled as a context for this research, critically address the multiple ways and extent to which students are labeled as part of the study, and report how principals are working to reduce the need for programs that require such labels.

Engage in Substantive Inclusion

DSE suggests that research and practice in educational leadership must focus on substantive inclusion, defined based on four interrelated parameters. These four parameters include (a) Applies to all students, (b) Transform the instruc-tional core, (c) Inclusion limits based on the school, and (d) Effective inclusion implementation

Applies to all students. First, substantive inclusion applies to all students in the school and not just to students labeled with disabilities, including, for example, students labeled English Language Learners, students struggling with reading, and students who are LGBTIQ – across literally all students and all student differences and their intersections. DSE scholars argue that the ways students identified with disabilities are excluded reflect larger exclusion issues across the school for other students who are marginalized (Erevelles, 2011).

According to Theoharis (2010), "Inclusive schooling is a necessary and enriching component to enacting justice" (p. 368). The social justice principals in Theoharis's (2010) study focused not only on students with disabilities, or students of color, or African American students. They discussed strategies that advanced the learning for literally all students, including students labeled with disabilities, students from low-income families, students of color, and students who were culturally and lin-guistically diverse and their intersections (the principals, however, did not mention gender, gender identity, or sexual identity). Theoharis explicitly defined what he meant by social justice leaders:

> These principals advocate, lead, and keep at the center of their practice and vision issues of race, class, gender, disability, sexual orientation, and other historically and currently marginalizing conditions in the United States. This definition centers on addressing and eliminating marginalization in schools. In doing so, inclusive schooling practices for students with disabilities, English language learners, and other students traditionally segregated in schools are also necessitated by this definition. (Theoharis, 2007, p. 222, cited in Theoharis, 2010, p. 333)

It is also implied that principals are responsible for literally all students in their schools, and that responsibility should not be passed off to special education teachers and administrators (DeMatthews & Mawhinney, 2014; Pazey & Cole, 2015).

Thus, when conducting research on inclusive practices in schools, DSE suggests that we include information about all students. This does not mean that we cannot learn from studies of principals' practices that zone in on a particular identity, for example, including students with significant cognitive disabilities (and their intersections of race and social class) across the curriculum. Such studies, however, should provide information on the context of this effort related to inclusive practices across the school for all students.

Transform the instructional core. Second, and related to this point, substantive inclusion concerns itself with transforming all aspects of the school, particularly the instructional core and culture of the school toward equity ends, working to "dissolve the normative center" (Baglieri et al., 2011c). Given this parameter, then, when educational leadership scholarship and practice address inclusive practices, such practices cannot and should not be considered an "inclusion program," an "inclusion model," or an "inclusion initiative" as doing so renders this work as something separate from the normative center of schooling – essentially a structural functional rendering of inclusive practices. This structural functional approach to inclusion, as DSE scholars point out, often yields "inclusion classrooms," "inclusion students," or "inclusion teachers" (Baglieri et al., 2011c).

These "inclusion classrooms" are frequently structured around a "co-teaching model" where a special education teacher is paired with a general education teacher (Baglieri et al., 2011c). Yet, Frattura and Capper (2015) point out how co-teaching perpetuates inequities. That is, from elementary through high school, students with disabilities are often segregated into these co-taught classrooms in numbers much higher than their proportional representation in the school. At the high school level, often these classrooms/courses include students without disability labels who are also struggling, constituting lower track classrooms. General education teachers become dependent on the special education teacher in the classroom. The goal of the special education teacher in these classrooms is usually one of supporting students, rather than further developing the capacity of the general education teacher to effectively teach all students to the point that the special education teacher is no longer needed in the classroom.

These references to inclusive practices ironically assume that inclusion is a separate program apart from the core of the school, or what I call "segregated inclusion." Thus, DSE suggests that research needs to move beyond questioning principals about their "inclusion program" or their "inclusion model" (as simply one ideologically neutral choice among many such choices) for students labeled with disabilities, as uncritically doing so perpetuates oppressive ideologies and structures. Instead, DSE suggests that research should consider how principals are addressing the normative core of schooling across student differences. They may find that principals are implementing inclusive practices in segregated, structural functional ways, and those findings should be problematized relative to DSE.

Inclusion limits based on the school. An uncritical special education perspective approaches the degree to which students are included based on "student needs" and "best interest of students" – again locating disability within the student. Instead, a third parameter of substantive inclusion assumes that any limits of inclusion are not because of the student, but are due to the not yet realized potential of educators and the school. Valle and colleagues (2011) argue, "Legitimizing widespread segregation as 'special' is both a misnomer and disservice to all children. And yet most teachers uncritically regard special education referrals as 'doing what is best' for students" (p. 2290). According to Erevelles (2011),

> Inclusive education is, now, no longer the radical idea it was once purported to be. In fact, most schools would say that they do some form of inclusive education in which students with disabilities are included in the least restrictive environment *best suited to their educational needs.* (emphasis added. pp. 2157–2158)

DeMatthews and Mawhinney (2014) describe the limits of inclusive practices and the complexities around inclusion from this "not-yet" perspective, with the limiting factor on how or to what extent students are included dependent on the unrealized capacity of the school and educators:

> Principals who choose to segregate students cannot promote inclusion and do not reflect values of social justice. School leaders are responsible for establishing a school culture that rejects segregation and inequitable treatment. Their daily work must reflect this responsibility. Yet, scholars must recognize the inclusion of all students may not be immediately obtainable during transitional reform periods (schools moving from segregation to full inclusion) because inclusive reforms often confront obstacles that cannot be remedied in the short term. (p. 851)

DeMatthews and Mawhinney's point is different from when educators believe that "our school cannot meet the students' needs" as a reason to not accept students into the school or segregate students. Instead, this parameter of substantive inclusion suggests that educators take the stance that they are unsure how to dissolve and transform the normative core of the school to integrate a particular student but are committed to do so, and committing to working continually toward that end.

Effective inclusion implementation. A fourth parameter related to substantive inclusion examines the complexities of inclusive practices without calling into question the effectiveness of the inclusion implementation that may have perpetuated the inclusion complexities in the first place. That is, in some educational leadership research related to disability, inclusion complexities are attributed to inclusive practices themselves, and not to poor implementation of inclusive practices related to the previous three parameters. It is beyond the scope of this chapter to delve into a deep diagnosis of the literature on the complexities of inclusion to determine the extent to which the identified complexities are attributable to implementation errors per the literature, rather than inclusion itself. Here, I identify a few examples to illustrate this fourth parameter.

DeMatthews and Mawhinney (2014) describe the complexities and contradictions of inclusive practices which two principals faced, both of whom were committed to inclusion. In one case, the district initiated inclusion of students with disabilities across the district, focused only on students with disabilities – singularly focused on place – and did not address the normative core of schooling across student differences. The "initiative" took place in a context of rampant district segregation, under three court orders, that included segregated schools only for students with disabilities and students with disabilities over-placed in residential and out of district placements.

The principal established co-teaching with particular classrooms identified as the "inclusion classrooms" with a general education teacher and special education teacher assigned to the classrooms, a practice which has been previously critiqued in this chapter (DeMatthews & Mawhinney, 2014). The principal also struggled to include students with behavioral issues and felt overwhelmed by the number of students with behavioral issues in her school; she thus advised some parents of students with behavioral challenges in the neighborhood that their children should attend a different school – in opposition to district policy. What we do not know from the case is the extent to which the principal attempted to work with the district office in ways to ensure that all students in the school's neighborhood could attend her school, regardless of disability.

Because some parents of students with disabilities protested the inclusion, the principal maintained segregated classrooms for four to five students labeled with disabilities whose parents did not want them included (DeMatthews & Mawhinney, 2014). What we do not know from the study is the extent to which the principal educated all parents about inclusive practices. We also do not know whether she planned for the inclusion process to take place over several years and how she would phase in the inclusion of all students, and thus the segregation of some students was part of a time-limited process in implementation.

The principal also wanted to hire another special education teacher and social worker but to do so required the principal to take funds away from an after-school tutoring program for all students (DeMatthews & Mawhinney, 2014). Relative to this point, we do not know the percentage of students with disabilities labeled in the school; thus we do not know whether additional staff were needed because students were over-identified with disabilities in the first place. Further, we do not know to what extent the principal sought to develop staff capacity to be effective with a range of learners in lieu of hiring more staff.

In sum, DSE suggests that substantive inclusion for educational leadership practice and research requires four parameters. First, substantive inclusion applies to all students, not only to students labeled with disabilities. Second, substantive inclusion concerns itself with transforming all aspects of the school, particularly the instructional core and dismantling pull-out, tracking, and other programs that segregate and marginalize students. Third, substantive inclusion does not make excuses about the degree to which students are included based on "student needs," but, instead, holds the educators and school responsible for the not realized potential of inclusive practices in the school. Fourth, the potential of substantive inclusion is based on effective inclusive implementation that relies on the three previously mentioned substantive inclusive parameters.

Critique Special Education

In addition to dissolving the hegemonic normative core, a denouncement of labeling and substantive inclusion, a fourth related implication of DSE for educational leadership and organizational theory requires a critique of special education. Without a doubt, the initial Public Law 94–142 that required all public schools to provide a free, appropriate, public education to students labeled with disabilities was with good intent, and without such a law thousands of children with disabilities may never have been provided or continue to be provided with access to public schools. At the same time, the research is clear that the public school outcomes of students labeled with disabilities can no longer be defended, including low achievement with 12 percent reading at or above proficient (Chudowsky & Chudowsky, 2009; National Assessment of Academic Progress, 2015), low graduation rates of a mere 61 percent (Stetser & Stillwell, 2014), and low post-school employment with a mean hourly wage of $9.40 (Sanford et al., 2011). Scholarship and practice in educational leadership related to special education and disability can no longer unquestioningly accept special education and the special education knowledge base as it is. From a DSE perspective, the goal cannot be to make special education better or more effective, but to work at changing the normative core of schooling across student differences. As Slee (2007) argues, inclusive schooling "is not the adaptation or refinement of special education. It is a fundamental rejection of special education's and regular education's claims to be inclusive. Inclusion demands that we address the politics of exclusion and representation" (p. 164, cited in DeMatthews & Mawhinney, 2014, p. 851).

Just as scholars in educational leadership could not defend uncritically including literature in their preparation programs that take a deficit view of students and families of color or students from low-income homes, from a DSE perspective, then, educational leaders cannot justify including literature in leadership preparation that takes an uncritical view of special education. Although a few publications over the past several decades have called for more attention to special education integrated throughout leadership preparation programs, I offer a different opinion. Given the uncritical view of special education in most of these publications, I oppose the suggestion of integrating uncritical special education into educational leadership preparation. To do so perpetuates all that we do not want schools to be related to deficit ideology, labeling and removing students, and ignoring the negative outcomes of special education. Uncritically including special education and disability in educational leadership preparation programs perpetuates the marginalization of students and an ideological system that reproduces unequal power relations (Leonardo & Broderick, 2011). As such, from a DSE perspective, educational leadership preparation programs are better off not addressing special education or disability at all than addressing these topics in uncritical ways as discussed in this chapter.

IMPLICATIONS FOR ORGANIZATIONAL THEORY

Given these implications of DSE for educational leadership, DSE offers several implications for organizational theory. One central implication is that though traditional organizational theory parses out leadership theory, change theory, and decision-making theory, with equity and social justice leadership, these theories are all intertwined and cannot be separated. Social justice leadership is anchored in change and decision-making toward equitable ends. Equity change requires a particular kind of leadership and decision-making as reflected in this chapter. All decisions are equity decisions, and require social justice leadership and understanding about change processes to implement equity decisions. I begin this discussion with change theory, as change theory related to equity change informs leadership and decision-making.

Change Theory

The DSE literature critiques current practices and at times mentions the possibilities of what could be, but this literature does not discuss the process of change toward equitable ends. As demonstrated in this chapter, the limited literature on social justice educational leadership and how principals and educators are changing schools toward those ends can inform the DSE literature.

DSE for social justice leadership suggests four implications for change theory. First, equity change, such as substantive inclusion, requires both ideological and technical change (Ferguson & Nusbaum, 2012). One without the other is not enough. As such, dissolving the normative core as part of the work of substantive inclusion requires a seismic internal and external shift – not only a shift of one's worldview of normativity, but also to learn new skills and new roles and responsibilities. Although educational leaders will face resistance at both the ideological and technical levels, technical resistance is most often due to ideological resistance. Educators are more apt to problem-solve proactively to implement substantive inclusion when they believe ideologically in such change – when their set of inner core beliefs align with substantive inclusion practices.

The ideological aspect of substantive inclusion also helps explain the resistance to such change that educational leaders can expect. Similar to the discussion on

resistance discussed in Chapter 7 on Critical Race Theory, leading to implement substantive inclusion means leading against literally centuries of exclusion and the normative core that anchors the founding history and development of public education in
the United States. All educators have been professionally prepared and licensed under
the assumptions of the normative core of schools; nearly all professional development
and all federal and state law and policy foster the normative core and work against
substantive inclusion. Education professionals and schools continue to be rewarded
and affirmed for sustaining the normative core. As such, most education professionals
hold tightly to their beliefs and practices – that these beliefs and practices are fundamentally the right beliefs and practices, and that changes in practice that substantive
inclusion demands will fundamentally harm students. Many educators hold these
beliefs even in the face of all countervailing evidence from their own equity data that
reveal stark inequities for students labeled with disabilities and inequities across student differences and from the research that supports substantive inclusion.

Second, DSE can inform change theory by considering who is required to make
the equity change. That is, what are the social identities of those being asked to
change toward equitable ends? In this case, the vast majority of public school educators are white, with the teaching profession dominated by white females and administrators mostly represented by white males. Thus, from an unconscious white
perspective, whites bear no personal consequences when we maintain the normative
core through our ideological beliefs and practices. If the normative core remains,
our personal and professional lives and the lives of our families without labels can
continue not only without harm and continue to be comfortable, but also continue
to prosper. Changing one's ideological beliefs and practices will be personally and
professionally difficult. Further, whites will question whether our own children or
loved ones will continue to prosper if the normative core dissolves.

At the same time, some urban school districts employ a majority of administrators of color (e.g., Milwaukee), or some districts in Texas include a majority of administrators who are Latino, as discussed in Chapter 7 (Alemán, 2009; Khalifa et al.,
2014). In such districts we would expect that the resistance to substantive inclusion
would be less formidable; that educators of color would be supportive and advocates for dissolving the normative core and its accompanying systems of oppression.
However, all of us, regardless of identity, are impacted by white racism and regimes
of oppression such that some people of color then also collude with the systems of
oppression in place (Alemán, 2009; Khalifa et al., 2014).

Third, as discussed in the section on the parameters of substantive inclusion,
change toward substantive inclusion informed by DSE means that such change is
always partial and incomplete, and thus lifelong and never finished. Such change
eludes the neat and tidy change process articulated in traditional change theory
from initiation, to implementation, to continuation (Fullan, 2007). McKenzie et al.
(2008) affirm that no perfect social justice school exists:

> A leader may be strong in some aspects of social justice, such as including
> students with disabilities, but weak in addressing the needs of students who
> are English-language learners inclusively. Nevertheless, our goal in preparing

leaders for social justice is that they become equally "expert" across student differences, that is, while striving toward this goal, a leader's area of expertise may be uneven. What we are aiming for is that the leaders realize their unevenness in the application of social justice and strive to close the gap between the ideal and the application. The same can be said of the instantiation of social justice in schools, that is, although students in these schools have made significant academic gains compared to other schools and although these leaders are determined to continue to make academic progress, the fact remains that not every single student in these schools is high achieving, although that is the goal. Thus, while persistently working toward the goal of high achievement for literally every single student, social justice may not be fully and completely accomplished, yet. (p. 116)

As a fourth implication for organizational theory, DSE suggests that the positionality of the change within schools and districts determines the extent to which the normative core is disrupted. For example, schools and districts often move forward with equity work and do not address disability or special education as part of that work. Often in these districts, directors of special education and student services are not centrally included on the district leadership team addressing inequities. Other districts initiate an "inclusion initiative" as detailed in DeMatthews and Mawhinney's study (2014), completely separate from other work in which the district is involved. Neither approach will lead to substantive inclusion. Substantive inclusion is only possible when special education constitutes a key aspect of the equity process.

In sum, DSE suggests four implications for organizational change theory: (a) equity change requires both ideological and technical change, (b) the identities of those involved in the changes impacts how and the extent to which change will take place; (c) equity change is non-linear, a lifelong process at the individual and institutional levels, and (d) the positionality of the change within schools and districts relative to other work in which the schools and districts are engaged determines the extent to which the normative core is disrupted.

Leadership Theory

DSE offers two implications for leadership theory. First, that leaders are responsible for literally all students in their school. Equity principals cannot only focus on race or social class, and ignore other dimensions of identity and difference and their intersections. Equity principals cannot make as their primary goal including students with disabilities and not address race, social class, sexual/gender identity, and their intersections. They must literally become responsible for all students in the school because they recognize that though identity histories are unique, the ideological systems of oppression in response to these differences are similar.

Second, leadership for equity must expect and anticipate resistance to this work given that leadership for social justice is pushing back centuries of historical, societal, and structural oppression – that this work is truly civil rights work. Hence this leadership demands the development of leadership teams at the school and district levels to lead the work forward in their settings in collaboration with the communities in which the school and districts are embedded.

Decision-making Theory

DSE suggests that all decisions are about equity. Theoharis states, "[The social justice principals] saw their commitment to the achievement of marginalized students, as one principal described, as 'permeating everything I did, every decision I made, every conversation I had, and every part of my leadership'" (p. 363). Not only are all administrative decisions about equity, but these decisions must be worked out in collaboration with demographically representative communities.

In sum, this chapter has reviewed the literature on disability, organizations, and leadership and explicated the major tenets of Disability Studies theory. The chapter then considered the implications of DSE for leadership practice and organizational theory, moving beyond and denouncing calls for consideration of special education for educational leadership. Next, Chapter 11 turns to Queer Theory and its implications for organizational theory and educational leadership.

LEADERSHIP DEVELOPMENT ACTIVITIES

After reading the chapter, leadership development activities that I describe next for Disability Studies in Education (DSE) include: (1) discussion questions for whole-class discussion; (2) critical analysis of the educator's own leadership, and (3) case study analysis. It is best to work through all the activities in the order they are presented here.

ACTIVITY 1:   Discussion Questions for Disability Studies in Education Epistemology

1. What are the organizational goals?
2. What does leadership look like?
3. How is the organization structured?
4. What does organizational culture look like?
5. What does decision-making look like?
6. What does change look like?
7. What aspects of education emanate from this epistemology?
8. What is the goal of education?
9. What does the curriculum look like?
10. What does instruction look like?
11. What does assessment look like?
12. What does evaluation/supervision look like?
13. How does this epistemology respond to differences and diversity?

ACTIVITY 2: Critical Reflection on Your Own Leadership from Disability Studies Theory and Epistemology

1. Discuss your leadership strengths relative to addressing the (a) hegemony of normalcy and dissolving the hegemonic normative core, (b) denouncement of labeling, (c) substantive inclusion, (d) critique of special education, (e) importance and critique of inclusion, (f) disability voice, and (g) intersectionality.

2. Discuss how your leadership for equity could be strengthened relative to addressing the (a) hegemony of normalcy and dissolving the hegemonic normative core, (b) denouncement of labeling, (c) substantive inclusion, (d) critique of special education, (e) importance and critique of inclusion, (f) disability voice, and (g) intersectionality.

ACTIVITY 3: Case Analysis Questions

1. Discuss how the problem(s) of the case is relate to the DSE tenets: (a) hegemony of normalcy, (b) denouncement of labeling, (c) disability is socially constructed, (d) critique of special education, (e) importance and critique of inclusion, (f) disability voice, and (g) intersectionality.

2. Discuss how the problem(s) in the case can be informed by the four implications of DSE for educational leadership and organizational theory toward equitable ends: (a) dissolve the hegemonic normative core, (b) denouncement of labeling, (c) substantive inclusion, and (d) critique of special education.

3. Discuss how the problem(s) in the case can be informed by (a) change theory, (b) leadership theory, and (c) decision-making theory as informed by DSE.

4. Discuss possible solutions to your case per the DSE tenets: (a) hegemony of normalcy, (b) denouncement of labeling, (c) disability is socially constructed, (d) critique of special education, (e) importance and critique of inclusion, (f) disability voice, and (g) intersectionality.

5. Discuss possible solutions to the case informed by the four implications of DSE for educational leadership and organizational theory toward equitable ends: (a) dissolve the hegemonic normative core, (b) denouncement of labeling, (c) substantive inclusion, and (d) critique of special education.

6. Discuss how the solution(s) in the case can be informed by (a) change theory, (b) leadership theory, and (c) decision-making theory as informed by DSE.

REFERENCES

Alemán, E., Jr. (2009). Through the prism of critical race theory: Niceness and Latina/o leadership in the politics of education. *Journal of Latinos and Education, 8*(4), 290–311.

Annamma, S., Connor, D., & Ferri, B. (2013) Dis/ability critical race studies (DisCrit): Theorizing at the intersections of race and dis/ability. *Race Ethnicity and Education, 16*(1), 1–31.

Baglieri, S., Valle, J.W., Connor, D.J., & Gallagher, D.J. (2011a). Disability Studies in education: The need for a plurality of perspectives on disability. *Remedial and Special Education, 32*(4), 267–278.

Baglieri, S., Bejoian, L.M., Broderick, A.A., Connor, D.J., & Valle, J. (2011b). Inviting interdisciplinary alliances around inclusive educational reform: Introduction to the special issue on Disability Studies in Education. *Teachers College Record, 113*(10), 2115–2121.

Baglieri, S., Bejoian, L.M., Broderick, A.A., Connor, D.J., & Valle, J. (2011c). [Re]claiming "inclusive education" toward cohesion in educational reform: Disability studies unravels the myth of the normal child. *Teachers College Record, 113*(10), 2122–2154.

Baker, B. (2002). The hunt for disability: The new eugenics and the normalization of school children. *Teachers College Record, 104*(4), 663–703.

Capper, C.A. & Frattura, E. (2008). *Meeting the needs of students of all abilities – How leaders go beyond inclusion.* Thousand Oaks, CA: Corwin Press.

Capper, C.A., Theoharis, G., & Sebastian, J. (2006). Toward a framework for preparing leaders for social justice. *Journal of Educational Administration, 44*(3), 209–224.

Chudowsky, N. & Chudowsky, V. (2009). State test score trends through 2007–2008, part 4: Has progress been made in raising achievement for students with disabilities. *Center for Education Policy.*

Connor, D.J. & Gabel, S.L. (2013). "Cripping" the curriculum through academic activism: Working toward increasing global exchanges to reframe (dis)ability and education. *Equity & Excellence in Education, 46*(1), 100–118.

Connor, D.J., Valle, J.W., & Hale, C. (Eds). (2015a). *Practicing disability studies in education: Acting toward social change.* New York: Peter Lang.

Connor, D.J., Valle, J.W., & Hale, C. (2015b). Introduction: A brief account of how disability studies in education evolved. In D.J. Connor, J.W. Valle, & C. Hale (Eds), *Practicing disability studies in education: Acting toward social change* (pp. 1–16). New York: Peter Lang.

Connor, D.J., Ferri, B.A., & Annamma, S.A. (2015). *DisCrit -- Disability Studies and Critical Race Theory in education.* New York: Teachers College Press.

Connor, D.J., Gabel, S.L., Gallagher, D.J., & Mortond, M. (2008). Disability studies and inclusive education – Implications for theory, research, and practice. *International Journal of Inclusive Education, 12*(5–6), 441–457.

Danforth, S. (2006). Learning from our historical evasions: Disability studies and schooling in a liberal democracy. In S. Danforth & S.L Gabel (Eds), *Vital questions facing disability studies in education* (pp. 77–90). New York: Oxford University Press.

Danforth, S. & Gabel, S.L. (Eds) (2006). *Vital questions facing disability studies in education.* New York: Oxford University Press.

DeMatthews, D. (2014). Deconstructing systems of segregation: Leadership challenges in an urban School. *Journal of Cases in Educational Leadership, 17*(1), 17–31.

DeMatthews, D. & Mawhinney, H. (2014). Social justice leadership and inclusion: Exploring challenges in an urban district struggling to address inequities. *Educational Administration Quarterly, 50*(5), 844–881.

Erevelles, N. (2011). "Coming Out Crip" in inclusive education. *Teachers College Record, 113*(10), 2155–2185.

Ferri, B.A. (2012) Undermining inclusion? A critical reading of response to intervention (RTI), *International Journal of Inclusive Education, 16*(8), 863–880.

Ferguson, P.M. & Nusbaum, E. (2012). Disability Studies: What is it and what difference does it make? *Research & Practice for Persons with Severe Disabilities, 37*(2), 70–80.

Fierros, E.G. & Conroy, J.W. (2002). Double jeopardy: An exploration of restrictiveness and race in special education. In D.J. Losen & G. Orfield (Eds), *Racial inequity in special education* (pp. 39–70). Cambridge, MA: Harvard Education Press.

Frattura, E. & Capper, C. (2007). *Leading for social justice: Transforming schools for all learners.* Thousand Oaks, CA: Corwin Press.

Frick, W.C., Faircloth, S.C., & Little, K.S. (2013). Responding to the collective and individual "best interests of students": Revisiting the tension between administrative practice and ethical imperatives in special education leadership. *Educational Administration Quarterly, 49*(2), 207–242.

Fullan, M. (2007). *The new meaning of educational change* (4th edn). New York: Teachers College Press.

Graham, L.J. & Slee, R. (2008). An illusory interiority: Interrogating the discourse/s of inclusion. *Educational Philosophy and Theory, 40*(2), 277–293.

Hattie, J.M. & Yates, G.C.R. (2014). *Visible learning and the science of how we learn.* New York: Routledge.

Hoppey, D. & McLeskey, J. (2011). A case study of principal leadership in an effective inclusive school. *The Journal of Special Education, 46*(4), 245–256.

Khalifa, M.A., Jennings, M.E., Briscoe, F., Oleszweski, M., & Abdi, N. (2014). Racism? Administrative and community perspectives in data-driven decision making: Systemic perspectives versus technical-rational perspectives. *Urban Education, 49*(2), 147–181.

Leonardo, Z. & Broderick, A.A. (2011). Smartness as property: A critical exploration of intersections between Whiteness and Disability Studies. *Teachers College Record, 113*(10), 2206–2232.

McKenzie, K.B., Christman, D.E., Hernandez, F., Fierro, E., Capper, C.A., Dantley, M., Gonzalez, M.L., Cambron-McCabe, N., & Scheurich, J.J. (2008). From the field: A proposal for educating leaders for social justice. *Educational Administration Quarterly, 44*(1), 111–138.

National Assessment of Educational Progress. (2015). *The nation's report card 2015 math & reading assessments.* Retrieved from www.nationsreportcard.gov/reading_math_2015/#reading/acl?grade=4.

O'Malley, M. & Capper, C. (2015). A measure of the quality of educational leadership programs for social justice. *Educational Administration Quarterly, 51*(2), 290–330.

Pazey, B.L. & Cole, H.A. (2013). The role of special education training in the development of socially just leaders: Building an equity consciousness in educational leadership programs. *Educational Administration Quarterly, 49*(2), 243–271.

Ryan, J. (2010). Establishing inclusion in a new school: The role of principal leadership. *Exceptionality Education International, 20*(2), 6–24.

Ryndak, D.L., Reardon, R., Benner, S.R., & Ward, T. (2007). Transitioning to and sustaining district-wide inclusive services: A 7-year study of a district's ongoing journey and its accompanying complexities. *Research & Practice for Persons with Severe Disabilities, 32*(4), 228–246.

Sanford, C., Newman, L., Cameto, R., Knockey, A., Shaver, D., Buckley, J., & Yen, S. (2011). The post-high school outcomes of young adults with disabilities up to 6 years after high school: Key findings from the national longitudinal transition study-2 (NLTSN2). Institute for Educational Sciences National Center for Educational Statistics.

Scanlan, M. (2006). Problematizing the pursuit of social justice education. *UCEA Review, 45*(3), 6–8.

Slee, R. (2007). Inclusive schooling as a means and end of education? In L. Florian (Ed.), *The SAGE handbook of special education* (pp. 160–172). London: Sage.

Stetser, M. & Stillwell, R. (2014). Public high school four-year-on-time graduation rates: School years 2010–2011 & 2011–2012. Institute for Educational Sciences National Center for Educational Statistics.

Taylor, S.J. (2006). Before it had a name: Exploring the historical roots of disability studies in education. In S. Danforth & S.L Gabel (Eds), *Vital questions facing disability studies in education* (pp. xiii–xxiii). New York: Oxford University Press.

Theoharis, G. (2007). Social justice educational leaders and resistance: Toward a theory of social justice leadership. *Educational Administration Quarterly, 43*(2), 221–258.

Theoharis, G. (2010). Disrupting injustice: Principals narrate the strategies they use to improve their schools and advance social justice. *Teachers College Record, 112*(1), 331–373.

Theoharis, G. & Haddix, M. (2011). Undermining racism and a whiteness ideology: White principals living a commitment to equitable and excellent schools. *Urban Education, 46*(6), 1332–1351.

Theoharis, G. & O'Toole, J. (2011). Leading inclusive ELL social justice leadership for English language learners. *Educational Administration Quarterly, 47*(4), 646–688.

Valle, J., Connor, D.J., Broderick, A.A., Bejoian, L.M., & Baglieri, S. (2011). Creating alliances against exclusivity: A pathway to inclusive educational reform. *Teachers College Record 113*(10), 2283–2308.

Waldron, N.L., McLeskey, J., & Redd, L. (2011). Setting the direction: The role of the principal in developing an effective, inclusive school. *Journal of Special Education Leadership, 24*(2), 51–60.

Williams, J. & Mavin, S. (2012). Disability as constructed difference: A literature review and research agenda for management and organization studies. *International Journal of Management Reviews, 14*(2), 159–179.

Zion, S. & Blanchett, W. (2011). [Re]conceptualizing inclusion: Can Critical Race Theory and interest convergence be utilized to achieve inclusion and equity for African American Students? *Teachers College Record, 113*(10), 2186–2205.

CHAPTER 11

Queer Theory[1,2]

Similar to the other chapters in this book, I examined the literature on Queer Theory as it relates to organizational theory and educational leadership. Referring to Figure 11.1, I position Queer Theory as originating from both critically oriented epistemologies and poststructuralism. Similar to the Disabilities Studies epistemology (Chapter 10), Queer Theory has been strongly influenced by poststructural epistemologies, in part because of when scholars developed Queer Theory after poststructuralism (O'Malley, 2013). Scholars also typically draw across critically oriented epistemologies to undergird Queer Theory conceptual applications to educational leadership. For example, Rottman (2006) relies on "poststructuralist, feminist and identity-based political foundations of Queer Theory to construct a conceptual lens which complements other critical, anti-oppression frameworks" (p. 1). O'Malley (2013) refers to poststructuralism, feminist, and gay/lesbian studies as antecedents to and scaffolding for Queer Theory.

In this chapter, I briefly review the educational leadership literature related to LGBT identities and the use, or not, of Queer Theory in that research. I identify and discuss tenets associated with Queer Theory which I gleaned from the literature. I review the history of Queer Theory in the organizational studies literature, and consider hetero-organizational culture and structures and resistance and queerness in organizations. Related to intersectionality, I also briefly discuss Queer of Color theory. I close the chapter with a discussion of applications of Queer Theory to leadership, change, and decision-making. The chapter includes questions for discussion and Queer Theory case analysis questions.

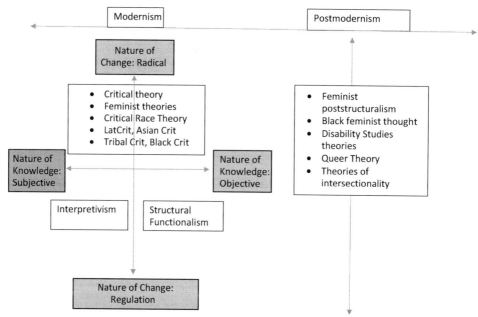

Modernism | Postmodernism

Nature of Change: Radical

- Critical theory
- Feminist theories
- Critical Race Theory
- LatCrit, Asian Crit
- Tribal Crit, Black Crit

- Feminist poststructuralism
- Black feminist thought
- Disability Studies theories
- Queer Theory
- Theories of intersectionality

Nature of Knowledge: Subjective | Nature of Knowledge: Objective

Interpretivism | Structural Functionalism

Nature of Change: Regulation

Figure 11.1 An Epistemology Framework

QUEER THEORY AND EDUCATIONAL LEADERSHIP

Payne and Smith (2017) categorized the lesbian, gay, bisexual, transgender (LBGT), and educational leadership literature into two central categories. One category includes studies that examine the leadership of LGBT identified leaders (Blount, 1996, 2000; Fraynd & Capper, 2003; Koschoreck, 2003; Lugg & Tooms, 2010), and studies of educational leadership practice related to student, staff, and family who identify as LGBT (cited in Payne & Smith, 2017). As to the former, Rottman (2006), who offered one of the first applications of Queer Theory to educational leadership, describes epistemological and practical conflict when studying educational leaders on the queer spectrum:

> [T]his literature is problematic in that it implicitly defines sexually-marginalized people as a 'species' (Foucault 1990) to be studied, while those in heterosexual relationships whose desires are publicly sanctioned continue to act as the implicit moral standard against which all others are measured. This practice of focusing on those most marginalized by sexual norms reifies a heterosexual/homosexual dichotomy, elevates the status of those who identify with the first category over those who identify with the second, and presents 'queer' as though it were an internally consistent category. (p. 2)

A second category of LGBT research in educational leadership includes studies that examine educational leadership preparation programs and LGBT identities (Allen, Harper, & Koschorek, 2009; Jennings, 2012; Marshall & Hernandez, 2013; O'Malley & Capper, 2015, all cited in Payne & Smith, 2017). To date, this literature across both categories remains limited and none of the studies Payne and Smith cite rely on Queer Theory for the conceptual framework. The few studies that view educational leadership from a Queer Theory epistemology are theoretically robust, though they are not as explicit in implications for practice (Lugg, 2003a, b; Lugg & Murphy, 2014; O'Malley, 2015; Rottman, 2006).

Unfortunately, the record of sexual identity in the field of educational leadership remains blemished. In a national study of social justice leadership preparation programs, sexual identity was the least included in these programs (O'Malley & Capper, 2015) among the range of identities. That is, though leadership programs claim to be social justice focused, fewer than half address sexual identity. This raises the question about how social justice leadership preparation programs define social justice if they exclude sexual identity in the program. Further, in the previous chapters in this text on critically oriented epistemologies and educational leadership, none substantively address the intersection with sexual identity.

QUEER THEORY TENETS

Similar to the Disability Studies in Education epistemology discussed in Chapter 10, queer theorists are reticent to articulate tenets of Queer Theory, since the epistemology itself works against categories and fixed meanings (O'Malley, 2013). For this chapter, I reviewed literature across education and educational leadership that relied on Queer Theory to identify key themes which authors referred to in their rendering of Queer Theory. These tenents include: (a) homophobia and heterosexism are pervasive and normal; (b) disrupt what is normal, (c) against the binary, social construction, and unstableness of identities; (c) pervasiveness and critique of heterosexuality; (d) anti-queer bias embedded in law and policy; (e) power is contested; (f) resistance/liberationist goal; (g) importance of language; and (h) intersectionality.

Homophobia and Heterosexism are Pervasive and Normal

Similar to Critical Race Theory (CRT) (Chapter 7), where racism is considered pervasive and normal, Lugg and Murphy (2014) convey similar dynamics with Queer Theory:

> As forms of CPA [Critical Policy Analysis], both QT [Queer Theory] and QLT [Queer Legal Theory] are interested in how power is used, negotiated, and subverted in organizational settings. Like other CPA forms of analysis, QT and QLT look at deep structures of oppression, particularly as they are woven into the woof and weave of institutions and professions like education. Furthermore, like one of its intellectual predecessors, Critical Race Theory (López, 2003) – that assumes racism to be a normal facet of life in the US – QT and QLT assume homophobia to be normal. Consequently, homophobia is expected to be a part of everyday life, no matter how enlightened the institution or particular individual might claim to be – even including queer people themselves. (Valdes, 1995, pp. 1186–1187)

Lugg and Murphy explain how homophobia continues to be perpetuated through stigma and erasure, historically in three ways: legally, psychologically, and religiously. Legally, homosexuality was illegal in all U.S. states until 2003, though, according to Lugg and Murphy, some states continued to seek legal enforcement of heterosexuality through 2013. Psychologically, homosexuality as a mental illness was removed from the American Psychological Association's list in 1973. However, to date, the religious form of queer erasure remains. Lugg and Murphy apply their arguments to the "no promo homo" laws. As explained on the website of the Gay, Lesbian Straight Educators Network (GLSEN), no promo homo laws are:

> local or state education laws that expressly forbid teachers from discussing gay and transgender issues (including sexual health and HIV/AIDS awareness) in a positive light – if at all. Some laws even require that teachers actively portray LGBT people in a negative or inaccurate way. These statutes only serve to further stigmatize LGBT students by providing K-12 students false, misleading, or incomplete information about LGBT people. There are currently 7 states that have these types of laws: Alabama, Arizona, Louisiana, Mississippi, Oklahoma, South Carolina, and Texas. (Retrieved on January 15, 2018)

Lugg and Murphy explain that these policies and laws are premised on:

> any form of gay tolerance in school is actually an insidious means of promoting homosexuality – that openly discussing the matter would encourage kids to try it, turning straight kids gay (Rubin Erdely, 2012, para. 20). Such an argument was and is ludicrous in light of the data on identity formation (Fausto-Sterling, 2000; Meyer, 2010; Wilchins, 2004). (p. 1188)

Disrupt What is Considered Normal

Similar to the Disability Studies in Education epistemology discussed in Chapter 10, Queer Theory centers on disrupting what is considered normal. Dilley (1999) explains: "the dominant culture's stronghold on proclaiming normality and deviance must be overthrown, or at least displayed as power-laden and repressive" (p. 466). Dilley (1999) further argues:

> The tenets of Queer Theory could be used, or adapted, in many varied areas of educational research as the underlying questions of what is normal, and how we know that, can enlighten our understanding of not only our human lives, but our teaching, our learning, and our questioning. (p. 470)

This tenet of Queer Theory remains most applicable across settings and identities compared to the other Queer Theory tenets, as this tenet extends beyond considerations of sexuality and gender.

Against the Binary, Social Construction, and Unstableness of Identities

Queer Theory moves against typical sex and sexuality binaries such as male/female and heterosexuality/queer (Rottman, 2006). Binary constructions reflect asymmetries of power, with one side of the binary (the first side) considered the norm and the other side the deviant from the norm and that which is deficient and inferior (O'Malley, 2015). Rottman extends Queer Theory beyond sex/gender binaries to interrogating binaries of any sort. She explains, "In this case the link [of educational leadership] to Queer Theory is in the 'queering' or the 'making strange' or the 'disrupting' of traditional dichotomous categories" (Rottman, 2006, p. 13).

Reflective of poststructuralism discussed in Chapter 6, Queer Theory also moves against the idea that identities are stable and fixed (Lugg, 2016 Lugg & Murphy, 2014), of which poststructuralism refers to as essentializing identities (O'Malley, 2015). Instead, Queer Theory asserts that sexual "identity is neither fixed nor unitary but multiple and shifting" (Kissen, 2002, p. 5) and that the self remains "partial, contested, and fluid" (O'Malley, 2013, p. 361). Queer Theory scholars assert that identities are multiple and complex, and according to Griffin (1996), researchers need to "not 'universalize' or essentialize the experiences of individuals" and need to "tak[e] into account the multicentered nature of identity, rather than focusing only on LGBT [lesbian, gay, bisexual, transgender] identity. We all have race, gender, class, religion, age, and able/disabled identities too" (p. 4) that, in and of themselves, are partial, intersectional (Crenshaw, 1991), incomplete, unstable, complex, fluid, and contested. Not necessarily focusing on the essentialized individual sexual identity of a person, scholars relying on Queer Theory examine instead the social construction of sexual identity, its multiplicities, and how this social construction reinforces power relations (see Beemyn & Eliason, 1996; Butler, 1993; Foucault, 1990; Fuss, 1991; Sedgwick, 1990; Seidman, 1996; Stein & Plummer, 1994).

Pervasiveness and Critique of Heterosexuality

Queer Theory reveals the pervasiveness of heteronormativity historically, structurally, culturally, and systemically. Queer Theory makes visible the ways "heterosexuality becomes normalized as natural" (Britzman, 1995, p. 153; Rottman, 2006). Queer Theory critiques the pervasive assumption of heterosexuality and critiques heterosexuality as a "privileged, compulsory, dominant mode of social organization" (O'Malley, 2013, p. 6). This critique of heterosexuality reveals the relationship of gender to heterosexism, because heterosexism depends on "the ongoing performance of hegemonic masculinity" (Rottman, 2006, p. 9).

Anti-queer Bias Embedded in Law and Policy

Similar to the foundations of Critical Theory (Chapter 5) and Critical Race Theory (Chapter 7), Queer Theory emerged in part out of Critical Legal Studies. Queer

Legal Theory (QLT) suggests how anti-queer bias is deeply embedded in law and policies in educational settings; for example, when schools require gender-specific uniforms for band, choir, or graduation, or prom courts that feature matched biological males and females (Lugg, 2015, p. 3), and classroom lessons that divide the class by biological sex or gender.

Power is Contested

Similar to the other critically oriented epistemologies, "power, status, and privilege are inequitably distributed, typically along lines of historic marginalization" (Lugg & Murphy, 2014, p. 1196). Thus, according to Lugg (2015), "Queer Theory and Queer Legal Theory also assume that *power*, that is, who has the power to shape the political culture and culture-bearing institutions, such as public schools, *is contested*" (p. 3).

Resistance/Liberationist Goal

Similar to the other critically oriented epistemologies, a tenet of Queer Theory includes resistance with a goal of liberation for those oppressed along the gender and sexuality continuum. Lugg (2015, p. 4) argues that:

> the most important outcome of any scholarly endeavor is to liberate queer people from political and cultural oppression as well as the oppression that occurs within institutions, whether it is the legal system, the health system and, in this case, the educational system. (p. 4)

The work of gay rights activists indicates that there is a political and social basis for resistance along the lines of gender and sexuality (Britzman, 1995; Koschoreck, 2003).

The Importance of Language

The importance of language as a Queer Theory tenet reflects the poststructural influence on Queer Theory as discussed in Chapter 6. Lugg (2015) explains that "Queer Theory and Queer Legal Theory are concerned with how language is used to classify, stigmatize and oppress" (p. 4). Lugg relies on the term "queer" in her writing, "which includes lesbian, gay, bisexual, transgender, intersexual, and queer-questioning people. I also made it normative, meaning that gender-typical heterosexuals are *non-queer* or are somehow lacking" (p. 4). Rottman (2006) traces the historical evolution of language related to queer, explaining how even the supposedly inclusive term "queer" can be marginalizing in its essentialist and assimilationist tendencies.

INTERSECTIONALITY

Similar to Critical Race Theory (Chapter 7), and LatCrit, Asian Crit, and Tribal Crit (Chapter 8), and influenced by its postmodern roots (Chapter 6), intersectionality of identities forms a key tenet of Queer Theory. As Lugg and Murphy (2014) explain,

> Both QT [Queer Theory] and QLT [Queer Legal Theory] use a combination of intersectionality and multidimensionality ... to decenter the legal and social structures that privilege and police heteronormativity, patriarchy, white supremacy, class advantage, and heterosexuality. QT's policy and political goal is to liberate sexual minorities without falling back on essentializing assumptions that demand historically marginalized groups assimilate – or leave. (p. 1183)

These Queer Theory tenets reveal how Queer Theory draws from critically oriented epistemologies like Critical Theory (Chapter 5) and Critical Race Theory (Chapter 7) with tenets such as the pervasiveness of homophobia and heterosexism, anti-queer bias in law and policy, and resistance with a goal of liberation. Likewise, some of the Queer Theory tenets are oriented toward poststructural epistemologies (Chapter 6): for example, the disruption of normal; against the binary, social construction, and unstableness of identities; and the importance of language.

QUEER THEORY AND ORGANIZATIONS

The history of sexuality and organizational theory began in the 1980s and early 1990s with European scholars writing on gender and sexuality and organizations. These scholars produced the most extensive work to date related to sexuality and organizations in the edited book *The sexuality of organization* by Hearn, Sheppard, Tancred-Sheriff, and Burrell (1990). The authors conclude:

> Different degrees of hierarchy in organizations are likely to be associated with different forms of sexuality, and moreover heterosexuality, in those organizations. This is because of the general eroticization of dominance ... and the more specific association of hierarchy and heterosexuality. ... This theme is so pervasive that we should perhaps have named this text *The Heterosexuality of Organization*. (p. 179)

Importantly, these scholars did not use Queer Theory as a lens for this scholarship. These scholars argued that the heterosexual culture of an organization controls behavior of all, regardless of sexuality. Although norms of heterosexuality are pervasive in organizations, these scholars suggest how postmodern theories can explore resistances and ruptures to these heterosexual norms, whether intentional or not. As such, studying the sexual culture and structure of schools as organizations can provide insight into how sexual norms, rituals, ceremonies, and other artifacts of culture and structure serve particular individuals at the expense of others and maintain heterosexual hegemony.

As this literature reveals, although researchers have given attention to sexuality and organization, the primary focus has been on heterosexual relationships. In this section, I consider organizational theory and heteroorganizational culture and structure, and resistance and queerness in organizations.

Hetero-organizational Culture and Structure

The study of organizational culture has proved fruitful for many scholars (Deal & Kennedy, 1990). Although typically not included in the organizational theory canon, several authors have deconstructed male-stream organizational culture theories and exposed their gendered (Mills & Tancred, 1992) and sexual (Burrell & Hearn, 1990) nature. The heterosexual culture of an organization controls the behavior of all individuals, regardless of sexual identity in subtle and powerful ways. A heterosexual-identified female student in one of my courses provides one example of how the heterosexual culture constrained her as a teacher:

> There just wasn't any discussion of gay, lesbian, or bisexual anything or anyone. Even though there wasn't discussion, however, the unwritten rule was always present. I remember when I first got my job, I wanted to take to school a few personal items for my desk. One was a picture of my best friend Andrea and myself. As I looked through the snapshots of us together I realized that there was not one photo of us where we aren't hugging or holding one another. The one picture I really loved was taken in my backyard at graduation. I picked her up and was holding her up in the air and we were laughing. As I looked at this picture, I knew it would cause speculation at my school so I didn't take it in. I didn't take any pictures of us in to put on my desk. I just didn't want to chance being thought of as a lesbian. Now I think back to that thought and I wonder what it was that intimidated me so badly and I begin to realize how strong those unwritten rules really are in people's lives.

Sheppard (1990) writes about the gendered nature of organizational structure, an analysis that could easily accommodate sexuality. Substituting sexuality in her analysis of structure, she argues,

> The notion of organizational structure as an objective, empirical and [nonsexual] reality is itself a [heterosexual] notion. … It masks the extent to which organizational politics are premised on the dominance of one set of definitions and assumptions that are essentially [heterosexually] based. (p. 142)

Noticing the sexual culture and structure of schools as organizations can provide insight into how sexual norms, rituals, ceremonies, and other artifacts of culture and structure serve particular individuals at the expense of others and maintain heterosexual hegemony. Critically reflective leadership questions could include: How is the heterosexual culture and structure of schools used to promote and maintain existing arrangements of power and control (Sheppard, 1990)? How is heterosexuality produced and reproduced in these organizational arrangements (Hearn, Sheppard, Tancred-Sheriff, & Burrell, 1990)? How does organizational culture contribute to the "construction and maintenance of [heterosexua] subjects" (Mills, 1990)?

Resistance and Queerness in Organizations

While norms of heterosexuality are pervasive in organizations, postmodern theories would suggest that we explore resistances and ruptures to these heterosexual norms, whether intentional or not. Burrell and Hearn (1990) suggest that though heterosexuality reflects the bureaucracy of organizations, queer expression of all forms is not absent.

QUEER OF COLOR THEORY

Anzaldúa (1998) challenged the racism and classism inherent in Queer Theory:

> White middle-class lesbians and gay men frame the terms of the debate. It is they who have produced Queer Theory and for the most part their theories make abstractions of us colored queers. They control the production of the queer knowledge in the academy and in the activist communities. … They occupy theorizing space, and though their theories aim to emancipate, they often disempower and neo-colonize. They police the queer person of color with theory. (p. 274, cited in Rottman, 2006, p. 7)

Pritchard (2013) conducted a Queer of Color analysis of bullying in K-12 schools and explains:

> Queer of color critique draws on theories of intersectionality to explore multiple oppressions and identities in ways that do not elide the specificity of difference but resist the undertheorizing of identities by acknowledging their complexities in our analysis of the everyday. (p. 371)

Brockenbrough (2016) offers a comprehensive yet concise explanation of Queer of Color (QOC) critique and its application to education. Brockenbrough defines QOC critique as "an interdisciplinary corpus of scholarship on the dialectics between hegemony and resistance that shape the lives of queer people of color across local, national, and transnational contexts" (p. 286). Brockenbrough notes the lack of scholarship on QOC in education, and argues that "educational scholarship that engages QOC critique could make important contributions to critical scholarship on QOCs, as well as to broader educational discussions on difference, power, and social justice" (p. 7).

Given the obvious dimensions of intersectionality in QOC critique, Brocken-brough identifies intersectionality in action as:

> the daily negotiations of multiple identities, noting how QOCs may make certain identities more visible at times (e.g., race, ethnicity, class, religion) while downplaying others (e.g., queer sexuality, gender non-conformity, immigrant status, HIV status) to strategically position themselves for participation in myriad social contexts. (p. 287)

Brockenbrough (2016) applies QOC to education with two examples from his own research. One of his studies focuses on the "politics of queer visibility" (p. 288) and recasts "coming out" research that has often focused on the white queer experience, and has typically framed coming out as a form of strategic justice. Instead, Brockenbrough describes queer invisibility itself as a form of strategic justice, "where queerness may be completely hidden, or, if visible, is not openly acknowledged – emerges as an agentive practice for some QOC's who prioritize connectedness with families and racial communities over coming out" (p. 288). In his study of black male teachers, which included five black queer men, Brockenbrough learned that these teachers were able to challenge homophobia and connect in meaningful ways to all their black students, "despite – and arguably because of – their closeted queerness" (p. 288).

Brockenbrough (2016) identifies three key tenets of QOC critique. First, QOC emphasizes institutional factors that produce marginality rather than focusing on the traditionally marginalized individual and locating "the problem" within that individual. Thus, the focus of change is at the institutional level rather than on expecting queer people of color to transform policies and practices. Second, QOC critique highlights the strategies of resistance and in so doing disrupts white renderings of the importance of queer visibility and the myth of "safe space" for queer individuals and other white queer agendas. Third, Brockenbrough (2016) emphasizes the importance of centering QOC individuals' lives and stories – similar to Critical Race Theory and counter-stories (Chapter 7) – and the critical importance of developing connections and relationships with QOC individuals that support honest, nuanced exchange. Brockenbrough acknowledges that nearly all the QOC research has focused on black males and that future research should consider QOC teachers and administrators.

QUEER THEORY AND CHANGE, LEADERSHIP, AND DECISION-MAKING THEORY

As with the other critically oriented epistemologies, Queer Theory implications for leadership, change, and decision-making converge. One central lesson of Queer Theory for change theory within organizational theory centers on how equity change oriented toward one area of marginality (e.g., culturally responsive curriculum) may continue to erase and stigmatize queerness and reinforce heteronormative hegemony. Lugg and Murphy (2014), for example, point out how the American Educational Research Association (AERA), though claiming political neutrality, nevertheless took clear political stands against federal and state immigration and racial policies, and continued to stigmatize and erase queerness in education. Queer Theory also uncovers the pervasiveness of homophobia and heteronormativity across policies, practices, and scholarship that address other marginalized identities. As discussed at the beginning of this chapter, though nearly all University Council for Educational Administration (UCEA) institutions claim to be social justice focused, fewer than half address sexuality. A recent study of social justice principals revealed how they continued to ignore queer identities in their schools (Payne & Smith, 2017). In an additional example from practice, a cisgender African American female district administrator described the vehement resistance of some of her black educator colleagues to her advocacy for gender identity and gender expression policy in a large urban district, pushing back on her that "why are we talking about this, when we should be talking about racism?" The district administrator exclaimed back, "in a district with 80 percent African Americans, what race do you think the transgender students are?," pointing out that advancing transgender/gender identity advocacy also acknowledged the racism in the district.

Similar to the other critically oriented epistemologies we have reviewed thus far in this text related to decision-making, in queering educational leadership, Rottman (2006) argues for decentering the educational leader and for representation in decision-making. She explains,

> If differently positioned people gain access to decision making structures and the power and resources attached to these structures, the resulting decisions will more likely resonate with multiply positioned educational stakeholders. Queering educational norms provides one avenue through which to challenge our current inclination to place the burden and authority of problem solving on the backs of individual leaders who cannot possibly represent the socially diverse group of students, staff or community members who live, learn and work in North American public schools. (Rottman, 2006, p. 14)

In each of the chapters devoted to critically oriented epistemologies and organizational theory thus far, we have addressed race (Chapters 7, 8, 9), gender (Chapter 6, 9, 11), social class (Chapter 5), sexual/gender identity (Chapter 11), and ability (Chapter 10) and, within each of these chapters, identity intersections. Thus, identity – no matter how fluid, multiple, fractured, and anti-esssentialist – matters. I close the book with Chapter 12, where I draw across the critically oriented epistemology chapters to consider identity development formation within individuals and organizations toward social justice.

LEADERSHIP DEVELOPMENT ACTIVITIES

ACTIVITY 1: **Queer Theory Discussion and Leadership Critical Self-reflection**

1. What are examples in your setting of a heterosexual culture and structure?
2. How are these examples used to promote and maintain existing arrangements of power and control (Sheppard, 1990)?
3. Heterosexuality is enforced partially through the enforcement of stereotypical gender roles.
    a. What are examples in your setting of how stereotypical gender roles are reinforced and supported?
    b. What are examples in your setting of how the stereotypical gender binary is reinforced? (E.g., boys vs girls groupings; male/female bathrooms; boys vs. girls uniforms, etc.)
    c. How does your setting (and you now/in the past) respond to individuals whose gender expression does not adhere to typical norms?
4. "Homophobia and heterosexism demand vigilant institutional maintenance of heterosexuality as a normative sexual identity. What educational policies and practices in your setting maintain normative heterosexuality?" (Rottman, p. 13). What changes could be made to remove (or at least lessen the impact of) the heterosexual norm?
5. Decision-making processes within heterogeneous queer communities are settled through inequitable contests for power and primacy. How are status and privilege assigned to individuals who are perceived as masculine, feminine, heterosexual, homosexual, bisexual, transsexual or transgendered in your context? How do issues of racism and classism intersect with these sexualized and gendered identities? What is the effect on [formal leaders], students and teachers in your school? How do you know? (adapted from Rottman, 2006, p. 13).
6. The work of gay rights activists indicates that there is a political and social basis for resistance along the lines of gender and sexuality. What examples of resistance have emerged in your [educational setting]? What structures have supported and constrained these efforts? (adapted from Rottman, 2006, p. 13).

ACTIVITY 2: **Queer Theory Analysis of Case Study**

Note: Individuals in your case do not have to be on the sexual/gender identity continuum (e.g., identify as LGB or transgender) for Queer Theory to be relevant to your case. As in all the epistemologies discussed in this book, each of the epistemologies calls you to reflect on what is not considered in your case and why it is not considered. What is left silenced or assumed in your case? What is considered normative and unquestioned in your case?

1. What aspects of the case issue could be informed by Queer Theory? Are there any possible solutions to the case from a Queer Theory epistemology?
2. How is the (hetero)sexual culture and structure of the situation used to promote and maintain existing arrangements of power and control (Sheppard, 1990)?
3. In what ways is heterosexuality assumed or presumed in your case?
4. In what ways is sexuality silenced in your case?
5. If sexuality or gender identity of the actors in your case does not seem salient, consider how the dynamics of your case would change should the sexual identity of one or more actors in your case shift toward the LGBT spectrum and its intersections.
6. How is heteronormativity produced, maintained, and reproduced in your case (Hearn et al., 1990)?
7. How does the organizational culture in the case contribute to the "construction and maintenance of [heterosexual] subjects" (Mills, 1990)?
8. How do the organizational structure, culture, practices, and policies serve to reinforce gender stereotypes?
9. How is sexual surveillance enacted, and how does it perpetuate existing discourses of power?

NOTES

1   Adapted from Capper, Colleen A. (Homo)sexualities, organizations, and administration: Possibilities for In(query)y. *Educational Researcher, 28* (5), 4–11. ©1999 Sage Publications. Reprinted by permission of Sage Publications. doi: 10.3102/0013189X028005004.
2   Adapted from Capper, Colleen A. (1998) Critical and postmodern perspectives: Sorting out the differences and implications for practice. *Educational Administration Quarterly, 34* (3), pp. 354–379. © 2018, Sage Publications. Reprinted by permission of SAGE Publications. DOI: 10.1177/0013161X98034003005

REFERENCES

Allen, J.G., Harper, R.E., & Koschorek, J.W. (2009). Fostering positive dispositions about LG-BTIQ matters: The effects of social justice curriculum on future educational leaders. In J.W. Koschorek & A. Tooms (Eds), *Sexuality matters: Paradigms and policies for educational leaders* (pp. 76–102). Lanham, MD: Rowman & Littlefield.

Anzaldúa, G. (1998) To(o) queer the writer: Loca, escritora y chicana. In C. Trujillo (Ed.), *Living Chicana theory* (pp. 263–276), Berkeley: Third Woman Press.

Beemyn, B. & Eliason, M. (Eds). (1996). *Queer studies: A lesbian, gay, bisexual and transgender anthology.* New York: New York University Press.

Blount, J.M. (1996). Manly men and womanly women: Deviance, gender role polarization, and the shift in women's school employment, 1900–1976. *Harvard Educational Review, 66,* 318–339.

Blount, J.M. (2000). Spinsters, bachelors, and other gender transgressors in school employment, 1850–1990. *Review of Educational Research, 70,* 83–101.

Britzman, D.P. (1995). Is there a queer pedagogy? Or, stop reading straight. *Educational Theory, 45*(2), 151–165.

Brockenbrough, E. (2016). Queer of color critique. In N.M. Rodriguez, W.J. Martino, J.C. Ingrey, & E. Brockenbrough (Eds), *Critical concepts in queer studies and education: An international guide for the twenty-first century* (pp. 285–298). New York: Palgrave/MacMillan.

Burrell, G. & Hearn, J. (1990). The sexuality of organization. In J. Hearn, D. L. Sheppard, P. Tancred-Sheriff, & G. Burrell (Eds), *The sexuality of organization* (pp. 1–28). Newbury Park, CA: Sage.

Butler, J. (1993). *Bodies that matter: On the discursive limits of sex.* New York: Routledge.

Crenshaw, K. (1991) 'Mapping the margins: intersectionality, identity politics, and violence against women of color', *Stanford Law Review, 43*(6), 1241–1299.

Deal, T. E. & Kennedy, A. A. (2000). The new corporate cultures: Revitalizing the workplace after downsizing, mergers, and reengineering. Cambridge, MD: Basic Books.

Dilley, P. (1999). Queer theory: Under construction. *International Journal of Qualitative Studies in Education, 12*(5), 457–472.

Foucault, M. (1990). *The history of sexuality, Vol. 1.* Translated by Robert Hurley. New York: Vintage Books.

Fraynd, D.J. & Capper, C.A. (2003). "'Do you have any idea who you just hired?!?" A study of open and closeted sexual minority K-12 administrators. *Journal of School Leadership, 13*(1), 86–124.

Fuss, D. (Ed.). (1991). *Inside/out: Lesbian theories, gay theories.* New York: Routledge.

Griffin, P. (1996). *A research agenda on gay, lesbian, bisexual, transgender administrators: What can we learn from the research on women administrators, administrators of color, and homosexual teachers and youth?* (Cassette Recording No. RA6–35.62). (Available from Teach'em, 160 East Illinois St., Suite 300, Chicago, IL 60611. American Educational Research Association Annual Meeting, NY.

Hearn, J., Sheppard, D. L., Tancred-Sheriff, P, & Burrell, G. (Eds). (1990). *The sexuality of Organization,* Newbury Park, CA: Sage.

Jennings, T. (2012). Sexual orientation topics in educational leadership programmes across the USA. *International Journal of Inclusive Education, 16*(1), 1–23.

Kissen, R. M. (Ed.). (2002). *Getting ready for Benjamin: Preparing teachers for sexual diversity in the classroom*. Rowman & Littlefield.

Koschoreck, J.W. (2003). Easing the violence: Transgressing heteronormativity in educational administration. *Journal of School Leadership, 13*(1), 27–50.

Lugg, C.A. (2003a). Our straitlaced administrators: The law, lesbian, gay, bisexual, and transgendered educational administrators, and the assimilationist imperative. *Journal of School Leadership, 13*, 51–85.

Lugg, C.A. (2003b). Sissies, faggots, lezzies, and dykes: Gender, sexual orientation, and a new politics of education. *Educational Administration Quarterly, 1*, 95–134.

Lugg. C.A. (2016). *US public schools and the politics of queer erasure*. New York: Palgrave.

Lugg, C.A. & Koschoreck, J.W. (2003). The final closet: Lesbian, gay, bisexual, and transgendered educational leaders. *Journal of School Leadership, 13*(1), 4–6.

Lugg, C.A. & Murphy, J.P. (2014). Thinking whimsically: Queering the study of educational policy-making and politics. *International Journal of Qualitative Studies in Education, 27*(9), 1183–1204.

Lugg, C. A. & Tooms, A. K. (2010). A shadow of ourselves: Identity erasure and the politics of queer leadership. *School Leadership & Management, 30*(1), 77–91.

Marshall, J.M. & Hernandez, F. (2013). "I would not consider myself a homophobe": Learning and teaching about sexual orientation in a principal preparation program. *Educational Administration Quarterly, 49*, 451–488.

Mills, A. (1990). Gender, sexuality, and organization theory. In J. Hearn, D. L. Sheppard, P.Tancred-Sheriff, & G. Burrell (Eds), *The sexuality of organization* (pp. 29–44). Newbury Park, CA: Sage.

Mills, A. & Tancred, P. (Eds) (1992). *Gendering organizational analysis*. Newbury Park, CA: Sage.

O'Malley, M. P. (2013). Creating inclusive schools for LGBT students, staff, and families: Equitable educational leadership and research practice. In L. Tillman and J. J. Scheurich (Eds). *Handbook of educational leadership for equity and diversity* (pp. 355–379). NY: Routledge.

O'Malley, M. P. & Capper, C. A. (2015). A measure of the quality of educational leadership programs for social justice integrating LGBTIQ identities into principal preparation. *Educational Administration Quarterly, 51*, 290–330.

Payne, E.C. & Smith, M.J. (2017), Refusing relevance: School administrator resistance to offering professional development addressing LGBTQ issues in schools. *Educational Administration Quarterly, 54*(2), 183–215.

Pritchard, E. D. (2013). For colored kids who committed suicide, our outrage isn't enough: Queer youth of color, bullying, and the discursive limits of identity and safety. *Harvard Educational Review, 83*(2), 320–345.

Rottmann, C. (2006). Queering educational leadership from the inside out. *International Journal of Leadership in Education, 9*(1), 1–20.

Sedgwick, E.K. (1990). *The epistemology of the closet*. Berkeley, CA: University of California Press.

Seidman, S. (Ed.). (1996). *Queer theory/sociology*. Cambridge, MA: Blackwell Scientific Publications.

Sheppard, D. L. (1990). Organizations, power, and sexuality: The image and self-image of women managers. In J. Hearn, D. L. Sheppard, P. Tancred-Sheriff, & G. Burrell (Eds), *The sexuality of organization* (pp. 139–157). Newbury Park, CA: Sage Publications.

Stein, A. & Plummer, K. (1994). I can't even think straight: "Queer" theory and the missing sexual revolution in sociology. *Sociological Theory, 12*(2), 178–187.

CHAPTER 12

Individual and Organizational Identity Formation toward Social Justice

We know that some leaders identify themselves as social justice focused (Theoharis, 2007), and that schools, districts, and universities exist that are more equitable than others (Smith & Brazer, 2016). Less is known about the evolution of these leaders and these educational settings toward social justice ends – that even in these exemplar settings some identities and differences are addressed more so than others. A few studies reveal the complexities of social justice leadership that result in leaders engaging in contradictory leadership practices (DeMatthews & Mawhinney, 2014). To date, no literature examines how the social justice identity of educational leaders evolves, how social justice change unfolds in educational settings, and how these aspects could help us understand further the contradictions in social justice leadership practice. Thus, this chapter addresses the relationship between the individual identity formation (e.g., racial identity formation) of educational leaders and the social justice identity formation of educational settings as organizations. The research question that anchors this chapter asks: How does the identity formation of the educational leader and other stakeholders at the individual level inform the organizational identity of the educational setting as it evolves toward equitable ends?

Most of the literature that grounds this research question refers to identity "development." I concur with the work of Adams (2016), who suggests the phrase identity "formation" versus identity "development." Identity development assumes a series of lock-step stages that individuals process through over time as their identity evolves relative to race, gender, social class, ability, sexual/gender identity, language, religion, and their intersections. Identity formation "acknowledge[s] the fluidity of identity, changes in salience of identity in different contexts, and the social and cultural communities within which identity is formed, challenged, and reworked" (Hurtado, Gurin, & Peng, 1994; Wijeyesinghe, 2001, cited in Adams, 2016, p. 36).

This chapter problematizes the contemporary use of social justice in the educational leadership literature that often erases race (Capper, 2015) and marginalizes sexual/gender identity (O'Malley & Capper, 2015). Instead, social justice identity formation within individuals and schools is conceptualized as explicitly addressing race, ethnicity, language, ability, gender, sexual/gender identity, social class, religion, and their intersections to eliminate inequities. This chapter is the first step in the theory's development by analyzing the existing literature to propose theory. Subsequent research will empirically test the theory via qualitative and mixed methods studies of social justice leaders and their schools.

LITERATURE REVIEW

To frame this chapter, I review three strands of literature: (a) organizational identity, (b) individual identity formation, and (c) social justice identity development.

Organizational Identity

The literature on organizational identity is fairly well developed with a special issue of *Organization* devoted to the topic in 2008 (Alvesson, Ashcraft, & Thomas, 2008). In the Introduction to this special issue, the authors trace the organizational identity lineage across three epistemologies of structural functionalism, interpretivism, and critical theory. The studies on organizational identity tend to focus on the individual's relationship to the organization. These scholars acknowledge that most of the research on organizations and identity emanates from the structural functional and interpretivist epistemologies. Importantly, none of the featured five empirical studies in the special issue addressed critically oriented epistemologies and none addressed the demographic identities of individuals and their relationship to their organizational work toward equity. Although the authors identify possible avenues for future research across the three epistemologies, their suggestion for critical epistemology remains severely limited.

Ashforth and Mael (1989) describe Social Identity Theory (SIT) and the organization. This literature focuses on the degree to which and in what ways individuals identify with an organization. Ashforth and Mael acknowledge that an individual's identity, such as age, gender, and political affiliation, may influence the degree and in what ways the individual identifies with an organization. Thus, an individual with a strong social justice orientation may identify more readily with an educational setting that also aspires toward these ends. This theory, however, does not consider how an individual's identity development along race, class, and other identities and their intersections influences the shift of an organizational identity toward equity ends.

In sum, though the empirical research on organizational identity remains robust, this literature focuses primarily on the relationship of the individual to the organization. No studies examine the evolution of an organization toward a social justice or equity identity, and the role of individual identity development in that process.

Individual Identity Formation

Identity development models have been developed across races, including white (Hardiman, 1982; Helms, 1990) African American (Cross, 1991), Latino (Gallegos & Ferdman, 2007), Native American (Horse, 2005), and Asian (Kim, 2012). By their name, these models focus only on racial identity, not on other identities (e.g., ability), and not on the intersection of race with other identities (e.g., black transgender). In addition to race, Adams (2016) describes additional social identity models, including:

> coming out models of gay liberation (Cass, 1996), feminist identity models (Bargad & Hyde, 1991), disability identity (Gill, 1997) … and ethnic and racial identity development models that reflect the ethnic/racial complexities of identity for immigrant communities of color (Hurtado, Gurin, & Peng, 1994). (pp. 36–37)

Adams (2016) further explains the similarities across these identity development models:

> 1) accepting and internalizing the dominant ideology and values that assume the superiority of the dominant group and the inferiority of the subordinated group; 2) questioning, rejecting, and resisting the dominant ideology and oppressive systems and thus the way their social group is characterized; 3) exploring, redefining, and developing a new sense of social identity that is not rooted in the norms and values of superiority and inferiority; and 4) integrating and internalizing the new identity along with a commitment to social justice. (p. 36)

One problem with the racial identity and other identity development models is the way they essentialize identity (Hernandez, 2005; Langdridge, 2008). For example, Helms's (1990) white racial identity development model focuses solely on race generically defined. It does not account for individuals who identify as white and may be at varying places in their racial identity development regarding races other than white (e.g., Latinx, African American, Asian, or multiracial as examples). In addition, these racial identity development models do not consider the complexities of racial identity with other identities (e.g., Latina transgender male). None of this literature discusses the social and organizational impact upon identity development, nor how this identity development could inform organizational development and vice versa toward social justice ends.

Social Justice Identity Development

Adams, Bell, and Griffin (1997) describe a social justice action continuum that moves from supporting oppression to confronting oppression. Adams and colleagues identify eight discrete points along this continuum (see Figure 12.1).

↑ Supporting Oppression

Stage	Description
1. Actively participating	Telling oppressive jokes, putting down people from target groups, intentionally avoiding marginalized individuals, discriminating against these individuals, or verbally or physically harassing these individuals.
2. Denying	Individuals enable oppression by denying that target group members are oppressed. These individuals do not actively oppress, but, by denying that oppression exists, collude with oppression.
3. Recognizing, no action	Individuals are aware of oppressive actions and their harmful effects, but take no action to stop this behavior. This inaction is due to fear, lack of information, or confusion about what to do. These individuals experience discomfort at the contradictions between awareness and action.
4. Recognizing/action	An individual is aware of oppression, recognizes oppressive actions of self and others, and takes action to stop it.
5. Educating self	When individuals seek to educate themselves about oppression and target group members.
6. Educating others	When individuals seek to not only educate themselves but to also educate others.
7. Supporting, encouraging	Individuals support others who are working against oppression and join a coalition or allies group as examples.
8. Initiating preventing	The individual takes even more action, and works to change individual and institutional actions and policies that discriminate against target group members, and plan educational programs and other events, work on policies, and being explicit about making target group members full participants in organizations or groups.

▼ Confronting Oppression

Figure 12.1 Continuum of Social Justice Identity Development

In relation to the epistemologies discussed in Chapter 2, the social justice action continuum of Adams et al. (1997) reflects movement from structural functional to critically oriented epistemologies. The last four stages of their model reflect a continuum of action within critical epistemologies. Their model illustrates that not only do leaders need to consider epistemological movement from interpretivist to critically oriented perspective but also to consider movement from less to more consciousness and action within critically oriented epistemologies.

The social justice action continua, such as the one promulgated by Adams et al. (1997) or the identity development models, can reflect the fluidity of movement from structural functionalist to critically oriented perspectives, and can reflect movement within critically oriented perspectives; at the same time, these models essentialize the practice of social justice. The continuum is presented as if an educator is equally adept at working across identities and difference in their educational settings, but our research and work with leaders in the field show this to be far from the case (Scanlan, 2005).

THEORY OF ORGANIZATIONAL AND INDIVIDUAL IDENTITY TOWARD SOCIAL JUSTICE

Garcia and Shirley's (2012) study that relies on Critical Indigenous Pedagogy illustrates and confirms the importance – as a prerequisite of social justice leadership – of deepening one's own identity development and understanding one's own cultural history (see Figure 3.1). In their study of Indigenous youth and Indigenous teachers, they discovered that when these individuals learned about Indigenous theory and Indigenous history, these learnings deepened their own Indigenous identity development. Their advancement in their own Indigenous identity development then, in turn, helped the youth and adults understand more clearly the nature of Indigenous oppression, their own role in perpetuating that oppression, and to understand more clearly how they could take steps to interrupt that oppression for themselves and other Indigenous individuals in their communities.

Leaders for social justice must advance their own identity development across race, gender, social class, language, ability, sexual/gender identity, religion, and their intersections to inform their social justice leadership practice. In turn, leaders must engage with their staff processes that can inform teachers' own identity development. In so doing, then, teachers can learn how to engage in this identity development work with their students. These identity development processes among leaders, staff, students, and community may in turn contribute to the social justice identity of an educational setting.

Six principles inform this theory of individual and organizational identity development toward social justice. First, identity development within a leader – along the dimensions of race, ethnicity, social class, gender, ability, gender identity, religion, language, sexual identity, and their intersections – comprises the internal foundation for a leader for social justice. That is, as Garcia and Shirley (2012) suggest, the development of identity along multiple and intersecting identities within individuals contributes to and is a prerequisite for the social justice identity of an individual. In addition, the leader's identity development can determine, in part, the degree to which a school evolves to being more socially just. The social justice identity development of an educational setting will always be limited by or open to possibility by the social justice identity development of the leader.

Second, the social justice identity development of individuals within the educational setting contributes to the social justice identity development of the organization. For this to make sense, we must ascribe to the idea that organizations hold an identity or associated underlying epistemology unto their own, informed by the multiple and shifting identities and epistemologies of individuals within the organization.

Third, though most literature attests to the power and influence of the leader on organizational identity, at the same time an organization's social justice identity could also be significantly informed by the staff, students, and educational community. Thus, the organization's social justice identity development process is a process of mutuality among all those involved: staff, students, community, and the leader in a continual process of influencing identity development within each other and within the school (see Figure 12.2).

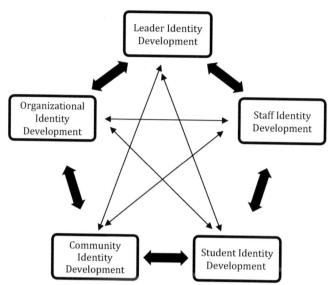

Figure 12.2 Theory of Individual and Organizational Identity Toward Social Justice

Fourth, this identity formation process does not have a concrete finish or end at the individual or organizational level. Instead, this social justice identity formation process is ongoing and lifelong at both levels.

In addition, evolution of identity across differences and their intersections within individuals and the organization will not be linear. Individuals shift forward and back at various levels in identity formation throughout their lives. Similarly, reflecting the aforementioned oftentimes meandering identity formation of individuals, the trajectory of educational settings may not always necessarily evolve toward social justice. An organization that has evolved toward social justice can retreat when the identity formation of individuals within the educational setting changes. For example, I have conducted research in schools that had evolved into inclusive communities ignited by a principal with these values and associated skills and a willing staff and community. Yet, when the principal was replaced by a principal without these same beliefs, the school evolved away from these inclusive ideals.

Fifth, the leader's own identity formation along multiple dimensions, in turn, influences leadership practices along these dimensions. For example, leaders who have addressed their own racial identity formation in limited ways will also be limited in how they address race in the school. In addition, leaders' typically uneven identity formation along these identities will be reflected in uneven leadership practice. For example, leaders who have progressed on their own racial identity development may in turn address white racism in their own schools directly and effectively. However, these same leaders may be limited in their sexual identity development and understanding, and thus their leadership practices associated with students on the Lesbian, Gay, Bisexual, Transgender, Intersexual, Questioning (LGBTIQ) spectrum may be more limited as compared to their racial practices. This unevenness in identity development can be reflected within identities and their intersections. For example, a leader may be effective in the proportional representation assignment of students with disabilities across the school; however, these same leaders may be less skilled in inclusive practices for students with significant intellectual disabilities. As a second example, a leader may strongly support the school's Gay/Straight Alliance (GSA), but may be less effective in supporting students and staff when addressing the racial injustices perpetuated by the GSA.

Identity development and practice inform each other and do not necessarily flow in one direction from identity development to practice. For example, as leaders learn more about eliminating segregated programs for students labeled with disabilities, learning about these practices will in turn inform their disability identity development.

Garcia and Shirley's (2012) Tribal Crit study suggests that learning about related theories can and perhaps should be part of this identity development process (see Figure 12.3). In their study, when students and educators learned about Tribal Crit theory along with the other aspects of decolonization, the theory contributed to their social justice identity development. The same may be said for this text. Individuals learning more about the range of critically oriented epistemologies can advance their identity across these epistemologies and their intersections.

Finally, a sixth principle of the theory suggests that as leaders deepen their identity development along one dimension of identity, such as race, doing so could contribute to their development along other dimensions of identity such as ability, though not necessarily so. However, further empirical study will reveal if this is necessarily so, and moves beyond the superficial impact of one aspect of identity development to another.

In sum, six principles emerge from this proposed theory of individual and organizational identity development toward social justice. This theory may help explain contradictions in social justice leadership practice and for exploring the evolution of school leaders in their own social justice leadership identity, and the linkage of this identity toward the evolution of socially just schools.

In sum, this chapter has discussed the relationship between our own identity development, our work as leaders for social justice, and the evolution of our schools

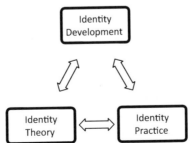

Figure 12.3 Relationship Between Identity Theory, Identity Development, and Identity Practice

as organizations toward socially just ends. Traditional organizational theory does not recognize personal identity development and its relationship to the organization, and remains neutral on organizational goals. In contrast, organizational theory informed by critically oriented epistemologies centers identity development in all aspects of organizational life – decision-making, conflict, structure, culture, motivation, leadership, politics, among others – anchored in the ultimate goal of organizational equity.

SIGNIFICANCE/CONCLUSIONS

This chapter proposes a theory that links individual identity development theories and their intersections to organizational identity and development toward social justice. I identified six key principles of this theory that may begin to help explain and inform leadership for social justice, contradictions in this leadership, and how schools evolve toward social justice. Beyond generic calls for leadership for social justice, the theory can inform the more nuanced details of social justice leadership practice than previous research.

LEADERSHIP DEVELOPMENT ACTIVITIES

ACTIVITY 1: The Example of Racial Identity Development

To further illustrate this theory, consider the example of racial identity development. Table 12.1 includes examples of racial identity development models for a range of races and for individuals who are multiracial. Undoubtedly, these models are limited in that they do not portray all racial possibilities. You should engage in these steps with the models.

1. Read through all the models to develop an understanding of racial identity development across races.
2. Select which model most closely corresponds to your own racial identity.
3. Read again the racial identity development model you selected and decide on the current status of your own racial identity development on that model.
4. Reflect on your own racial life experiences that influenced the current status of your racial identity development.
5. Consider the usefulness and limitations of this model.
6. Find a partner to share responses to steps one through two to five.

In this example we engaged in examining our own racial identity development. Where we are in our own racial identity development will determine how we engage with race as leaders in our schools, with our staff, community, and students, and will influence how our school evolves in its own racial identity development as an organization.

ACTIVITY 2:   Identity Formation across Differences and Our Education Practice

To further illustrate the relationship between identity formation at the individual level and its relationship to the identity formation of the school as an organization, please complete Appendix 12.1 to assess your own individual identity formation across different identities and then, in turn, consider the formation of that identity at the school level. Classroom teachers can also assess the identity formation within your classroom on the scale. While completing the scale, consider how where you locate yourself on the identity development scale is reflected in the school identity development in that same area (see Appendix 12.1).

SAMPLE IDENTITY DEVELOPMENT MODELS (ADAPTED FROM HERNANDEZ, 2005)

Table 12.1: Black Identity Development Model – Cross's (1991) Model of Nigrescence (Nigrescence means the process of becoming black)

Stages	*Features*
Pre-encounter	- Low salience attitude toward being black. - Blacks in this stage do not deny being black but do argue that their blackness is in no way connected to how others interact with them. - "[P]lace value in things other than their Blackness, such as their religion, their lifestyle, their social status, or their profession" (Cross, 1995, p. 98).
Encounter	- Blacks begin to seek identification with black culture. - Characterized by a crisis that causes blacks to question their worldview and that brings them closer to Nigrescence. - Plummer (1995) argues that this crisis is a "critical incident in one's life that leads the individual to reconceptualize issues of race in society and to reorganize racial feelings in one's personal life" (p. 169). - Involves two steps: "first experiencing the encounter and then personalizing it" (p. 105).
Internalization	- Blacks begin to experience a comfort level with being black and to acknowledge their African American background. - This is the stage when the person internalizes the new identity, "which now evidences itself in naturalistic ways in the everyday psychology of the person" (Cross, 1995, p. 113).
Internalization-Commitment	- A repeat of the activities, behaviors, and attributes of what was shown in the previous four stages (Torres, Howard-Hamilton, & Cooper, 2003). - Cross (1995) describes this stage by comparing blacks who "fail to sustain a long-term interest in Black affairs" to those who "devote an extended period of time, if not a lifetime, to finding ways to translate their personal sense of Blackness into a plan of action or general sense of commitment" (p. 121). - It is the latter people who embody the final stage of Nigrescence.

Table 12.2: Asian American Racial Identity Development Model (Kim, 2012)

Ethnic Awareness	- Generally comes from family and relative interactions and first occurs prior to a person's entrance into school. - Asian Americans who are raised in "predominantly Asian or mixed neighborhoods have greater exposure to ethnic activities and experience more ethnic pride and knowledge of their cultural heritage" (Torres et al., 2003, p. 72). - Asian Americans living in mostly white neighborhoods are uncertain about what it is to be Asian and have far fewer experiences with ethnic activities.
White Identification	- Begin to adopt white "societal values and become alienated from self and from other Asian Americans" (Torres et al., 2003, p. 60). - "[A]re not sure what makes them different from their peers" but "try at all costs to fit into White society in order to avoid publicly embarrassing themselves" (p. 73). - While whites are the reference point during this stage, many Asian Americans feel isolated from them and often get involved in school activities, such as being class officers, and excel academically to "compensate" for this isolation (p. 74). - Stage two is characterized by Asians' growing awareness of how different they are from their peers and is often associated with painful encounters in which Asians are made fun of during socialization.
Awakening to Social Political Consciousness	- See themselves as a distinct cultural group and begin to shed their white societal values. - "[A]re able to shift their worldview and realize that they are not personally responsible for their situation and experiences with racism" (Torres et al., 2003, p. 74). - The political awareness of white racism provides alternative perspectives, a new paradigm for Asian Americans. This new worldview allows Asian Americans to reinterpret their lives and lets them know that things could be different. - Reject white societal values as the only reference point or standard available. - Do not become anti-white but work at not being or acting white. - Involvement in social political movements and campus politics, in which Asian Americans identify themselves as a minority in the United States who do not wholly accept white values.
Redirection to an Asian American Consciousness	- Identify and embrace the Asian American identity and immerse themselves in the Asian American experience. - Can result in negative feelings toward whites that are based on introspective reflection on white racism in the United States and the impact it has had on their views of themselves and of others. - Racial pride is displayed during this stage and a "positive self-concept as Americans with Asian heritage" is accepted (Torres et al., 2003, p. 79). - The primary reference group is other Asians at the same stage. - Immersion in the Asian American community and a sense of self and belonging.
Incorporation	- Reach a level of balance and confidence that "allows Asian Americans to relate to many different groups of people without losing their own identity as Asian Americans" (p. 80). - Begin to understand commonalities with whites but do so on their own terms by using an Asian American perspective to ground their own views. - Understand culture better and do not see one culture as better than another.

Table 12.3: Native American Identity Development Model (Horse, 2005)

Influences and Features

- How well one is grounded in the native language and culture.
- Whether one's genealogical heritage as an Indian is valid.
- Whether one embraces a general philosophy or worldview that derives from distinctly Indian ways, that is, old traditions.
- The degree to which one thinks of oneself in a certain way, that is, one's own idea of self as an Indian person.
- Whether one is officially recognized as a member of a tribe by the government of that tribe.

- At the core of Indian identity is the fact that Indians "are engaged in a cultural struggle that is becoming more and more one-sided in favor of non-Indian influences" (Torres et al., 2003, p. 104).
- "[I]n those cultures, ultimately, lies our identity as native people. As individuals too, we draw much of our personal identity from those cultures" (p. 104).
- Most Americans do not recognize diversity within the Native American community.
- Although "risky" to generalize about Indian identity, "there are identity issues that affect most, if not all, American Indians" (p. 91).

Table 12.4: Latino and Latina Racial Identity Orientations (Gallegos & Ferdman, 2007)

Orientation	Lens	Identify as/Prefer	Latinos are seen	Whites are seen	Framing of race
White Identified	Tinted	Whites	Negatively	Very positively	White/black, either/or, one-drop or "mejorar la raza" (i.e., improve the race)
Undifferentiated/ Denial	Closed	People	"Who are Latinos?"	Supposedly color-blind (accept dominant norms)	Denial, irrelevant, invisible
Latino as Other	External	Not White	Generically, fuzzily	Negatively	White/not white
Subgroup Identified	Narrow	Own subgroup	My group OK, others maybe	Not central (could be barriers or blockers)	Not clear or central; secondary to nationality, ethnicity, culture
Latino identified (Racial/Raza)	Broad	Latinos	Very positively	Distinct; could be barriers or allies	Latino/not Latino
Latino Integrated	Wide	Individual in a group context	Positively	Complex	Dynamic, contextual, socially constructed

Table 12.5: Multiracial/Biracial Identity (Root, 1990)

1. Acceptance of the identity society assigns.	Family and a strong alliance with and acceptance by a (usually minority) racial group provide support for identifying with the group into which others assume the biracial individual most belongs.
2. Identification with both racial groups.	Depending on societal support and personal ability to maintain this identity in the face of potential resistance from others, the biracial individual may be able to identify with both (or all) heritage groups.
3. Identification with a single racial group.	The individual chooses one group, independent of social pressure, to identify him- or herself in a particular way (as in resolution 1).
4. Identification as a new racial group.	The individual may move fluidly among racial groups but identifies most strongly with other biracial people, regardless of specific heritage backgrounds.

Root, M.P.P. (2003). Racial identity development and persons of mixed race heritage. In M.P.P. Root and M. Kelley (Eds), *Multiracial child resource book: Living complex identities*. Seattle, Washington, DC: MAVIN Foundation.

Table 12.6: White Racial Identity Development (WRID) (Helms, 1990)

Stages	Features
Contact Status	- Describes someone who is oblivious to his or her own racial identity. - Whites in this status are satisfied with the racial status quo. - Racial factors have very little influence on life decisions. - Believe it is best to be "color-blind", to see people for being "human."
Disintegration Status	- Whites acknowledge their own white identity. - A time when "anxiety is provoked by unresolvable racial moral dilemmas that force one to choose between own-group loyalty and humanism" (p. 185).
Reintegration Status	- The field in which whites are idealized and blacks are denigrated. - Whites acknowledge their historical racism but justify it with a comment such as *that was then but this is now*. - Believe we live in a "post-racial" society, using examples of prominent people of color as proof that racism is no longer an issue. - Whites believe there is such a thing as reverse discrimination, and that this hurts whites.
Pseudo-independence Status	- White people intellectualize acceptance of their own and others' races. - Life decisions are made at times to support other racial groups, and this status may be the first sign of a positive white identity.
Immersion/ Emersion Status	- Whites begin to replace white and black myths and stereotypes with correct information about what it means to be white in the United States. - Whites in this status understand that they benefit from a racist society and begin to explore ways to work against it.
Autonomy Status	- Whites are integrated into black communities and work against generalizations about blacks. - Whites are consistently learning from other races and becoming acutely aware of other forms of oppression and the relation of these forms to racism.

This theory is based on the attitudes, behaviors, and feelings white people have developed.

All the above models are adapted from the work of Hernandez, F. (2005). *The racial identity development of selected Latino school principals and its relation to their leadership practice.* Unpublished doctoral dissertation, University of Wisconsin-Madison.

IDENTITY DEVELOPMENT INVENTORY

Identity Development Inventory of Yourself, Your Teaching/Immediate Sphere of Influence, and Your School/District/Organization Adult Version

Directions:

1. First, read through the description for each item on the rating scale 1–6.
2. On the following pages, mark your identity for each area:
   - Mark in the box where you are in your own identity development.
   - Mark in the box that identity area where you believe you are in your own teaching/immediate sphere of influence
   - Mark in the box that identity area where you believe your school/district/agency to be in its own identity development.

NOTE

This scale measures only one identity at a time, such as race, gender, ability, etc. Yet, all of us comprise multiple identities based on our gender, race, social class, ability, sexual identity, gender identity, language, and their intersections. Thus, for example, we may be further along the identity development scale for race, yet we may not be as far along the identity development scale for African American transgender females. Thus, though the scale only measures one identity at a time, it may be possible to also consider our identity development along intersecting identities by combining identities on the scale.

IDENTITY DEVELOPMENT INVENTORY OF YOURSELF, YOUR TEACHING/IMMEDIATE SPHERE OF INFLUENCE, AND YOUR SCHOOL/DISTRICT/ORGANIZATION ADULT VERSION ADAPTED FROM THE RIDDLE SCALE

1 = Repulsion or Fear

Identity is seen as a crime against nature. For example, someone who is gender nonconforming or transgender is considered sick, crazy, immoral, sinful, psychologically unstable. There is a level of fear at times with this identity based on stereotypes (e.g., fear of black males), fear/discomfort interacting with someone with a significant cognitive disability, etc.

(Continued)

2 = Pity

This identity is to be pitied and felt sorry for. Education is viewed as charity. For example, students from low-income homes are considered less fortunate and to be felt sorry for. Students with physical disabilities are pitied or felt sorry for, and seen as weak. A focus on deficits and lower expectations.

3 = Neutrality/Ambivalence

Not repulsion, fear, or pity. A feeling of distance from this identity, that it does not really have anything to do with you. Live and let live. Do the best you can. Treat everyone the same. All are equal. All are human.

4 = Acceptance

A respect and celebration of differences/diversity. The "it's a small world after all" view. Emphasis on getting along. Still implies that there is something to accept. The existing societal history and systems and structures of oppression and discrimination are ignored or believe there is nothing really that can be done about these systems. This view ensures the comfort of someone in the majority.

5 = Admiration

It is acknowledged that being any of the particular identities and their intersections takes strength. People at this level are willing to truly examine their own racism, classism, homophobia, transphobia, sexism, among other oppressions, yet they are unsure at times how to make a difference or question their ability to do so. It is easy to fall back into privileged comfort and to be timid about taking on the task of dismantling oppressive structures. No sense of urgency.

6 = Ally

Understand that one can never fully stop working on one's own oppressive attitudes/beliefs/behaviors, that it is a lifelong task. Work diligently and urgently as an ally with typically marginalized individuals toward justice. Do whatever it takes to dismantle systems that perpetuate oppression. Be clear at the core of being about the critical importance of social justice work and one's role in it.

IDENTITY DEVELOPMENT INVENTORY OF YOURSELF, YOUR TEACHING/IMMEDIATE SPHERE OF INFLUENCE, AND YOUR SCHOOL/DISTRICT/ ORGANIZATION ADULT VERSION

Table 12.7: Identity Development Inventory

	1 Repulsion/ Fear	2 Pity	3 Neutrality	4 Acceptance	5 Admiration	6 Ally
Race						
My view of persons of color						
How I address race in my teaching/immediate sphere of influence						
How race is addressed in my school/district/ organization						
Social Class						
My view of individuals of poverty						
How I address poverty in my teaching/ immediate sphere of influence						
How poverty is addressed in my school/district/ organization						
Biological Sex						
My view of females						
How I address females in my teaching/ immediate sphere of influence						
How biological females are addressed in my school/district/ organization						

(Continued)

	1 Repulsion/ Fear	2 Pity	3 Neutrality	4 Acceptance	5 Admiration	6 Ally
Linguistically Diverse						
My view of individuals for whom English is not the first language						
How I address linguistically diverse in my teaching/ immediate sphere of influence						
How linguistically diverse is addressed in my school/district/ organization						
Ability						
My view of persons with disabilities						
How I address disability in my teaching/immediate sphere of influence						
How disability is addressed in my school/district/ organization						
Sexual Identity						
My view of lesbian, gay, bisexual individuals						
How I address LGB in my teaching/ immediate sphere of influence						
How LGB is addressed in my school/district/ organization						
Gender Identity						
My view of transgender individuals						

How I address transgender in my teaching/immediate sphere of influence.

How transgender is addressed in my school/district/ organization

Religion

My view of different religions other than ones I am most familiar with.

How I address the range of religions in my teaching/immediate sphere of influence.

How the range or religions are addressed in my school/district/ organization.

Ethnicity (e.g., Latino, Slovenian)

My view of different ethnicities.

How I address different ethnicities in my teaching/ immediate sphere of influence.

How are different ethnicities addressed in my school/district/ organization?

Identity notes:

In which identity areas and their intersections have you made some progress with yourself and your immediate sphere of influence?

In which identity areas and their intersections would you like to develop further within yourself and your immediate sphere of influence?

REFERENCES

Adams, M. (2016). Pedagogical foundations for social justice education. In M. Adams & L. Bell (Eds), *Teaching for diversity and social justice: A sourcebook* (pp. 27–54). New York: Routledge.

Adams, M., Bell, L., & Griffin, P. (1997). *Teaching for diversity and social justice: A sourcebook.* New York: Routledge.

Alvesson, M., Ashcraft, K.L., & Thomas, R. (2008). Identity matters: Reflections on the construction of identity scholarship in organization studies. *Organizations, 15*(1), 5–28.

Ashforth, B.E. & Mael, F. (1989). Social identity theory and the organization. *The Academy of Management Review, 14*(1), 20–39.

Bargad, A., & Hyde, J. S. (1991). Women's studies: A study of feminist identity development in women. *Psychology of Women Quarterly, 15,* 181– 210.

Capper, C.A. (2015). The 20th anniversary of Critical Race Theory in education: Implications for leading to eliminate racism. *Educational Administration Quarterly. 51*(5), 791–833.

Cass, V. (1996). Sexual orientation identity formation: A Western phenomenon. In R. P. Cabaj & T. S. Stein (Eds.), *Textbook of homosexuality and mental health* (pp. 227–251). Arlington, VA, US: American Psychiatric Association.

Cross Jr, W. E. (1991). *Shades of black: Diversity in African-American identity.* Temple University Press.

DeMatthews, D. & Mawhinney, H. (2014). Social justice leadership and inclusion: Exploring challenges in an urban district struggling to address inequities. *Educational Administration Quarterly, 50*(5), 844–881.

Gallegos, P. V. & Ferdman, B. M. (2007). Identity Orientations of Latinos in the United States. *The Business Journal of Hispanic Research, 1*(1), 26–41.

Garcia, J. & Shirley, V. (2012). Performing decolonization: Lessons learned from Indigenous youth, teachers and leaders' engagement with Critical Indigenous Pedagogy. *Journal of Curriculum Theorizing, 28*(2), 77–91.

Gill, C. (1997). Four types of integration in disability identity development. *Journal of Vocational Rehabilitation, 9,* 39– 46.

Hardiman, R. (1982). *White identity development: A process model for describing the racial consciousness of White Americans.* Dissertation Abstracts International, 43, 104a (University Microfilms, No. 82–10330).

Helms, J.E. (1990). Toward a model of White racial identity development. In J.E. Helms (Ed.), *Black and White racial identity: Theory, research, and practice* (pp. 49–66). Westport, CT: Greenwood Press.

Hernandez, F. (2005). *Latino K-12 principals on leading and leadership: Racial identity development and its impact on leadership practice.* Unpublished dissertation, University of Wisconsin-Madison.

Horse, P. G. (2005). Native American identity. *New Directions for Student Services, 109*(1), 61–68.

Hurtado, A., Gurin, P., & Peng, T. (1994). Social identities—A framework for studying the adaptations of immigrants and ethnics: The adaptations of Mexicans in the United States. *Social Problems, 41*(1), 129–151.

Kim, J. (2012). Asian American identity development theory. In L. Charmaine & B. W. Jackson (Eds). *New perpectives on racial identity development: Integrating emerging frameworks* (pp. 138–160). New York, NY: New York University Press.

Langdridge, D. (2008). Are you angry or are you heterosexual? A queer critique of lesbian and gay models of identity development. In L. Moon, (Ed.), *Feeling queer or queer feelings? Radical approaches to counselling sex, sexualities and genders* (pp. 23–35). New York: Routledge.

O'Malley, M. & Capper, C.A. (2015). A measure of the quality of educational leadership programs for social justice: Integrating LGBTIQ identities into principal preparation. *Educational Administration Quarterly. 51*(2), 290–330.

Scanlan, M. (2005). *Epistemologies of inclusion: Catholic elementary schools serving traditionally marginalized students.* Unpublished dissertation, University of Wisconsin-Madison.

Smith, R.G. & Brazer, S.D. (2016). *Striving for equity: District leadership for narrowing opportunity and achievement gaps.* Cambridge, MA: Harvard University Press.

Theoharis, G. (2007). Social justice educational leaders and resistance: Toward a theory of social justice leadership. *Educational Administration Quarterly, 43*(2), 221–258.

Wijeyesinghe, C. L. (2001). Racial identity in multiracial people: An alternative paradigm. *New perspectives on racial identity development: A theoretical and practical anthology,* 129–152.

Index

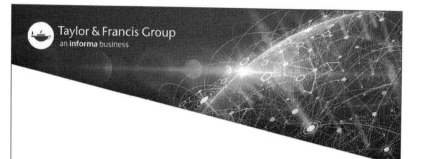

Made in the USA
Middletown, DE
15 July 2020

12814854R10144